DATE DUE

I Am Right —
You Are Wrong

EDWARD DE BONO

I Am Right —
You Are Wrong

FROM ROCK LOGIC TO WATER LOGIC

VIKING

VIKING
Published by the Penguin Group
Viking Penguin, a division of Penguin Books USA Inc.,
375 Hudson Street, New York, New York 10014, U.S.A.
Penguin Books Ltd, 27 Wrights Lane,
London W8 5TZ, England
Penguin Books Australia Ltd, Ringwood,
Victoria, Australia
Penguin Books Canada Ltd, 10 Alcorn Avenue, Suite 300,
Toronto, Ontario, Canada M4V 3B2
Penguin Books (N.Z.) Ltd, 182–190 Wairau Road,
Auckland 10, New Zealand

Penguin Books Ltd, Registered Offices:
Harmondsworth, Middlesex, England

First American Edition
Published in 1991 by Viking Penguin,
a division of Penguin Books USA Inc.

10   9   8   7   6   5   4   3   2   1

LIBRARY OF CONGRESS CATALOGING IN PUBLICATION DATA
De Bono, Edward, 1933–
I am right, you are wrong: from rock logic to water logic / Edward de Bono.
p.   cm.
ISBN 0–670–84231–1
1. Perception.   2. Thought and thinking.   I. Title.
BF311.D384   1991
153—dc20   91-20969

Printed in the United States of America
Set in Melior

Contents

Foreword

Ivar Giaever

Dr Edward de Bono is a man with a mission; he wants to teach people how to think creatively. He is the originator of the 'lateral thinking method', a conceptual tool used to enhance creative thinking. I must confess that I was very sceptical when I was first introduced to this system, but after reading this fascinating book I have become a convert. There are many stories circulating about scientists who have sudden flashes of insight seemingly coming from nowhere. The fact is that scientists often become so engrossed in their ideas that they constantly turn them over in their minds whether they drive, eat, sleep or make love. This ruminating process allows unrelated impulses to trigger associations in the brain, and *eureka!*—An unexpected solution suddenly appears. In 'lateral thinking' this haphazard way of gaining insight is replaced by a deliberate method that, in a prescribed and systematic way, solves the problems.

In *I Am Right — You Are Wrong* Dr Edward de Bono emphasizes various concepts about human behaviour. For example, even though humour is to a large extent neglected in philosophy, de Bono considers it to be of central importance in understanding creative thinking. His point can perhaps best be captured by paraphrasing Descartes: 'I laugh, therefore I am.' (In a recent movie a robot told a joke to convince its human owner that it was conscious!) Humour may be missing from philosophical thoughts, but it is not missing from this book. It is very clearly written and easy to read because it is full of stories, metaphors and anecdotes that vividly illustrate de Bono's points. At first glance the writing may appear somewhat simplistic because of this style, but upon reflection it is very deep and perceptive. Complex matters can indeed be explained in simple terms if the expositor has a thorough understanding of the subject. De Bono is a master in this art, and he describes in clear terms why and how humans think. *I Am Right — You Are Wrong* is of great importance to anyone who wants to understand human thought and behaviour.

In addition to discussing fully many aspects of the human mind, de Bono manages actively to engage the reader. For example, he cleverly states that if the brain were understood, it would have enormous consequences for human affairs. Next he surprises, and maybe shocks, the reader with the seemingly contradictory statement that we do, in fact, know how the brain works. Of course, he is wrong, but he is also right. For although we will not understand the details of how the mind functions for a long time, de Bono argues that it does not matter, since we understand it in principle. He emphasizes that the brain is not inherently logical; it is rather a pattern-recognizing machine that moves from one state to the next in an unpredictable fashion. For example, on one hand, when you smell newly baked bread (or whatever else may jar your particular memory) you are suddenly seven years old and transported back to your mother's kitchen. On the other hand, de Bono states: 'Every valuable creative idea must always be logical in hindsight.' Scientific papers are good examples of this; they are written in a wonderfully logical way, but the progress of real science that precedes the papers depends on hunches, accidents, imagination and luck.

Many discussions have taken place recently in artificial-intelligence circles over whether or not computers can ever learn to think like humans. Computers are, of course, experts in algorithms (i.e. logical manipulations). But algorithms cannot be equated to creative thinking, as Roger Penrose emphatically points out in a book entitled *The Emperor's New Mind*. There are, however, new approaches to computers — the so-called neural networks — that in a very rudimentary way try to emulate the nerve cells in the human brain. A superb and amusing description of this method can be found in de Bono's book, in which the brain is described by analogy as a beach full of octopuses. Although computer neural networks are in an elementary stage at present, the fact that they are self-organizing makes them reminiscent of the brain.

Another memorable point made by de Bono is the unique, yet limiting, role that language plays in human communication. He feels that we are trapped by our language, and states: 'In a sense language is a museum of ignorance.' An example is that words tend to polarize and categorize situations: you are either guilty or innocent, right or wrong, happy or sad. De Bono names this 'knife-edge discrimination'. Our traditional system of logic both relishes and depends on this dichotomy, and he refers to it as 'rock logic'. This is in contrast to 'water logic', which is not absolute but changes with circumstances and contexts. Perceptions, memories and life experiences play a much larger role in human communication and expression than people realize. For example, most works of art are culturally dependent, while great art may have universal appeal if it touches only upon common human factors.

If we are trapped in our language, how can I best describe *I Am Right — You Are Wrong*? It is much more than a catchy title, and it calls for no less than a revolution in our thinking (de Bono courageously intones 'a New Renaissance'). These are big and bold words, and they may sound pompous to some, but we live in a very exciting and unusual time. The train of thought that guides us into the future has already left the station, and a few brave people are on board. Dr Edward de Bono is certainly one of the passengers and he recognizes President Mikhail Gorbachev as a fellow traveller. If you would like to board this train, read the book!

Foreword

Brian Josephson

Edward de Bono's thesis in this book is that we give too much weight to conclusions that are based on logic. Logical thinking is thinking based on propositions and on consideration of the truth or falsity of propositions. Its primary usefulness is in situations where facts can be relied on to remain facts — in other words, in circumstances where nothing really new or unexpected is likely to happen.

The other side of things, according to Dr de Bono's scheme, is perception. When we look at the world around us we see (if we are attentive enough) what is actually there, even if what is actually there is not the same as what we expected to see there. When we turn our attention from the world around us to the world of possibilities that we can imagine with our minds, however, perception does not work nearly so well. We often fail to see the obvious until it is too late or until somebody else sees it and points it out to us. And very often something that we think is the case is not the case at all.

What is the cause of this? According to Dr de Bono, it is our rigid beliefs, our 'rock logic'. This takes control over our minds and determines how we will end up perceiving things. Much of the author's previous work, expounded in a number of books and taught in various courses, has been about how to persuade the mind to operate in a different, 'lateral thinking', mode. This book is more in the nature of an analysis and a diagnosis of the kinds of situation to which rigid thinking patterns lead, pointing out how things can go wrong and how they could be done differently. For example, once the thought comes to us that an idea that just has been suggested to us seems to be the same as an idea that we have heard of before we tend to think, 'this is nothing new,' and then give it no further thought. Different habits of thinking would veto this automatic response, so as to let the mind stay with the new idea for a while till it could be seen clearly.

I do not believe that there was no such thing as lateral thinking before Edward de Bono invented the term. There are many people who think in unconventional ways, often with great success, making no use of any special 'lateral thinking' techniques in order to do so. There are other approaches (such as meditation) to the problem of realizing the hidden potential of the mind. But our culture (or perhaps one should say instead, that part of our culture associated, according to some, with the masculine aspect of our being) is suspicious of any kind of thinking that works in ways other than through logic; and, to a very large extent, logical thinking is the only kind of thinking that is encouraged in our educational system. Dr de Bono does well to expose so clearly the faults in a system that places exclusive reliance on one aspect of the mind alone.

The book also proposes models, explained in non-scientific language, of how the brain works. These models are used as a means of expounding the 'logic' of the processes of perception that underlie aspects of mind that are intelligent despite being non-logical. One can see antecedents to these models in the pioneering work of Donald Hebb, but until recently conventional scientists did not, as Edward de Bono has done, apply such models to understand processes of thinking other than the logical ones. Now things are changing. Workers in the cognitive sciences are starting to see that there is much more to the way we think than merely following specific learnt procedures (algorithms) that tell us on all occasions how we should think.

But all this is very much on the theoretical side, and Dr de Bono's 'New Renaissance', where this kind of expanded knowledge of the nature of thought will be put to use in practice, still lies very much ahead of us. One hopes that this book will be studied and appreciated by those to whom it will be of the most value.

Foreword

Sheldon Lee Glashow

'The last Renaissance was clearly based on the re-discovery of ancient Greece (about 400 BC) thinking habits of logic, reason, argument, truth and the importance of man,' says Dr de Bono, physician and master teacher of creative thinking. Are these patterns still applicable to today's changing world? The old habits seem confining, inadequate and perhaps even dangerous, since our social conflicts are as primitive as ever while our technical ability to pursue them is unconstrained.

I Am Right — You Are Wrong (whose title signifies the gist of old thinking patterns) issues a clarion call for a New Renaissance. Today's thinking habits cannot be based on word-play or belief systems but must be attuned to the latest developments in neuro-science and matched to 'the way the human brain creates perception'. Dr de Bono is motivated because 'in democracies, it is everyone's business that everyone should think better'. However, he is ultimately led by his own logic to denounce our form of government as 'an excellent way of ensuring that nothing much gets done', an apt remark in view of America's political paralysis as the incredible Eastern European revolution unfolds.

Dr de Bono argues that perception-based 'water logic' must supplant the confrontational 'rock logic' we are accustomed to. He believes that the time is ripe for the New Renaissance because of what we now know of the brain as a self-organizing system. (With a charming model involving multitudes of music-loving octopuses, Dr de Bono tells us about some of these developments.) Surely our thinking processes should mimic the mechanisms of our own brains rather than the old and pernicious modes that have led us to wars, misery and the despoliation of our planet? New Computers based on neural networks promise to think as we do. Dr de Bono addresses the converse problem of the brain's operating system, which is traditionally based upon language rather than on how the brain works. He would like to design 'better software for the brain'.

Dr de Bono is not alone in attacking the language-based logical strategies that we have inherited. Feminist sociologists, especially Sandra Harding, despair of the aggressive and repressive tendencies inherent in conventional thought. They too seek a gentler paradigm based on perception rather than a questionable 'objective reality'. However, they view male dominance as the root of the problem, while Dr de Bono's analyses are not explicitly gender-specific. Ms Harding advocates the revolutionary reconstruction of our social, economic and educational institutions. Dr de Bono is not nearly so radical. He suggests the term 'provolution' to describe a gradual but cumulative introduction of values and perceptions into a society where rock logic and water logic may work hand in hand. The very idea of revolution (or the question of whether Ms Harding is right and we are wrong) he sees as an artefact of outmoded ways of thought. Yet he and they seek similar goals: new thinking modalities that may serve us better.

I can recall an earlier but futile quest for a new logical system. In *Science and Sanity* Alfred Korzybski, basing his analysis on what we had learned of the brain by 1933, claimed that 'present-day theories of meaning are extremely confused, ultimately hopeless, and probably harmful to the sanity of the human race . . . We face a complete methodological departure from two-valued "objective" orientation to general infinite-valued "process" orientation . . . The problem is whether we deal with scientific methods of 350 BC or AD 1933.' His non-Aristotelian world view did little to stave off a decade of death and destruction, but since then we've learned a lot more about the nature of mind and brain.

But have we learned enough to formulate an effective new method of thought that is based upon perceptions and not words, one that is adaptive but not confrontive, imaginative and creative but not repetitive and stylized? Certainly we cannot yet build an artificial brain. Super-computers are as dumb as they are fast. The proudest accomplishment of the promising new science of neural networks is a mere toy that reads aloud from a text without too many 'slips of the tongue'. It adapts, it recognizes patterns, but it does not think. When Dr de Bono says 'we do, right now, understand how the brain works', he speaks more as a clinician than as a research scientist. From the vital realization that the brain is a self-organizing rather than a pre-programmed system we can derive useful new habits and methods of thought. The purpose of conceptual models has always been to suggest and implement changes that have a practical impact, which is just what Dr de Bono sets out to do in this book.

Granting that we may understand the principles underlying the brain as a system in which information organizes itself, how may we use this knowledge to think better? Magic, humour and creativity, Dr de Bono insists, depend upon the deliberate subversion of the brain's normal pattern. 'Lateral thinking' helps us to leap from a well-travelled neural rut to a more productive sidetrack whose benefit is seen only in hindsight. His thinking tools are designed to lead us from the vicarious 'Why didn't I think of that?' to the triumphant 'Eureka!' They include, among others, the provocative intervention (which can play the role of Newton's proverbial apple), the concept of learning backwards (which I know to be the only way to read most physics research papers) and his exchangeable 'six thinking hats' (which managers begin to don now that 'business as usual' is failing).

Dr de Bono's innovative thinking methods have been tried and tested by many pupils and professionals, and they do seem to help people to be more creative and original. I saw the system in action at an impasse during a seminar of Nobel laureates. When a random word was injected into the discussion (another of Dr de Bono's thinking tools), the problem was quickly resolved. Perhaps it is time for the New Renaissance, and perhaps it will lead us towards the sane and benevolent society.

Author's Note

I am often asked to explain the connection between my background in medicine and my work in the field of thinking. At first these seem to be two very different fields. Yet the connection is very direct, and I probably would not have been able to develop my ideas without this background in medicine.

As a biological system the human brain handles information in a way that is quite different from traditional information systems. In traditional information systems we store information symbolically and then operate on these symbols according to certain rules (logic, mathematics, grammar etc.). Traditional computers store information in memory and then act upon it with the processor. In biological systems the information and the receiving surface act together as a self-organizing system — which means they produce patterns and arrangements on their own. In biology information triggers the next stable state of the system.

When I wrote the book *The Mechanism of Mind* about twenty years ago, many of the ideas seemed crazy to many people. Today these ideas are mainstream for all those working on self-organizing systems. Even mathematics has begun to enter into consideration of non-linear systems. There is a field of mathematics dealing with self-organizing systems.

So the connection between medicine and thinking is quite direct. Indeed it is difficult to see how anyone working in the field of thinking in the future can do so without an understanding of the underlying biological processes.

Civilization has done a marvellous job in taming thinking by putting it into a symbol and rules game — without reference to the underlying information system. Today — for the first time in history — we can look at the underlying system. We can begin to examine the impact of that understanding on our traditional thinking habits. For example lateral thinking and provocation are mathematically necessary in self-organizing patterning systems.

Since every valuable creative idea must always be logical in hindsight (otherwise we could not appreciate its value) we have believed that logic is sufficient. This is totally wrong in a patterning system.

Introduction: The New Renaissance

Humour is by far the most significant behaviour of the human mind.

You may find this surprising. If humour is so very significant, why has it been so neglected by traditional philosophers, psychologists and information scientists?

Why humour is so significant and why it has been so neglected by traditional thinkers together form the key to this book. Humour tells us more about how the brain works as mind, than does any other behaviour of the mind – including reason. It indicates that our traditional thinking methods, and our thinking about these methods, have been based on the wrong model of information system. It tells us something about perception which we have traditionally neglected in favour of logic. It tells us directly about the possibility of changes in perception. It shows us that these changes can be followed by instant changes in emotion – something that can never be achieved by logic.

There are probably no more than two dozen people in the whole world who would really understand (at the most fundamental, system level of brain mechanisms) why I claim such significance for humour. After reading this book there may be some more who come to understand the basis for the claim – and its implications for the future of society.

*

There are those who hope to be able to hope that – somehow – the world will become a better place. There is a hunger for such hope. As we proceed along the countdown to the year 2000, is there much cause for such hope? There is no mystical significance about the year 2000, but it does provide a unique focal point, one that will not recur for another thousand years. It could become a turning-point if we tried to make it a turning-point. But how and why?

There are those who feel that the pressures of evolution, the emergence of new values and the application of collective good sense must ultimately make things better. Surely if everyone goes about their own business and exercises a sharp criticism of their governments and their fellow beings, all will be well.

There are those who see a real need for a sort of New Renaissance. They are tired of arguments, polemics, confrontations, conflicts and problems that cannot be solved. They see serious threats to the environment; third-world debt and poverty; the spread of drugs and new diseases; and house prices that no young couple can afford. They are tired of the excuse that all these things arise from the rate of progress and from the innate defects of human nature, which will always be short-sighted, selfish, greedy and aggressive.

Maybe we are doing our best and there is nothing more to be done. Maybe the world is actually far better off than it has ever been and that we are just made more aware of the problems by the effectiveness and energy of modern media.

There are also a few who sense that a New Renaissance may already have begun. The train is pulling out of the first station. There are only a few people on board. Most people will get on at much later stations, as the direction becomes clearer. There are those who see that the conscious attempts at new thinking brought about by Mikhail Gorbachev in the USSR (for whatever internal needs and reasons) signal a change in thinking from confrontational habits to more constructive habits. President Gorbachev is not the engine driver of the train but he is one of the first people to have boarded the train.

*

There is a time and a place and a courage for saying something. The New Renaissance needs a formal announcement in order that people may notice it and focus upon it with hope and resolve. That is the purpose of this book.

To announce a New Renaissance will always seem presumptuous and provocative, whoever makes the announcement and with whatever justification. Surely such things just happen without anyone making a formal announcement. Is the purpose of such an announcement to create a self-fulfilling prophecy in that if we believe in a New Renaissance we shall make it happen?

We do need to believe in the possibility of a New Renaissance – because it is possible. There is always value in recognizing something that is already happening. Why delay recognition? There is, however, a much more substantial basis to the New Renaissance than hope and the year 2000.

*

On what is the New Renaissance to be based?

The last Renaissance was clearly based on the re-discovery of ancient Greek (about 400 BC) thinking habits of logic, reason, argument, truth and the importance of man. Before the last Renaissance the thinking habits of the Western world were derived entirely from dogma and theology. Maps of the world had to show large land masses with Jerusalem at the dead centre – not because the experience of navigators had suggested such a disposition of land but because dogma said that was how it had to be.

'I am right – you are wrong' is a short-hand crystallization of the thinking habits that both formed the last Renaissance and were further developed by it. The search for truth – as distinct from dogma – was to be made through the exposure of falsity by means of argument, reason and logic. This reason, not dogma, was to decide what was right and what was wrong.

In this way there developed the thinking habits that have served us so well in certain areas. The legalistic application of principles through the use of argument and reason can be said to be the basis of the civilization we know. Technical affairs have progressed to the point that we can get men to the moon and back, transmit instant television to 300 million people across the world, and use the ultimate form of energy (nuclear).

Is it possible that these excellent thinking habits are somewhat limited and inadequate? While we have made so much progress in technical affairs we have made less progress in human affairs. Our habits of conflict are as primitive as ever, even though the weapons we use have benefited from our technical excellence.

Is it possible that these thinking habits are, in some respects, even dangerous? Is it possible that they have reached their limit, that they are unable to cope with the problems we face, that they prevent further progress? Is it possible that the time has come to improve upon them? If so, on what are the new thinking habits to be based?

*

The new thinking habits of the New Renaissance are to be based on the most fundamental of all bases, more fundamental than philosophical word-play or belief systems. They are to be based directly on how the human brain works, and, in particular, the way the human brain creates perception.

For the first time in history we can now have an idea of how the brain is organized to give rise to mind. We may not know all the details, but we do know enough about the broad system behaviour to re-examine our traditional thinking habits and to be able to develop new ones. We can come to see how the thinking habits of the last Renaissance emphasized some of the worst habits of mind. We can come to see why the thinking and language systems we developed and now esteem so highly are good at logic but poor at perception. We can see how that failure to deal with perception gives rise to the inadequacies and dangers of our current thinking. We can see how these habits were responsible for much human misery in the past and why they are not adequate for the constructive steps that are necessary in the future.

*

'I am right – you are wrong' condenses the essence of our traditional thinking habits that were set by the last Renaissance.

Here we find 'argument', which is the basis of our search for truth and the basis of our adversarial system in science, law and politics. Here we have absolutes and finality and judgement –and the confidence (sometimes arrogance) which comes from these. Here we have the mutually exclusive incompatibility which is the very essence of our logic. Each party cannot be both right and wrong at the same time. The essence of logic is identity and contradiction. In language we deliberately create mutually exclusive categories such as right/wrong and friend/ enemy in order to operate this logic of contradiction. Yet there are cultures – as I shall show in this book – which find no contradiction in a person being both friend and enemy at the same time.

The last Renaissance revived and polished the methods of Socrates and the other thinkers of the golden age of Greek philosophy. It is possible that the argument method was in use before, but Socrates developed it into a formidable procedure. There is a remarkable paradox in how the revival of Greek argument thinking in the last Renaissance served a dual purpose. On the one hand, humanistic thinkers used the system of logic and reason to attack the dogma that suffocated society. On the other hand, Church thinkers led by the genius of Thomas Aquinas of Naples developed the same argument logic into a powerful way of defeating the numerous heresies that were forever surfacing.

For the purpose of defeating heresy the system was highly effective because a thinker could proceed from common agreed concepts (axioms), such as the omnipotence of God, to logically derived conclusions. The same methods were used to proceed from assumed principles of justice to the regulation and judgement of human conduct. This system of principle, logic and argument is the basis for our much used – and often beneficial – legalistic thinking. Where it breaks down is in the assumption that perceptions and values are common, universal, permanent or even agreed.

This argument/logic type of thinking became standard in seminaries, universities and schools. This was because such establishments were largely run by the Church at that time and also because the free humanistic thinkers esteemed the same methods. The paradox is that both Church thinkers and non-Church (humanistic) thinkers found equal value in the methods. Perhaps this is not so surprising, since the new methods were such an obvious advance on existing thinking habits.

Central to this type of thinking is the underlying notion of 'truth'. By means of argument which manoeuvres matters into a contradictory position, something can be shown to be false. Even if something is not completely false, the garbage has to be chipped away by the skilled exercise of critical thinking in order to lay bare the contained truth.

Thus arose the pre-eminence of critical thinking as the highest form of civilized thinking – and the defence of civilization itself. Any intrusion was to be subjected to an intense scrutiny and fierce criticism within existing frameworks, since these were assumed to be eternal.

That critical thinking is so highly esteemed in our civilization has had some unfortunate consequences. Critical thinking lacks the productive, generative, creative and design elements that are so needed to tackle problems and find our way forward. A high proportion of politicians are lawyers and are only accustomed to this manner of thinking.

Is thinking that is free from error good thinking? Is driving that is free from error good driving? If you wanted to avoid all errors in driving a car, the best strategy would be to leave the car in the garage. As in critical thinking, the avoidance of errors in driving presupposes the generative, productive and creative aspects of thinking. These elements are essential for the progress of society. Where are these things to come from? This may not have mattered much in the stable city states of ancient Greece, where the perfection of existence (except for women and slaves) suggested that any disturbance was likely to be bad or at least unnecessary. It may not have mattered much in the relatively stable society of the Middle Ages, when happiness was to be achieved in the next world rather than in this one. But it does matter today. That is why the American tendency to want to teach only 'critical thinking' in schools is appalling in its medieval inadequacy.

Whether this argument style was responsible for our confrontational style of politics is more open to question. The Greeks bequeathed us both argument and democracy and we have wanted to keep the two together, since we do not know how to operate democracy without argument. Yet there were many cultures which had developed the notion of clash between good and evil (Manichaeism, Hinduism etc.) quite independently of Greek thinking.

Hegel's notion of historic opposition and tension gave rise to the dialectical materialism of Marxism and the energy for its revolutions. Unfortunately this 'clash' system of change is making very difficult the constructive and creative thinking that is so needed in order to make perestroika work in the USSR.

In summary, our traditional thinking system is based on 'truth', which is to be uncovered and checked by logic and argument (supplemented by statistics and other scientific methods). The result is a strong tendency towards negativity and attack. Negativity is seen to be a powerful way of uncovering the truth, resisting disturbing intrusions and giving a personal sense of satisfaction to the attacker.

The most powerful case for the value of argument as a thinking method is that it encourages the motivated exploration of a subject. Without the personal gratification of argument (win/lose, aggression, cleverness, point-scoring) there might be little motivation to explore a subject. There is merit in this justification, except that beyond a certain level of motivation the actual exploration of the subject starts to suffer: argument becomes case-making, point-scoring and ego-strutting. No person is going to bring to attention matters which would benefit the opposing side of the argument, even when such matters might greatly extend the exploration of the subject.

In the book I shall return to these matters, in more detail and in different contexts.

*

We can now return to the significance of humour.

Humour is so significant because it is based on a logic very different from our traditional logic. In our traditional (Aristotelian) logic there are categories that are clear, hard-edged and permanent. We make judgement decisions as to whether something fits into a category, does not fit into the category or cannot fit into the category (contradiction). In contrast, the logic of humour depends directly upon patterns, flow, expectations and context.

In our traditional thinking we have what I call 'rock logic'. In humour we have what I call 'water logic'. A rock has a shape of its own. It is hard, hard-edged, permanent and unchanging. We can see and feel its shape. We can say that a rock 'is'. It is not going to let us down and change into something else. There is the sense of an independent absolute. Water is very different from rock, but just as real. It flows. The emphasis is on 'to' rather than 'is'. Water flows according to the gradient (context). It takes the form of the vessel in which it is placed (circumstance).

You can analyse and describe a pen in terms of its component parts: metals, hard plastic, soft plastic, pieces of differing shapes. You can describe the mechanism by which the pen works and its function as a writing instrument. But what is the 'value' of a pen? That depends on circumstance and a perception of circumstance. If a person cannot write, it has little value. If a person can write, it has more value. If the person has no other pen or writing instrument, it has yet more value. If a person has to write down an important telephone number or an urgently needed medical prescription, it has even more value – not just to the writer but also to other people. The pen may have value as a gift. It may have a high historic value (even to someone who cannot write) if it has been used to sign a historic treaty.

If you add one rock to another, you get two rocks. But if you add water to water you do not get two waters. Poetry is based on water logic. In poetry we add layer after layer of words, images, metaphors and other vehicles for perception. It all builds up into one holistic perception.

You can empty water out of a glass a few drops at a time if you wish. With a rock you do not have the choice – the rock is either in the glass or all gone. In our legal system we make a sharp distinction between 'guilty' and 'innocent'. If guilty there is punishment to follow. In Japan half the arrested offenders are released by the prosecutor, who has power to let them go if they apologize and seem intent on behaving better in the future. The emphasis in the Japanese system is not on a judgement category but on what comes next. The crime rate in Japan is very low. There is one lawyer for 9,000 people compared to one lawyer for 400 in the USA.

Rock logic is the basis of our traditional processing logic, with its permanent categories, identities and contradictions. Water logic is the basis of the logic of perception. Until quite recently we have had no idea how perception works. We are now beginning to understand perception in terms of how the brain works.

*

A horse is different from a car, although both are land transport systems. A bird is different from an aeroplane, although both fly through the air. Tennis is different from chess, although both can be two-person games with a winner and a loser. Soup is different from spaghetti, although both are food and are often eaten at the start of a meal.

In the same way there are two distinct types of information system. There is the traditional 'passive' system in which pieces, symbols or information of any sort are recorded and stored on some surface. The information does not change on the surface. The surface does not change. There is a need for some outside operator who manipulates the information according to some rules. Imagine a chess-player. The pieces sit passively and inertly on the chess-board until the player moves the pieces around according to the rules of chess and with some strategy in mind.

Traditional computers are passive information systems. The information is stored on tapes or discs and then used (according to particular rules and for a particular purpose) by a central processor. A schoolboy doing arithmetic in an exercise book is also an example of a passive information system. In passive systems there is a clear distinction between the passive storage of the information and its manipulation by an outside operator. Our use of language and symbols is based on the behaviour of passive information systems. We use the stored pieces according to the rules of mathematics, grammar and logic.

The other type of system is the 'active' system. There is no outside logical operator. All the activity takes place within the recording surface. The information is active. The surface is active. The information interacts with the surface to form organizations, sequences, patterns, loops etc.

A very simple example of an active (self-organizing) patterning system is given by rain falling onto a virgin landscape. In time the rainwater forms itself into streams, rivulets and rivers. The landscape has been altered. There has been an interaction between the rain and the landscape. There has been activity. Future rainwater will flow along the channels that have been established.

Passive systems record only place or shape on a surface. This place or shape has a meaning because it refers to a pre-defined situation. Active systems record place, time, sequence and context. It is all these things that determine how patterns form and which things link up with which.

Active systems are sometimes called 'self-organizing systems' because they do not rely on an outside 'organizer' but organize themselves. The whole subject of self-organizing systems is rapidly becoming of great importance in thermodynamics, biology, mathematics and economics.

*

In 1968 I wrote a book called *The Mechanism of Mind* (published in 1969 by Jonathan Cape in London and by Simon &

Schuster in New York; it is currently still in print in Penguin Books). It was not much noticed at the time because the time was not yet ready for such ideas.

In the book I described how the nerve networks in the brain behave as a self-organizing system that encourages incoming information to organize itself into a series of stable states that follow one another – the formation of sequences and patterns. I described this pattern-forming behaviour as the natural behaviour of quite simple nerve networks.

Today the principles set out in that book are well accepted. They form the basis of the latest developments in computers: neural net machines and neuro-computers. Various models and computer simulations of this type of system have subsequently been proposed, for example by Gerald Edelman (1977) and John Hopfield (California Institute of Technology). I would not claim that these later developments were based on the concepts I expressed in 1969, because other people were also working on the behaviour of nerve networks. What I do claim is that ideas and concepts which seemed strange, crazy and irrelevant at that time are now mainstream thinking. There are now branches of mathematics dealing with the behaviour of such systems. As a matter of interest the model I proposed in 1969 was simulated on computer by M. H. Lee and colleagues and behaved as predicted.* This is important because conceptual models sometimes fail to operate as predicted.

*

When you get dressed every morning you have a number of pieces of clothing to put on. If you are wearing eleven items of clothing there are theoretically over thirty-nine million different possible sequences of which about five thousand are practical (for example you could not put on your shoes before putting on your socks). Even then you would need to choose among the five thousand in order actually to get dressed.

* M. H. Lee and A. R. Marudarajan, *International Journal of Man-Machine Studies* (1982), vol. 17, pp. 189–210.

The mathematics that give such a huge range of choices are simple and will be mentioned later. The point is that if our brains were to work like traditional computers it would take us about two days to get dressed, a week to make breakfast and a week to get to work. You would have to figure out how to hold a glass each time you picked one up, how to fill it and how to drink from it.

But we get dressed in normal time and drink normally from a glass because the brain behaves as a self-organizing system that sets up routine patterns. Once the patterns are established we just use them. We should be immensely grateful for such patterning behaviour because without it life would be utterly impossible.

Does it really matter that we should understand the way the brain actually works? Does it really matter that we should understand the type of information system that is involved?

It does matter. Philosophy and psychology have always suffered from descriptions chasing descriptions in a complex dance to the music of words. A description matches only what it describes. In order to move forward we do need to understand the underlying mechanisms. There is no mechanism more basic than the operation of the nerve networks in the brain. Once we can understand these mechanisms, we are freed from endless description. We can build on this understanding to devise new thinking tools (as in the processes of lateral thinking). We can recognize the faults and bad tendencies in the system and see how these are encouraged by some of our traditional thinking habits. We can begin to see a need for new thinking habits.

In this book I shall be looking, in some detail, into how the brain comes to form and use patterns. I shall be looking at how this patterning behaviour is the basis of perception and at how it gives rise to such aspects of perception as recognition, discrimination, polarization, centring, humour, insight, creativity, and the benefits and problems of language.

I shall be exploring how the mechanism of mind actually

affects our thinking. Most people working in these areas have been interested in designing computers that might think like the human brain – to produce artificial intelligence. My own interest has been to consider the behaviour of these types of system in order to detect their faults and to be able to make better use of them. I would like to build on the strengths of the system and to minimize its weaknesses. I would like to design better 'software' for the brain.

Our traditional thinking systems are based on language rather than on how the brain works. As a result they sometimes tend to encourage the bad points of the system (such as sharp polarizations) and to neglect the strong points (creativity and perception changes).

*

The patterns formed in the brain are not symmetric. This is a crucial point for the understanding of brain mechanisms. But what does it mean?

In driving to a new restaurant you go along the road with which you are most familiar. The journey may be quite long. After dinner one of the friends with whom you have been dining points out that there is a much more direct route home. You take this route and suddenly realize that you could have saved a lot of time by taking this route in the first place. So the route you take to the restaurant is not the same as the route you take back. If the pattern sequence from A to B is not the same as the sequence from B to A, the patterns are not symmetric.

If the brain as consciousness flows along the main highway patterns, we are not even aware of the potential side-tracks, because these have been temporarily suppressed by the dominant track (this is the simple and natural behaviour of a nerve network, as I shall describe). If 'somehow' we can manage to get across from the main track to the side-track, the route back to the starting-point is very obvious. This moving sideways across tracks is the origin of the term 'lateral' thinking (cutting across patterns instead of moving up and down them). The 'somehow' with which we might cut across patterns is the essence of humour and is provided in deliberate creative thinking by the actual techniques of lateral thinking, such as provocation.

The significance of humour is precisely that it indicates pattern-forming, pattern asymmetry and pattern-switching. None of this can occur in a passive information system. That is why traditional philosophers, psychologists and information scientists have had to ignore humour – humour cannot occur in passive information systems. Creativity and lateral thinking have exactly the same basis as humour.

The sequence of our personal experience (historic and at the moment), the words and concepts provided by culture, the context provided by the immediate environment, determine the main highway pattern. If 'somehow' we can get across to a side-track we then find a creative idea that is perfectly logical – after we have found it. This is the basis of insight and the result of deliberate lateral thinking. Now we come to the crucial point which explains why we have never been able to take creative thinking seriously.

Every valuable creative idea (concepts and perceptions, not artistic expression) must always be logical in hindsight. If it was not, we could never recognize the value of that idea. It could only seem a 'crazy idea'. We might catch up with it in twenty years time – or never, for it might truly be a crazy idea.

When I first wrote about lateral thinking many people thought it crazy because it was contrary, at some points, to our usual thinking. Today lateral thinking is seen to make sense – and to be mathematically necessary in self-organizing systems. Unfortunately, because all valuable creative ideas must always be logical in hindsight if we are to accept them, we have supposed that better logic would have reached the idea in the first place and that there is therefore no need for creative thinking. This apparently 'logical' line of thought is why we have never paid serious attention to creative thinking.

It is only today that we know that an idea which is obvious in hindsight may be invisible in foresight, in a patterning system. In order to understand this point it is necessary to understand – even superficially – the nature of patterning systems. Since the huge majority of our thinkers, today and historically, have considered only passive information systems, they cannot see this point. In this traditional system there is no place, no need and no mechanism for creative thinking. In patterning systems there is an absolute need, a place and mechanisms for creative thinking.

That is one example – and a very important one – of how our failure to understand the information system of the brain can seriously limit our thinking. That is why we have been so poor at the creative thinking that is so needed to solve those problems that will not yield to analysis.

How might we actually skip laterally across to the side-track to give us a creative insight? We can wait for insight, intuition, accident, mistake, chance or someone's crazy idea. These have been traditional sources of new ideas – and they do work from time to time. We can also devise and then use methods that are more deliberate and systematic. For example we can use 'provocation', signalled by the new word 'po', which I suggested to indicate a deliberate provocation. Such a signal is required because otherwise such a statement as 'cars should have square wheels' will seem utter rubbish or madness. A provocation is a statement that lies outside our normal experience patterns. So we are forced to leave those patterns. We can then move on from the provocation to a new pattern and so create a new idea. So the provocation of 'po cars have square wheels' led many years ago to the concept of suspension which adjusted to the bumpiness of the ground so that cars would 'flow' over the ground instead of bump over it. This concept is now being put into practice.

These are the sort of deliberate techniques that were used by Peter Ueberroth, who made such a success of the 1984 Olympic Games in Los Angeles through the introduction of new concepts. At that time there was a risk that the Olympic movement would come to an end, since no city wanted the huge financial losses that had occurred with previous Olympic Games. As a result of Mr Ueberroth's creativity (and leadership) many cities today compete to get the Games. Mr Ueberroth had learned the techniques of lateral thinking at a talk I had been asked to give to the Young Presidents Organisation, nine years before (in Boca Raton, Florida). This story was told by Peter Ueberroth in the *Washington Post* (30 September 1984).

There are other techniques of lateral thinking, such as the 'random entry' technique. This would be total nonsense in a passive information system but is perfectly logical and mathematically sensible in a self-organizing system.

*

What else can we learn from the behaviour of active information systems that create and use patterns?

Drop a steel ball on the beach and it will embed itself in the sand directly under the point at which you released it. Drop the same ball into the wide end of a funnel. No matter where you release it (within the radius of the funnel), it will always come out of the funnel at exactly the same place. Water falling anywhere in the wide catchment area of a river will end up in that river. Patterns in a self-organizing system behave in the same way. They have a wide catchment area. This means that many unstable patterns will all lead to the main stable pattern. This catchment behaviour is what we call 'centring'.

Centring is a most useful property of perception because it means that we can recognize things and situations even when they are not exactly in the form that we know them. We can recognize a dinner plate from any angle even when a photograph would show it to be oval from that angle.

Language is based on this centring and catchment property of patterns. While this is most useful in general, there are some problems. We can perceive things only through established patterns. English is probably the world's richest language because there is such an abundance of words and nuances. It is excellent for description, but very poor for perception. (This may surprise – and even upset – those who treasure the sufficiency and variety of the language.) In English there are not many gradations in use between 'friend' and 'enemy' and between 'like' and 'dislike'.

There are many ways we can describe in-between gradations but that is description after the event. An Innuit language in Northern Canada might have twenty gradations between 'friend' and 'enemy'. There is even one word to convey: 'I like you very much but I would not want to go seal hunting with you.' Such a word allows the observer to perceive another person in that way.

The mind can see only what it is prepared to see. The brain has to use existing patterns and catchments. When we believe that we are analysing data we are really only trying out our stock of existing ideas to see which one might fit. It is true that if our stock of possible ideas is rich then our analysis will be adequate.

But the analysis of data will not by itself produce new ideas. This is a rather important point, because the whole basis of science and progress is based on the belief that the analysis of data will produce all the ideas we need in order to move forward. In fact, the creator of new ideas must do a lot of 'idea work' in his or her mind and then check out these ideas against the data. Just analysing the data is not enough.

*

To learn to play tennis, to execute a new dance routine, to handle a sailboat, usually requires a lot of repetition and practice. We know from experience that learning takes time and repetition.

How many times do you have to hold your finger in a flame in order to learn not to do it? Just once. How can the learning be so very quick? The finger in the flame may be the simplest example of a 'belief' system. A belief system is a way of perceiving the world that prevents us from testing the validity of the belief. Belief systems create perceptions that reinforce the belief system. They can be so powerful that people are prepared to give up life itself for their beliefs.

The mind has to form belief systems because without them it could never connect up all its different experiences. They are practical and necessary. The nerve networks in the brain very easily set up the circularities that probably form the basis of our belief systems. This 'connecting' function of the brain arises directly from the way the nerves are wired up and allows us to believe in cause and effect and other relationships (as Kant supposed).

How true are belief systems? What does truth mean in perception, in belief and in logic? Outside the particular game of mathematics is 'truth' itself a belief system? No doubt some truths are indeed true. Others are usable as 'true'. Maybe the social value of truth is as a destination – so long as we do not assume we have arrived there. These are some of the things that I set out to examine in more detail in this book.

*

What will happen if we prefer not to have a New Renaissance but to continue to be satisfied with our traditional thinking habits?

All our current problems might just fade away and the world will become a better place. Why? Because this might be the cycle of destiny or development.

We might become much more adept at dealing with the problems with our existing thinking skills. Why? Because we become more experienced and more information becomes available.

Changes in values may be sufficient to drive our existing thinking skills to solve all problems. Why? Because the defect is not in our thinking skills but in our value frames.

We might be satisfied with the above possibilities or we might not.

Perhaps we ought to assess the adequacy of our existing methods for making progress. These methods include: the concept of intelligent behaviour; the concept of evolution; the to and fro of political argument; the analysis of problems; the analysis of data to produce new ideas; lessons from history; and fundamental shifts in value. We might summarize our existing methods as: 'the intelligent operation of traditional logic on existing information within a values frame'.

I believe these methods to be inadequate. Intelligence is certainly not enough. There are many highly intelligent people who are poor thinkers. For example an intelligent person may use his or her thinking simply to defend a point of view. The more skilled the defence the less does that person ever see a need to explore the subject, listen to others or generate alternatives. This is poor thinking.

The relationship between intelligence and thinking is similar to that between a car and the driver. The horse-power and engineering of the car represents a 'potential'. But the way the car actually performs also depends on the skill of the driver. A powerful car may be driven badly. A more humble car may be driven well.

We put great faith in evolution as a path to progress. This is because we believe that it works well – and also because we are highly suspicious of the opposite of evolution, which is 'design'. We are suspicious of designed ideas and designed futures because we believe that all designs are from a particular point of view. We believe that designs cannot take into account all the relevant factors, do not fit human nature and human needs, and cannot foretell the reaction to the designs. We immediately think of the design of tower blocks. Many of these points are valid. But we do design things: constitutions, legal systems, medicines, cars and carpets.

We prefer to put our trust in evolution. This is because evolution is gradual and allows the pressure of needs, values, reactions and events to mould ideas. It allows the shaping force of criticism. Bad ideas will die. Good ideas will survive and become even better. We really like the method of evolution because it fits our traditional thinking habits. Change has its own energy and we can modify and control this by the use of our critical faculties because criticism is the basis of our thinking tradition. Evolution is also collective and seems democratic, whereas design always seems autocratic.

In spite of all these excellent reasons for preferring and trusting evolution, there is a serious flaw in the evolutionary process.

Suppose you were handed some geometrically shaped wooden blocks (square, rectangle, triangle etc.) one at a time and instructed to try to arrange the blocks to give a larger geometric shape with every addition. As you are given the next piece you build on what you have, if this is possible. Where you are at the moment determines what you do next. Only if it is completely impossible to build on what you have do you separate out all the pieces to start again. The point will come when the arrangement you get by building on what you have is barely adequate. At this point you should really go back and separate out all the pieces in order to make the best possible use of them, without regard to the sequence in which they were handed to you.

The flaw in evolution is that the sequence of development will determine the ideas and structures we can use. If the line of development is adequate we proceed along that line. Only if it is disastrous do we go back and think again. So the ideas and structures we use may be far short of what can be done with available knowledge. Evolution is by no means an efficient mechanism (because of the dependence on sequence). At best it is just adequate.

In a sense language is a museum of ignorance. Every word and concept has entered language at a stage of relative ignorance compared to our present greater experience. But the words and concepts are frozen into permanence by language and we must use these words and concepts to deal with present-day reality. This means we may be forced to look at things in a very inadequate way.

The word 'design' should be a very important word because it covers all aspects of putting things together to achieve an effect. In fact language usage has made it into a word with a restricted meaning. We think of design only in terms of graphics, engineering and architecture. To many people it simply means visual appearance, as in fashion.

Language by itself could never evolve the word 'po' because this does not lie along a line of evolution. But 'po' is needed, both mathematically and socially. When I was teaching at School 57 in

Moscow, one of the students said that young people had a real
need for 'po', otherwise they could see things only as they were,
not as they could be.

If evolution is not enough, should we then have revolution?
This is the usual answer to a required change that is so radical
that evolution will not bring it about. In most societies the usual
style of revolution no longer makes sense. Revolutions are dangerous, wasteful and highly disruptive. In the end the revolution
may simply replace the group of people who are running the
system, without much change in the system.

We almost need a new term – 'provolution' – to imply change
that is more radical than evolution but more gradual than revolution. It is change of this sort that I intended in my book *Positive
Revolution for Brazil*. The weapons are not bullets but perceptions
and values. The steps are small but cumulative. There is a steady
working towards making something better, not towards destruction of an enemy. It is based on water logic not rock logic.

The media, art and culture may be powerful mechanisms for
changing values. Not too long ago non-smokers had almost to
apologize for not smoking. Today it is the smokers who are in
retreat and apologizing. The growing concern for the environment
and ecological values show how cumulative and powerful expressed opinion and pressure groups can be in changing social values.
Politicians go along with the mood because otherwise votes
might be lost. In some societies the position of women and
minorities have been changed by the same mechanisms.

We must also remember that sometimes value changes can be
harmful. Apparent value changes gave power and cohesion to
Nazi Germany. The encouragement of hostility and warlike values
has been responsible for much aggression. Prejudice and persecu-
tion have also arisen in the past from encouraged values.

General goodwill and mounting pressure of value changes do
make a significant contribution to progress. The 'slow growth'
movement in California, even if it is sometimes based on selfish
motives ('not in my back yard'), may lead to re-consideration of
urban growth for the sake of growth.

No matter how powerful the value changes there is always a need for new concepts in order to put the value changes into effect. Sometimes it is enough just to be against something. Pressure groups can be powerful in bringing something to an end. But in many cases there is also a need for constructive ideas. If you cannot transport oil because of the danger of pollution, what do you do? If you do not want more people to move to big cities, what do you do?

To some extent pressure groups partake of our traditional confrontational thinking habits. It is enough to be against something – let the other side figure out what to do. This places far too much confidence in the constructive abilities of the 'other side'.

*

The to-and-fro of political argument has little constructive or creative force. This is because argument was never intended to be creative or constructive. Argument is meant to reveal the truth, not to create it. Argument can oppose a bad idea and can modify, and thereby improve, a good idea. But it does not design new ideas any more than garden shears grow a garden. Politicians, however, do not have to be creative. For ideas they listen to their advisers and analysts.

We are good at analysis. All institutes of education – especially at the highest level (the Harvard Business School, the Grandes Écoles in France) – put almost all the intellectual emphasis on analysis. Surely if you correctly analyse a situation or problem you will know what to do about it? This is obviously true and yet, at the same time, it has been a major fallacy of Western thinking.

Should you analyse your discomfort and discover that it is due to sitting on a pin, you remove the pin and all is well. Find the cause and remove it. Some problems are of this type. Some illness is due to a bacterial invasion: kill the bacteria and effect a cure.

In many problems we cannot find the cause. Or, we can find it but cannot remove it – for example human greed. Or, there may be a multiplicity of causes. What do we do then? We analyse it further and analyse the analysis of others (scholarship). More and more analysis is not going to help, because what is needed is design. We need to design a way out of the problem or a way of living with it.

We are much better at analysis than at design because we have never put enough emphasis on design. In education we have felt that design was necessary in architecture, engineering, graphics, theatre and fashion but not in other areas because analysis would reveal the truth, and if you have the truth action is easy. For design we need constructive and creative thinking and to be conscious of perceptions, of values and of people. It is this traditional emphasis (part of our thinking heritage) on analysis rather than design which makes some problems (like drug abuse) so difficult to tackle.

We have always depended on analysis not only to solve problems but also for our source of new ideas. Most people in education, science, business and economics still believe that the analysis of data will give us all the new ideas that we need. Unfortunately, this is not so. The mind can see only what it is prepared to see. That is why after a breakthrough in science we look back and find that all the needed evidence was available a long time before but could be seen only through the old idea (Kuhn's paradigm shift). There is a desperate need for the sort of 'idea work' or conceptual effort that Einstein provided in his field and Keynes in his. We know this is important, but we are content to let it happen by chance or genius because our traditions of thinking hold that analysis is enough.

*

What about lessons from history as a contribution towards change? Our thinking culture puts a great deal of emphasis on the study of history, deeming it to be the true laboratory of human behaviour and system interaction.

At the time of the last Renaissance, the thinkers of society could move forward very much faster by looking backwards than by looking forwards. This was a highly unusual state of affairs.

Through looking backwards the thinkers discovered the stored wisdom and knowledge of Greek, Roman and Arabic thinking. This was excellent in itself and even more excellent when contrasted with the stifled thinking of their own medieval society.

This accumulated wisdom of ages could be unlocked through the exercise of 'scholarship'. So scholarship became a key ingredient of the intellectual tradition when this tradition was being established. Scholarship was perfectly appropriate at the time. Today it is much less appropriate, because we can get more by looking forward than by looking backwards. Scholarship has its value and its place, but it pre-empts too large a slice of intellectual resources and effort.

There is an obsession with history. History is there and increasing in quantity, both because we are learning more about it and because we create it every day. We can get the 'teeth' of our minds into it. History is attractive because it is always possible to find a niche and there is always a reward for effort – in contrast to many subjects in which years of endeavour may produce nothing. It is attractive to minds with a preference for analysis over design (only in Russia can history be re-designed). It may also, sometimes, be a refuge for minds that would not achieve much elsewhere.

History does have an important part to play. But Western thinking traditions, established by the last Renaissance, are far too obsessed by history. About twenty times as much emphasis is put on history as on design. Yet design thinking is at least as important as history. History is easy to write about. That is why the literary culture sometimes seems to be a culture of corpses, with the bulk of attention being given to the dead and to the past.

Education has, historically, always been concerned with knowledge. You learned cultural values from your family and the Church. You learned operating values in a long apprenticeship to your father or master. The purpose of education was to give knowledge to the knowledge users. Knowledge is easy to teach because it can be presented in books. Knowledge is easy to test.

Is knowledge enough? When a student leaves school he or she has to start operating in the future: decisions, choices, alternatives, plans, initiatives. Even if we could have complete knowledge about the past, the use of that knowledge for future action requires 'thinking'. To the knowledge base we must add the thinking skills of doing. It was to describe these skills that I suggested the term 'operacy' many years ago. Operacy involves such things as an examination of the consequences of action, a consideration of relevant factors, the assessment of priorities, attention to other people's interests, a definition of objectives etc. All these things can be taught specifically in schools – for instance in the CoRT thinking programme.* Many countries (the USA, Canada, China, the USSR, Australia, Bulgaria, Malaysia, Venezuela, Singapore etc.) are now using the programme. It is mandatory in all schools in Venezuela and used in the top schools in China. There is rapidly growing use in the USA, and the government of Singapore is planning to introduce it into all schools, having carried out extensive testing. The important point is that the thinking skills of operacy are very different from those of debate and critical thinking. Critical thinking skills are included as one part of the programme – but only as a part.

Knowledge and critical thinking skills are not enough. It is taking most people in education a very long time to realize this. This is partly because education easily becomes a world unto itself – choosing, setting and satisfying its own priorities without too much regard for the outer world.

*

Should we condemn our traditional thinking methods, which were set in place by the last Renaissance? Surely they have served us well in science, in technology, in democracy and in the development of civilization itself?

There is no doubt that our existing thinking culture has taken us very far. It is pointless to speculate that a different thinking culture might have taken us even further – especially in human

---

* CoRT (Cognitive Research Trust) is a sixty-lesson programme published by S.R.A. for the direct teaching of thinking as a school subject.

affairs – because such speculation can never be tested. We can be duly appreciative of our traditional thinking culture and also realize that it is inadequate. It may have been adequate for the period in which it was developed (ancient Greece and medieval Europe), but at that time there were stable societies, agreed perceptions and limited technical change. Today there are problems caused by rapidly accelerating change and the uneven nature of that change. In part these things are caused by the 'cleverness' of our traditional thinking systems and a lack of 'wisdom'.

The inadequacy of our traditional thinking culture may be pinpointed as follows:

We need to shift from a destructive type of thinking to a much more constructive type.

We need to change from argument to genuine exploration of a subject.

We need to lessen the esteem in which we hold critical thinking and to place it below constructive thinking.

We need to match skills of analysis with an equal emphasis on the skills of design.

We need to do as much idea-work as we do information-work. We need to realize that the analysis of data is not enough.

We need to shift from an obsession with history to a concern for the future.

We need to emphasize 'operacy' as much as knowledge. The skills of doing are as important as the skills of knowing.

We need, for the first time, to realize that creative thinking is a serious and essential part of the thinking process.

We need to move from our exclusive concern with the logic of processing to the logic of perception (from rock logic to water logic).

We need to shift from cleverness to wisdom. Perception is the basis of wisdom.

*

Even if our existing thinking culture is limited and inadequate, does that make it dangerous? An inadequate cook is just inadequate. An inadequate car driver is dangerous. There are some dangers that arise directly from the nature of our traditional thinking culture. There are others arising from the complacency and arrogance with which we hold to be adequate a thinking culture that is clearly inadequate.

The direct dangers include crude perceptions, polarizations, misleading effects of language, unnecessary confrontations, righteousness and aggressive beliefs. Many of these things are directly responsible for much of the human misery that man has inflicted on man. It is only fair to say that the same thinking methods may also have protected man from much misery – as with law and medicine.

Perhaps the greatest dangers are those of arrogance, complacency and the ability to defend that arrogance and complacency. An acknowledgement of inadequacy is a prelude to change. A defence of arrogance is a denial of any need to change. If we believe our thinking habits to be perfect – as many people do – we shall never see the need to supplement them with further thinking habits (creative, constructive, design etc.). We can always defend our existing thinking culture because, fundamentally, it is a particular belief system based on concepts of truth and logic. Every belief system sets up a framework of perception within which it cannot be attacked. The arrogance of logic means that if we have a logically impeccable argument then we must be right – 'I am right – you are wrong'.

Yet the value of any conclusion depends on both the validity of the logic and also the validity of the starting perceptions and values. A faulty computer will produce rubbish. A computer working flawlessly will also produce rubbish if the input is rubbish. Every junior student in logic knows this.

Every junior logic student knows that the excellence of logic can never make up for inadequacies of perception. Then we ignore this point. There are three reasons for this. In the stable societies in which the rules of logic were developed it could be assumed that certain axioms or perceptions were common and agreed. For example it was only very much later that the axioms on which Euclid built his geometry were shown to be rather particular and to apply only to plane surfaces. The second reason is that we have supposed that logic itself could be turned round to justify the perceptions – this has been a dangerous and misleading illusion. The third, and perhaps most important, reason is that we have not known how to tackle perception.

An intelligent person can always win an argument by choosing perceptions, values and circumstances to fit the logic.

The greatest danger is perhaps not the arrogance with which we defend our existing thinking system but the complacency with which we hold onto it – because we cannot conceive of anything else. This complacency means that we have channelled so much of our intellectual effort, resources, education and esteem into the existing methods that the more needed habits of thinking do not get a chance. There are no resources left, and many educators have told me that there simply is no time to teach thinking in schools.

We are as locked into our institutions and structures as we are to beliefs. The paradox is that as we move forward into the future there is more need for change than ever, yet there is less room for change because everything is locked into position. We rely so much on the excellence of argument for attack and defence that we fail to see that something may be 'right' but inadequate in a larger framework. For defence, we refuse to see or accept the larger framework. We fail to see that the arguments with which we defend argument lack the constructive and creative aspects of thinking that we need so badly. That is why there is a real need to suggest, propose, announce and work towards a New Renaissance.

*

There are those who have turned away from the rigidities, arguments and word-play of traditional thinking and have turned away from thinking altogether. They have turned to spirituality, emotions, holistic feelings, mysticism, a general goodwill concern for humanity and nature. This inner directedness has always been a valuable ingredient in the development of both individuals and society. Can it be enough?

There are bridges to be designed and built. There are economic systems that need to be made to work. There are health services to be delivered. Are the right attitudes and the right values enough to get such things done? The spirituality of the East is accompanied by a passivity and acceptance that can provide a complete philosophy only if the acceptance also includes those things which some cultures find unacceptable (poverty, ill-health). Furthermore the reliance on goodwill works best in a small community where the majority have the same perceptions and values. Nor should we forget that 'inner feelings', 'truth' and 'rightness' may be no protection from the dangers of 'righteousness'.

Useful as these New Age directions may be, I do not believe that we should abandon the use of that most excellent resource: the human mind and its thinking. Instead we should seek to develop thinking habits that are more constructive and more creative than those we now have. That is why we need not just New Age values but also New Renaissance thinking. Values are not enough. Thinking is not enough. We need perceptions, values and thinking.

*

It is not a case of just being a bit more positive and constructive in our thinking. If that were so, I would not be writing this book. Exhorting people to be more constructive and positive is well worth doing, but others can do this much better than I can. We are dealing with something more fundamental and more serious than exhortation.

If this book seems to be attacking much of the basis of our traditional thinking culture (identity, contradiction, dichotomies, logic, language, argument, data analysis, history etc.), it is because that is what it set out to do. Now that we know so much more about self-organizing information systems, we can indeed start to question the accepted sufficiency and perfection of these traditional habits of thinking. Does this mean that our traditional thinking methods are 'wrong' or 'false'?

I do believe that our traditional thinking methods are based on the wrong model of information system, but a method may have a false foundation and yet be very valuable in practice. Indeed, a method may be totally artificial and be valuable. To categorize something as 'wrong' or 'false' is usually required in our existing thinking culture, but for my purposes it is enough to regard our traditional thinking methods as limited, inadequate and dangerous in some respects.

A saw is a marvellous tool for cutting wood but if you want to put pieces of wood together you may need a hammer and nails, or glue, or screws and a screwdriver. In the same way, analysis has its place but there is also a need for constructive design.

I suspect that we could design a better thinking system than the current one, even to serve those purposes the current system serves quite well. As a simple example, instead of arguing one case against another, both parties could lay out both cases in parallel and then make comparisons. We could also design new operations, new concepts, new words for our existing languages and even totally new languages for thinking (a project I am working on). All that will take time. For the moment we can continue to saw wood with the saw even while we become aware of its limitations.

The central purpose of this book is to signal the start of a New Renaissance, not just in terms of hope, need and attitude, but also in terms of a fundamental re-examination of the thinking culture set up by the last Renaissance. The basis of this re-examination is a consideration of how the brain works as a self-organizing information system.

*

I suspect that the ideas put forward in this book will be received with rage and outrage. Ideas such as these can be expressed only in book form. That is one of the key justifications for the continued existence of books and a justification for reading. But the guardians of culture are language-based. Any book has to pass through this 'literary' gateway. Since much of this book questions the sufficiency of our traditional language-based argument and logic, I do not expect a very objective response. So readers will need to come to their own conclusions.

We have probably reached the stage where progress in philosophy or psychology does require an understanding of the underlying information system and its basis in neuro-physiology. This is something which will be fiercely resisted by those who have an 'arts' background and believe that traditional word-games are sufficient. This is a dilemma that will impede the progress of society. Yet in our concern for the environment, goodwill has to be allied to scientific understanding at some point.

Cyberneticians, mathematicians and information scientists will have much less trouble with the book than those with a 'literary' or 'legalistic' frame of mind. People in business and those involved in doing things (as distinct from describing things) will also see the need for 'operacy' and for constructive and creative thinking. There are also many who have always felt that 'design' is as important as 'analysis'.

It will, of course, be said that if we abandon the decisive 'right' and 'wrong' of traditional thinking, how would society deal with a phenomenon like Hitler? The simple answer is that society would deal with Hitler in the same way as it deals with a mad dog, a runaway truck, a polluting oil spill, or a meningitis epidemic – appropriately. A move away from the simplistic 'right/wrong' framework does not mean that everything is always right any more than it means that everything is always wrong. The extremes of 'always' and 'never' are part of our traditional need for the absolute on which is based our identity/contradiction logic. For example, we have a general precept that trying things out is a good policy in order to broaden experience. Does this mean that you should try jumping out of a twelfth-floor window or try the taste of cyanide?

There are so many areas in which we badly need new ideas. We need new ideas in economics (for example a 'care loop' which intertwines with the 'productive loop'); in politics (for example power that is consumable rather than absolute); in ecology (for example 'ecological tariffs'); in the quality of life; in organizations and behaviour; in the use of technology; in education etc., etc. Our traditional thinking habits are not providing these new ideas. Too many good minds have been limited and sterilized by these habits.

We need a New Renaissance and I believe that it has already begun. I am just putting up one signpost among the many that will eventually be erected. It is up to individuals to ignore a signpost or to look at it.

The New Renaissance will be constructive and creative in its thinking. It will be concerned with perceptions, values and people. There is a basis to the new thinking of the New Renaissance. That is what the book is about.

Edward de Bono
Palazzo Marnisi
Malta

OUR THINKING SYSTEM

Some of the topics that are covered in this book are listed below:

Why humour is the most significant characteristic of the human brain and why humour has always been neglected by classical philosophers.

Why, contrary to our traditional view, the brain may be a very simple mechanism acting in a highly complex way.

The very important difference between our usual 'passive' information systems and 'active' information systems.

Why the very excellence of language for description has made language so crude and inefficient for perception.

Why we are able to see only what we are prepared to see.

Why it may be much easier to learn things backwards rather than forwards.

How patterns have both broad catchment areas and also knife-edge discrimination.

Why the classical thinking traditions of truth and reason that we inherited from the Greeks may have set civilization on the wrong track.

How we became, and remain, so very obsessed with history.

Why I call our traditional reasoning 'table-top' logic.

How we can have been so successful in technical matters and yet made so little progress in human affairs.

Why the analysis of data cannot by itself produce new ideas and is even unlikely to discover the old ideas in the data.

How we can move from the behaviour of a neurone in a neural network to the behaviour of the mind in politics, economics and world conflict.

How we can have a patterning system and yet enjoy free-will.

Why we have completely failed to understand creativity and why something that is logical in hindsight may be inaccessible to logic in foresight.

Why logical argument has never been successful at changing prejudices, beliefs, emotions or perceptions. Why these things can be changed only through perception.

How beliefs are cheap and easy to set up in a self-organizing system and how they provide the only perceptual truth.

How traditional logic has trapped us with the righteousness of its absolutes.

How we can design specific creative tools that can be used deliberately to generate new ideas.

Why there may not be a reason for saying something until after it has been said – the logic of provocation which is mathematically necessary in a patterning system.

How a simple, randomly obtained, word can be so powerful a creative tool.

Why there is an urgent need to create many new words to help our thinking.

Why there is a need for the functions (such as zero-hold) carried by the new word 'po'.

Why the established scientific method and its call for the most 'reasonable' hypothesis is perceptually faulty.

How the Laffer curve (more is better) is such a problem in our traditional thinking.

Why our cherished argument mode sets out to provide motivated exploration of a subject but soon loses the 'exploration'.

Why our underlying model of progress – evolution through muddling along – is bound to be ineffective.

Why philosophy can never again be more than a word-game unless we take into account the system behaviour of the human mind.

Why the false dichotomies we constructed in order to operate the logic principle of contradiction have been so especially disastrous.

Why poetry and humour both illustrate so well the logic of perception, which is different from the logic of reason.

Why we left perception to the realm of art and why art has done such a poor job.

Why truth is best described as a particular constellation of circumstances with a particular outcome.

How we may eventually derive a new ideology from information technology just as Karl Marx derived one from the steam-engine technology of the industrial revolution.

Human Affairs

I want to return to a matter I touched upon earlier. The very excellence of our technological achievements serves to highlight our lack of progress in human affairs. We can communicate instantly with billions of people at once via television and satellites in orbit. We can fly faster than sound. We have the nuclear power to annihilate all civilization (several times over).

I happen to believe that had we not been constrained by some aspects of our thinking system we would have made even more progress. I believe that by now we should have achieved control of ageing, cancer and virus infection; cure for most mental illnesses; unlimited pollution-free energy from nuclear fusion; abundant food supply; much more effective means of transport; and a superb education capacity. I shall discuss later in the book why I feel that our scientific system is not as perfect as it might be and how it has also been held back by our traditional thinking habits. Nevertheless, I am as much in admiration as anyone else of our technical accomplishments to date.

If, however, we look at the area of human affairs we see poverty, wars, racism, prejudice, ecological disasters, violence, crime, terrorism, greed, selfishness and short-term thinking. Our habits of war are the same, only the weapons are more powerful. We spend, worldwide, about £1,000 billion a year on arms. Our habits of government (both democracy and tyranny) were used in the same way by Greek civilization. Much is the same. Why? I shall look first at our traditional excuses:

Basic human nature will not change. Human nature is selfish, greedy and aggressive and will always be so. There is also a claim that the older and basic 'animal' parts of our brain dominate emotional behaviour.

The world has become too complex and we just cannot cope. Ecology, economics, politics are all now a complex of interacting factors all of which affect each other in direct and indirect ways. We just do not have the systems for dealing with such complexity.

We cannot cope with the rate of change brought about by technology. Curing childhood diseases causes population explosions. Industrial development threatens the environment through local pollution and global effects (ozone layers and greenhouse effects).

The rate of progress in the world is uneven. Some countries have stabilized their populations, others are victims of explosive population growth. In some countries (Sweden, Canada, the USA) there is a great concern for ecology. Yet between 27 and 29 million acres of rain forest are destroyed annually and three life forms disappear every day. In some parts of the world there are medieval attitudes towards war.

Our structures are inadequate to cope with the situation. Political thinking by its very nature is short-term and selfish (especially in a democracy).

We have developed beyond the capacity of our brains to cope.

Now all these excuses, except the first one, explain only how recent explosive developments have made matters worse. We then need to ask why things had not got very much better even before these developments took place. Only the first excuse actually answers this question: it is all due to human nature, with its unchangeable aggression and greed. Our only way of changing this has been religion, which has made some very worthwhile changes but also created many of the problems (hatreds, prejudices, wars and persecutions).

There is a further explanation and it is the one I intend to pursue. It was Einstein himself who said that everything had changed except our way of thinking. It is my contention that our failure to make progress in human affairs is due to our traditional thinking habits. This failure can be seen in two ways. The first way is an inadequacy in dealing with human affairs. The second way is the actual creation or exacerbation of problems and conflicts in human affairs. So on the one hand there is inadequacy and on the other a directly harmful effect.

Experience has shown that reason and logic can never change perceptions, emotions, prejudices and beliefs. Yet we continue in the pious hope that if everyone would 'see reason' the world would be so much better. As we shall see later, there are very good reasons why logic will never affect emotions and beliefs. The only way to do this is through perception. But we have totally failed to develop an understanding of perception.

Our logic system carried through into language (and particularly the false dichotomies necessary in order to operate the principle of contradiction) have created and crystallized perceptions that are crude and polarized – of the 'right/wrong' and 'us/them' type. Logic cannot change beliefs and prejudices but can be used to reinforce them and solidify the perceptions.

Because we have never understood patterning systems we have not been able to understand the strong 'truth' of belief systems and how perception has no other truth. We have obsessively concerned ourselves with critical thinking and argument as our instruments of change. They are virtually useless for change because they lack a truly creative element. We have not begun to understand creativity and paradigm changes.

We can get men to the moon with astonishing mathematical precision but we cannot predict tomorrow's weather. This is because we have mainly been successful with static systems in which the variables do not change and do not interact (space is a perfect example of this).

Now all the faults I have listed above arise directly from our traditional thinking habits of logic, reason, truth, language, identity, contradiction, categories, etc. Exactly how these faults arise I shall explain in the book. I shall also show that if we move forward, not from a constructed language system (Greek heritage), but from the actual way the brain works as a self-organizing patterning system, we can get a very different perspective.

Perception

For twenty-four centuries we have put all our intellectual effort into the logic of reason rather than the logic of perception. Yet in the conduct of human affairs perception is far more important. Why have we made this mistake?

We might have believed that perceptions did not really matter and could in the end be controlled by logic and reason. We did not like the vagueness, subjectivity and variability of perception and sought refuge in the solid absolutes of truth and logic. To some extent the Greeks created logic to make sense of perception. We were content to leave perception to the world of art (drama, poetry, painting, music, dance) while reason got on with its own business in science, mathematics, economics and government. We have never understood perception.

All these reasons are valid, but the last one is the most important. Perception does have its own logic. This logic is based directly on the behaviour of self-organizing patterning systems totally different from the table-top logic of traditional reason and language. Perceptual truth is different from constructed truth.

Never before in history have we been in a position to understand the system and neurological basis for perception. Never before in history could we understand the logic of perception. That is why we have had no choice but to neglect perception.

Whenever we have had to confront perception we have sought refuge in the certainties of classical logic. That is why a book such as *The Closing of the American Mind* is so old-fashioned and retrogressive. It seeks to advocate a return to those very habits of thinking that wrecked civilization, rather than face the complexity of perception. A language-based philosopher has no choice, because the understanding of perception involves the understanding of self-organizing systems.

Because we have not understood perception we have allowed the crudities of language to distort and then fix our distorted view of the world. The very excellence of language as a descriptive medium has made it crude as a device for perception. Because we can describe complex situations we have not needed to enrich our patterns of perception. The false dichotomies and fake certainties of language do not help either.

Our category habit which is the basis of language logic automatically flavours perception. All 'criminals' are seen first as criminal.

We have left perception to the world of art. Has art done a good job? Changes of mass sentiment have certainly come about through art, as have revolutions. At its best art is dogmatic, eccentric and propagandist. It presents perceptions – which may be new and valuable – but has never presented the tools for changing perceptions. It can continue on its course with its valuable contributions to culture, but let us not pretend that it fulfils the perceptual role. We need to learn the logic of perception and tools for broadening and changing perception. Being on the receiving end of perceptual propaganda, no matter how worthy, is not enough.

In time computers will come to do all the logic and processing that we need. This will put more demands than ever on our perceptual skills. What we feed into the computer depends entirely on our perceptual choices and craftsmanship. No matter how brilliant the computer, the result can never be better than our perceptual input. The worth of any econometric model depends on what it includes, the linkages and the parameters. These are a matter of perception backed up by measurement once the perception has been made.

If we do develop really intelligent computers we shall be in grave danger unless we develop our perceptual skills to a much greater extent. That computer will give us dangerously logical answers based on our faulty perceptions.

Humour

Humour is by far the most significant phenomenon in the human mind. Why then has it been so utterly neglected by classical philosophers, psychologists and information theorists – not to mention logicians?

In system terms reason is a cheap commodity. Reasoning can be obtained with boxes, cog-wheels and simple linear computers. Any sorting system run backwards is a simple reasoning system. Humour, however, can happen only with the asymmetric patterns created in a self-organizing patterning system. So humour is significant because it tells us a great deal about the information system acting in the brain. Even in behavioural terms humour tells us to beware of absolute dogmatism because suddenly something can be looked at in a new way.

So classical philosophers, psychologists and information theorists have not been able to look at or understand humour because they have been dealing in what are called 'passive' information systems (essentially, table-top symbol manipulation according to rules). Humour occurs in 'active' information systems (self-organizing). I shall be discussing the key difference between the two broad classes of information system.

Poetry is also a 'logical' process and partakes of the logic of perception but cannot be fitted into traditional logic. The 'water logic' of perception is indeed different from the classic 'rock logic'.

Practical Outcomes

There is an apocryphal story about an American ambassador who had a race with a Russian ambassador. The American ambassador won. The race was reported in the local press to the effect that there had been a race and the Russian ambassador had come second and the American ambassador had come just one before the last person in the race. There was no mention that this was a two-person race.

In that absurd story the details of the report of the race are true, but something important has been left out. Of course this sort of thing would not happen with a serious newspaper – but it does. The *Independent* regards itself as one of London's most serious newspapers. In a review of one of my books there was a comment that I was claiming creative credit for the 1984 Olympic Games on the basis that the organizer, Peter Ueberroth, had once attended a seminar of mine. This seems preposterous. What had been left out was the fact that in an interview in the *Washington Post* (30 September 1984) Mr Ueberroth had himself attributed the new concepts needed to make a success of the Olympic Games to his deliberate use of 'lateral thinking'. In that interview he goes into some detail about the specific techniques which he had first learned from me in 1975. The direct Ueberroth attribution in that interview was mentioned in the book but deliberately ignored by the reviewer, who presumably wished to make the claim seem preposterous. Surprisingly this deliberate omission and distortion was defended by the editor of the *Independent*.

There can be no truth in the media and in this respect the media are a good model for perception. There is no truth in perception. It is always from a point of view. It is never complete.

Understanding perception has a very high practical value because it covers most of our thinking outside technical areas. The above comment on the media is one example. We should never expect the media to be objective because perception does not work that way.

The only truth in perception is the 'truth' of belief systems. As we shall see, beliefs arise very easily from the circularity phenomenon in the underlying system. As we understand how beliefs arise and how they are sustained we can see why logical arguments will not touch beliefs, but how changes in perception are the only way to alter beliefs, prejudices and faulty perceptions. This is of great practical value, since various belief systems are a major component of human affairs. We shall also see why we should value belief systems.

We shall also look at the severe limitations of language as a perceptual and as a thinking system. This also has a high practical importance because language is our major instrument of communication and thinking. When we understand why we have created artificial dichotomies (us/them, right/wrong, innocent/ guilty) and how powerful they are in perception through the knife-edge effect, we can try to remedy the matter.

There is a need for many new words in language in order to allow us a richer perception. Once we understand that the adequacy of hindsight description with language is not the same as initial perception, then we might reduce our strong resistance to creating new words. That can have a very high practical value.

Our understanding of the symmetry of patterns will allow us, for the first time in history, to understand the phenomena of humour, of insight and of creativity. Through understanding the logical necessity of provocation (to cut across patterns) we can devise specific creative thinking tools.

Understanding perception and the nature of hypotheses will explain why we can only see what we are prepared to see. This in turn will show why the analysis of data as such is unlikely to produce new ideas – unless they are half there already. It will also show why the single most 'reasonable' hypothesis as the basis of the scientific method is inadequate. Again these are highly practical matters.

Critical thinking and argument have been our basic attempt at progress in the classical thinking system and permeate society (law, politics, science, etc.). Critical thinking and argument are based on the notion of 'getting to the truth'. There is a total lack of the design and constructive element needed for progress. The needs of today are different from the needs of Greek discourse or medieval theology. An appreciation of the weakness of critical thinking and argument as instruments for progress is also of high practical value.

We shall see that art has a value in offering new perceptions, insights and more detailed perceptions. But these are offered with great certainty. Art does not equip people with the tools to form and alter their own perceptions. Art is not a course in cooking but the presentation of excellent dishes. We cannot assume that perception is safely left to the 'art world'.

In all these matters we are looking at the very fabrics of civilization as we know it: belief, truth, reason, argument, science, art, etc. In all these areas a better understanding of perception has a direct impact. Until now we have had no base on which to build this understanding. Now, our developing understanding of self-organizing systems provides just such a base.

THE HUMAN BRAIN

. . . if only we could understand the human brain.

. . . it will be a long time before we can understand the brain.

. . . when we do understand how our minds work then everything will become clear.

One day I was having lunch at a little restaurant high up on the Col de Frêne, near Annecy in France, and looked out across the valley at the beginning of the Alps. I noticed a hawk circling overhead. For twenty minutes the hawk glided without once flapping its wings. The hawk knew the system perfectly and moved from one thermal up-draught to another. Human para-gliders descended to the valley floor in just two minutes. Knowing the system makes a difference.

Suppose that one day we did understand how the brain worked, what would we do?

1. We would immediately set out to design computers that worked like the brain.

2. We would seek to manipulate the brain for specific purposes.

3. We would examine the relevance of our existing 'software' for the system and try to design better software.

Well, we do, right now, know how the brain works. This claim will be resisted by those who hold a dogmatic ignorance ('The brain is so important that we shall never understand it') and by those who are obsessed by complexity. The latter believe that only a very complex system can achieve the complex behaviour of the brain. This was the stance of early workers in artificial intelligence. There are others who have always believed that certain types of very simple system can operate in a highly complex way. Mathematicians now know full well that in chaos theory a very simple expression will create immense complexity.

The claim will also be resisted by specialists who feel that unless we know the exact connections of every neurone and the nature and distribution of every chemical neuro-transmitter, we cannot claim to know how the brain works.

The claim will be accepted by those who know that understanding of a broad class of system (never mind the detail) will allow us to say very useful things about the behaviour of the system. We are most definitely at the stage of realizing that the brain belongs to the broad class of self-organizing systems. Once we understand this we can go on, in some detail, to examine the behaviour of such systems and to build forward from that behaviour. Details will be filled in later. Such understanding of the nature of the system is even more important when we realize that the system is very different from our traditional view of the brain (as a sort of telephone exchange with an operator at the switchboard).

We can no longer afford to be held back by dogmatic ignorance. So if we do understand the way the brain works, what are we doing about it? We are indeed designing computers that work like the brain. These are the neuro-computers that are already in action. We shall seek to manipulate the brain with more and more skilled propaganda, as in political packaging.

When I wrote *The Mechanism of Mind* in 1968 I did not set out to build a computer with these features. Others have taken that line. My own interest is in the software (thinking system) side. Can we devise better software for the brain? How good is our existing software?

The software area is that of 'perception', which is the most important part of thinking but it is not touched by our existing thinking habits of logic. So, as I mentioned earlier, I devised practical methods of teaching thinking that are now in use around the world with millions of students.

Our traditional view of the brain has made creativity a mystery and completely impossible to understand. Every valuable creative idea must be logical in hindsight (otherwise we could not appreciate the idea), so we have assumed that better logic should have reached the idea in the first place. An understanding of the brain as a self-organizing patterning system with pattern asymmetries (as I shall explain later) provides the logical basis for provocation, random entry and the other deliberate tools of lateral thinking which are used for cutting across patterns.

We need to know what practical effects might come from understanding the brain system. We can show why our existing thinking habits are inadequate and dangerous. We can suggest some practical new software. These are precisely the matters I intend to cover in this book. I shall be looking at such areas as truth, logic, reason, language and above all perception.

Can we really move forward step by step from the behaviour of a neurone in a network to understand – and improve – our thinking behaviour in such great matters as politics, economics, world conflict and belief systems?

We can, and that is the exact purpose of this book.

Validity of the Model

How can we be absolutely sure that the explanation of the way the brain works put forward in this book is the right one? The answer to this question is in ten parts.

1. The purpose of science is to put forward concept models of how the world works. Science can never 'prove' anything. Newton's view of the mechanics of the universe seemed perfect until Einstein came along. Very soon Einstein's views will be changed. Sometimes a concept model is updated, sometimes different models are shown to apply over different ranges of effect, sometimes the model has to be changed completely.

Here, I am putting forward a model of a self-organizing neurone-based information system. That is the concept model. It seems clear that our understanding of the brain is not going to arise from measuring what each individual cell in the brain does. This sort of measurement will not give us an idea of how the brain is 'organized' to work. Examining the design of railcars and the metallurgy of the rails will not give us an organizational concept of how a railway works. We need a function concept which shows how the interactive behaviour of neurones gives rise to a whole variety of mental activity: humour, insight, perceptions, emotions, etc.

As I have said, dogmatic ignorance has no place in science: 'The brain is far too complex to understand, therefore we can never understand it.'

2. Essentially we are concerned with a very broad class of self-organizing systems, as compared with passive systems (traditional computers). Within this broad class of system there may

be other models. The details will almost certainly vary. For example where I suggest a nerve connection there may be a chemical connection.

The trick in science is to make the class of system as broad as possible and yet be able to predict definite types of behaviour. The simple contrast between passive information systems and self-organizing ones provides plenty of differences in behaviour.

There are those who say that the brain stores information like a hologram. Maybe it does, but this description does not say how the brain moves from one state to another to give us thinking. The hologram concept, like many others, is functionally compatible with the model used here.

3. Our model is of a very simple system that is capable of behaving in a highly complex way. This is immediately more satisfying than a highly complex system, because biology tends to work through simple systems with complex behaviour (the encoding of the genes is simply a string of different proteins). Most important of all, the behaviour of the system that gives rise to such phenomena as pattern-making, insight and humour arises directly from the natural behaviour of the system. The system could not behave in any other way. This is quite a different matter from saying: 'Now let us program humour into this model.'

Descriptive models which simply say 'it happens' or 'some mechanism connects up this process' have very little value. They are like a child's drawing showing a box and the label 'it all happens in here'.

4. Our basic model has indeed been simulated on computer and does behave largely as predicted. This is important, because sometimes complex models can 'freeze' or 'blow up' when run in practice. Most important of all, the great amount of work that has now been done on neuro-computers or neural net machines (since I published the book *The Mechanism of Mind* in 1969) shows that such systems do work and do learn very fast. Although not yet in commercial production, such machines are up and running every day. So it is clear enough that this type of information

system does work and is powerful. In a sense this is proof of design. The neuro-computers are designed to work as we think the brain works and by their success they show that this type of system does really work.

5. Our self-organizing system is fully compatible with what we know about neurones and about nerve networks. Advances in neurology will fill in the details. For example the discovery of the effect of the enzyme 'calpain' in providing the 'connectedness' of association came after the prediction of some mechanism to carry out this function. Neurology may eventually show that there are several brains or layers of brain working independently and in parallel with some way of co-ordinating the output. Neurology may show a very powerful effect of both neuro-transmitter and background chemicals. Nevertheless the organizational 'type' of system will not be changed by these discoveries.

6. The effects predicted by the model (such as humour, insight, creativity, effect of emotion on perception) fit in with our normal experience. There is nothing that is contrary to empirical experience, although there may be much that is contrary to our traditional view of the brain as a telephone switchboard.

7. Darwin's concept model of evolution has never been proved and probably can never be proved. We accept and use the model because it is plausible, because it explains phenomena in a more or less feasible way, and because we have no better model. All these factors apply to our self-organizing model. It has as much functional validity as Darwin's theory of evolution. It is up to anyone to put forward a better model that also builds forward from the simple behaviour of neurones. In fact the model is probably a good deal stronger than Darwin's because Darwin's theory of change through random mutation is very weak.

8. The most important aspect of any concept model is that it should produce practical outcomes. The model put forward here has produced an understanding of the process of creativity in concept changes. From this has come the logic of provocation and the design of deliberate creating thinking tools (lateral thinking) that have been used widely with measurable effects. Simple ways

of teaching perceptual thinking in schools have also been derived from the model and have been shown to be effective. In addition to practical outcomes (like learning backwards) there is an understanding of such phenomena as insight and humour.

Throughout this book are scattered various practical points that arise directly from the self-organizing patterning model. All these effects are summarized at the end of the book on page 269.

9. Euclid's system of geometry is both a brilliant mental construction and a very practical system from which we can derive real benefit. The first step was to define the universe. For Euclid's geometry does not work on spherical and some other surfaces. The next step was to define some axioms. These axioms were derived from the behaviour of simple elements, like lines, in the defined universe: for example, parallel lines will never meet. Then from these axioms was built up the whole system of theorems and proofs.

We could forget all about the brain and regard the model put forward here as defining a certain type of 'self-organizing' universe. The elements need no longer be neurones. We could define this universe as 'pattern space'. We would then explore behaviour in this space and derive some very basic principles. This is what I have done in part of this book. Finally we see what happens when these principles or 'axioms' work together. We get a result that is remarkably similar to the human mind. We can still choose to ignore this similarity.

10. Finally, it seems to me – and the reader does not need to agree – that our concept model explains certain behaviour of the brain (like humour, insight and creativity) a great deal better than any other existing model. This is also the case for the broad area of 'perception', which is what is of interest to me. Now it may be that there are certain parts of the brain that behave in a different way (types of algorithmic sorting) and I would not want to rule that out. My task is to provide a feasible model for perception that arises from and is compatible with what we know about neurone behaviour. Anyone who believes that the

system is not basically a self-organizing system should come up
with a model that is different and better.

So, in my view, there are very sound and practical reasons for
working with the self-organizing model. The practical understanding and insights that come from such a model (or broad class of
model) can be very valuable and can serve to alter our thinking
system. For example the limitations of the evolutionary model of
change and the great difficulty in changing paradigms arise
directly from the basic nature of self-organizing systems.

We can certainly have a better understanding of how the brain
works than we do of how 'gravity' works.

Different Universes

In an Islamic country if someone owes you money and hands you a bundle of notes, you must count them, one by one, in front of this person. If you did the same in a Western culture the person handing you the money would be extremely offended. The Islamic universe is different from the Western universe.

At work Japanese women are treated appallingly (though it is beginning to change). As soon as they marry they are expected to leave their jobs. Even if they do not marry they are thrown out at the age of thirty and younger women are brought in because the younger ones are cheaper (wages rise each year of employment). Women very rarely attain senior positions in larger companies. At home, however, the Japanese woman is almost totally in charge. She makes all decisions and looks after the family finances. The husband, no matter how senior, hands over all his salary to his wife. She hands him a little pocket money for day-to-day expenses — that is why corporate expense accounts are so huge. The Japanese mother has total control over the education of the children. There are two distinct universes: the work universe and the home universe.

There are living creatures on this earth that do not live on oxygen. We are so used to the oxygen-breathing universe (which includes fish as well) that we take it for granted that this is the only universe. It is not. In the deepest parts of the ocean, in the Pacific, there are strange worm-like creatures that do not live on oxygen but on the hydrogen sulphide bubbling out of volcanic vents in the ocean floor. At that depth there is very little oxygen in the water. Again this is an example of a different universe.

Most young Frenchmen now learn to speak English but you

may find yourself in a situation where people only speak French. So you speak English more loudly and more slowly and it seems incomprehensible to you that your listeners do not understand what you are saying. You are in a different universe and what is obvious in your universe has no meaning in this different universe.

Each of three people is holding a small block of pine wood. The first person releases the block and it falls to the ground. The second person releases the block and it moves upwards. The third person releases the block and it remains in exactly the same place. Someone is reporting this to you over the telephone. In the first case the behaviour is as expected. In the second case the behaviour is bizarre. In the third case the behaviour is simply unbelievable. This is because you assume that all three cases are taking place in the same universe.

It turns out that the first person is standing on the surface of the earth, so the wood falls to the ground. The second person happens to be standing under water, so naturally the wood floats upwards. This is perfectly normal and logical in that situation. The third person is in an orbiting spacecraft with zero gravity, so the piece of words stays just where it has been released. This is also normal and logical in that universe.

Once we understand the universe difference, we at once understand the behaviour. But if we did not know there was a universe difference and we assumed that all three people were standing on the surface of the earth, we would have had a very hard time understanding what was going on.

Euclid's famous geometry works only on a plane surface but not on a spherical surface (where parallel lines can meet).

In all these examples we see that the behaviour in a different system or different universe is indeed different. What is important to realize is that behaviour in a different universe may be incomprehensible until we realize that the universe is different.

Imagine that you are dropping some small balls onto a tray full of sand. Each ball embeds itself in the sand directly under the point of release. If we now look at the positions of the balls on the surface of the sand we have a good record of all the starting positions. The balls remain where they are. They do not move about. The surface of the sand remains as it is, with no change. This is a typical passive system. It represents all those information recording systems in which the information is recorded on some neutral surface and remains as recorded. This type of system ranges from the marks made by a schoolboy in his exercise book to the electronic marks made by a super computer on a magnetic hard disc. If we want to use that information, some outside operator (the schoolboy's brain or the computer's central processor) will carry out some logical operation on the stored information.

Let us now look at a different system, a different universe. This time instead of sand in the tray we have a latex rubber bag filled with a very viscous oil. We drop the first ball onto the surface. The ball is more dense than the oil so gradually it sinks down pushing the rubber surface ahead of it. The ball comes to rest on the bottom of the tray. The surface of the tray is no longer flat but slopes downward towards the first ball. We drop other balls onto the surface. They roll down the slope and end up against the first ball.

In the sand tray the balls stayed exactly where they were dropped. In the viscous tray the balls do not stay where they were dropped but move about. In the sand tray the surface remains flat. In the viscous tray the shape of the surface has been altered by the first ball. Because the balls move about, because the surface changes, we call this an active surface.

In the (passive) sand model the balls stayed where dropped. In the (active) viscous model all the balls come to cluster together at one point in the tray. In effect the surface has permitted the balls to 'organize themselves' into a group. This is a simple example of a self-organizing system. The organization of the balls into a group is not brought about by some outside agency – the organization is a natural characteristic of the system itself. This is a very important point and marks the key difference between passive systems (which require an outside operator to move things around) and active systems (in which the information moves itself around).

Consider another pair of models. The first model is a small towel taken from the bathroom and placed on a table. Alongside is a bowl of ink. You take a teaspoonful of ink and empty it onto the towel at some point. An ink stain is formed as a record of your activity. At the end this passive system gives a good record of your activity. The ink stays where it was placed.

For our 'active' model we replace the towel by a shallow dish containing gelatine (Jell-o or table jelly as served at children's birthday parties). This time you heat up the bowl of ink. When you place a spoonful of the heated ink on the gelatine the hot ink dissolves the gelatine but stops dissolving it as the ink cools. You now pour off the cooled ink and dissolved gelatine and are left with a shallow depression in the surface of the gelatine. This is your mark on the surface and corresponds to the ink stain on the towel. You place another spoonful of hot ink onto the surface. If this second spoonful is anywhere near the first depression the ink will flow into that depression. If you continue in this way with further spoonfuls you will find that a river or channel has formed in the surface of the gelatine (this will not happen if the placements are far apart). What has happened is that the first input has altered the way the surface receives the next input and so on.

As in the preceding viscous model the gelatine model has provided an environment in which the incoming 'information' can organize itself. In the case of the viscous model the information organized itself into a group. In the case of the gelatine model the information organized itself into a channel, a sequence, a pattern. Once the pattern has been established, anything nearby will flow into and along that pattern.

With these models we see a sharp contrast between two very different systems or universes. In the passive system information stays exactly where it has been put and we move that information around as we wish and according to whatever rules we want –

for example the rules of logic or mathematics. In the active system the surface and the information allow the information to organize itself in some way, for example into patterns or sequences.

The importance of this difference between the two systems is that in virtually all our information systems we have used the passive model. We store information in a passive way and then move it around according to some rules. All our thinking systems are based on this model. It now seems increasingly likely that the brain does not work like this at all, but as a self-organizing system in which information organizes itself into patterns.

In traditional computers there was information storage and information manipulation. In the very latest computers (neural net machines) the wiring is arranged to imitate the nerve networks in the brain. These are active self-organizing systems in which information organizes itself.

Traditional Table-Top Logic

Imagine a child sitting in front of a table on which are a number of blocks of different shapes, sizes and colours, like the 'attribute blocks' supplied to kindergartens. There are also boxes of different shapes, sizes and colours.

The child is free to pick up the blocks and move them round according to some rule, putting all the red blocks together irrespective of shape, or putting them into the red box, and so on. Once they are in the red box, any block taken out of that box must be red. The blocks can be grouped according to shape or according to both shape and colour. The child may find two blocks that are identical in shape, size and colour or two that have nothing at all in common, and quickly understands that if something belongs in the red box, it cannot belong in the green box at the same time. The child sees immediately that if something is inside one box which itself is inside a bigger box, the first object is also inside the bigger box. The blocks are static. They do not move of their own accord but can easily be moved round. They do not change.

In this simple table-top behaviour we can see several mental operations at work. There are attributes to be noticed and to be looked for. There is judgement. There are categories. There is inclusion, exclusion and contradiction. There is identity and mismatch.

This simple system illustrates the basic thinking system that we inherited from Aristotle, Plato and other Greek thinkers. The system was polished up by medieval theologians who needed a logic on which to base their defence of the true theology. It was further polished up in the Renaissance to provide a basis for reason, as distinct from religious belief and acceptance. The system is simple and powerful and it has been useful.

Instead of coloured blocks we use the words of language, which to some extent represent what we experience. To some extent we deliberately set out to construct words to carry the meanings we want them to carry. At the base of the system is the powerful word 'is' and its opposite 'is not' (leading to the powerful principle of contradiction).

This has been the basis of our reasoning. Let us now consider a different universe, a different system.

The table top now consists of a miniature landscape made of a special sort of sand. Water is sprinkled randomly over the surface. As in real life little streams form and then join to give bigger streams and finally small rivers develop. The landscape has now been shaped. Any water dropped at any point will now follow the established flow patterns.

Having seen how the flow patterns are formed we shall now change the model. We copy the landscape in rubber (possibly we could just make a latex mould of it). When inflated with air from below, the model will resemble the landscape. But if we inflate the model in a different way the landscape will be different and the flow patterns different. These different patterns of inflation will depend on where the water is placed. So there is not just one set landscape but a variety of possible landscapes, each with its flow patterns.

A child watching the flow patterns will observe how the coloured areas (representing towns) get linked up in one way in one flow pattern and in another way in another flow pattern.

The child does not consciously control the input of the water but notices that, if he or she looks in a certain direction, the water input will occur at a certain point. Sometimes the input will flow along the channels in the existing landscape and sometimes it will trigger a change in the landscape and will flow along channels in the changed landscape. In time the child gets to learn some of the patterns (in landscape A this is followed by this, then this, etc.) and might say: 'If I look in that direction, the landscape will change and the flow pattern will go this way . . .'

In this second system the flow paths represent patterns that have emerged (at the sand stage). The changing landscape (inflated rubber) represents the changing background, for the patterns will change depending on this background (later we shall see how 'emotion' changes the background in the mind). In this second system the child is not deliberately manipulating the effects as was the case with the blocks. But just as a person looking at a different picture will trigger different thoughts, so the child can trigger effects by looking in a different direction.

In a little while we shall see how this crude landscape model can be described much more precisely in terms of the behaviour of neurones in nerve networks in a structure like the brain. For the moment it is enough to appreciate that the table-top model is very different from the landscape model. They are two different universes.

The Nerve Network of the Brain

I shall describe here a much simplified model of a nerve network that is, however, compatible with what we know about real-life nerve networks as in the brain. For the sake of simplicity I shall not be using the neurological terms because a reader unfamiliar with neurology would constantly have to refer back to an explanation of the terms. What matters is the functional behaviour of the system.

This functional behaviour will cover a very broad class of systems of this type. Details may change and it may be shown that an effect may be brought about in a different way, but the effect is the same. The details of different types of electric light switch may vary but the over-all effect is the same. The model put forward is essentially that proposed in 1969 in *The Mechanism of Mind*. Computer simulation of this model has shown that it does work largely as predicted.

With any model of this sort the actual mode of behaviour will depend very largely on the parameters, that is to say the quantities assigned to the various interactions. I have not included these and will therefore be describing the model behaviour with the optimal parameters (whatever these might be). I also believe that in the brain, as elsewhere in the body, there are layers of local feedback systems which keep parameters within the optimal band-width.

Imagine a neurone as an octopus with a large number of tentacles (not the usual eight). Some of these tentacles may be very long. Each of them rests on the body of another octopus and can transmit to that octopus an electric shock. This transfer is done by means of a release of a chemical from the end of the tentacle (corresponding to a neuro-transmitter). If an octopus receives a sufficient number of shocks it wakes up and proceeds to shock others. The beach is covered with a larger number of octopuses all linked up in this way. Any octopus may actually be linked up, by means of long tentacles, to an octopus quite far away, but for the sake of convenience we shall assume an octopus is linked to its physical neighbours.

Now if we stimulate a group of octopuses, for example by shining a bright light from a helicopter above, they become active and start sending out shocks along their tentacles. In order to see what is happening we shall suppose that when an octopus is awake its colour changes from a grey-green to a vivid yellow. So now we see a patch of yellow spreading outwards from the group we stimulated with the bright light. Now that yellow patch could go on spreading until it covered the whole beach of octopuses. This would be somewhat equivalent to an epileptic fit in the brain, with all systems activated.

Let us now add another feature. When an octopus is awake (and vivid yellow) it gives off a pungent smell – a sort of cross between decaying fish and ammonia. This smell is so unpleasant to all octopuses that if the strength of the smell reaches a certain level they refuse to be woken up. So when the spreading yellow patch of activated octopuses has reached a certain size the smell will have reached a certain level of strength. At this point no further octopus will wake up, so the patch stays limited to that size.

In neurological terms we have a spreading activation and also a build-up of inhibition. This inhibition could be brought about through a build-up of chemicals or direct negative feedback carried by another set of nerves. The function is the same.

If this was all there was to it, the patch of yellowness would always be circular around the octopuses on whom the helicopter light had first shone. So let us add another effect. If an octopus is already awake when it receives an electric shock through a tentacle, that patch of skin under the tentacle gets rather sore. This soreness means that the octopus is much more likely in future to respond to a shock from this particular tentacle. This means that if two spots of helicopter light awake two groups of nearby octopuses, in the future the connection between those two groups will be stronger than with other octopuses.

This effect gives rise to the important phenomenon of association and also to reconstruction. In 1969 I predicted that this was a necessary part of the system. Subsequent research by others has shown that there is indeed an enzyme change (calpain) which ensures that the 'connectedness' between neurones that are excited at the same time is higher than with other neurones.

Back to the octopuses. If two helicopter lights have been used in this way and in the future only one light is used, the yellow patch is more likely to spread to the group that is better connected than anywhere else. So the situation is re-created as if there were two spots of light this time, and the yellow patch does not spread as a simple circle round the stimulus point but follows the track of increased connectedness which itself depends on past experience. In this way the crowd of octopuses can repeat or reconstruct a pattern. Even if the input is not exact this time, the same shape of yellow patch can be produced.

We now have pattern repetition or reconstruction – which is an immensely important part of the system.

What happens next? The yellow patch is no longer spreading but is limited (by the stink). It has followed previous experience. Now the active octopuses (like today's television addicts) have only a short attention span, so they start to get bored or tired. As they start to get bored the stink they are giving out drops sharply. This means that other octopuses outside the first yellow patch who are receiving enough shocks to be awakened but have been discouraged by the stink can now wake up and get active. The original group now fall asleep, so their yellow patch disappears. The yellow patch shifts to the new group of recently awakened octopuses.

So now we get a shift in the yellow patch from one group to another. The patch, always limited in size by the stink, will continue to shift across the beach. If one group is well connected by long tentacles to a distant group, the patch may disappear in one area and appear in a distant area. The way one area after another becomes yellow is a sequence or pattern. For a given set of conditions that pattern will be constant.

For any single octopus, whether it awakes and becomes active will be determined by the number of shocks the octopus is receiving from already awakened octopuses (in other words the number of tentacles from that group resting on its body) and the degree of 'soreness' under these tentacles (in other words the past history of how often the octopus has been active when the other group has been active). Working against these stimulating effects is the overall level of pungent stink which inhibits the octopus and also the tiredness or boredom factor.

At this point I should point out that the relationship between the awakening or stimulating factors and the octopus awakening is not linear. It is what is called a threshold effect and is absolutely typical of the nerve system. It means that up to a point a growing stimulation will have no effect at all, but beyond that point the octopus will spring into full activity. Later in this book I use the analogy of tickling. You can tickle someone more and more strongly with no effect but, suddenly, the person bursts out laughing. This non-linear effect is a very important part of the behaviour of nerve networks and should not be left out in calculations of their behaviour. It is like increasing pressure on a trigger which, suddenly, is enough to release the full force of the gun.

What happens to the bored group of octopuses who were initially stimulated? Do they remain bored and drop out for ever? After a while the boredom passes. Not only does the boredom pass but it is followed by a short period of increased wakefulness.

The tiredness, refractory period and increased excitability are all normal behaviour of nerve systems.

The increased wakefulness of the first stimulated group means that the yellow patch of activity may well return to this group, since it now has a slight edge over other groups. This would lead to a circularity of the pattern. The yellow patch would start under the direct stimulus at one part of the beach, wander off around the beach, then return to the original spot and repeat the circuit. In the brain it is this circularity which probably constitutes a thought.

What happens if there are two helicopters both shining lights onto different parts of the beach at the same time? Both yellow patches would start and try to spread. The pungent smell would increase. The stronger group (in terms of greater connectedness, greater size) would continue to spread and the smaller group would be suppressed by the smell. So at any point there would be only one area of activity, one yellow patch. In the brain this would correspond to one area of attention at a time.

Next it turns out that these octopuses sprawled on the beach are more cultured than we thought. Some of them respond to music. Of those who respond to music some appear to like jazz, others appear to like country and western music and some respond only to Mozart. The response takes the form of an increased wakefulness.

It happens that further down the beach a picnicking group has a ghetto-blaster at full blast. For the moment the machine is playing jazz. Those octopuses sensitive to jazz are livened up. This means that they are more 'ready' to go active than any other group. This music-induced readiness is added to the other 'readiness' factors which have already been mentioned (connectedness, degree of current stimulation, boredom etc.). It means that the yellow patch of activity will be more likely to shift to this half-awakened group. If the ghetto-blaster had played country and western music, that group of octopuses would have been favoured. If it had been Mozart, the up-market octopuses would have been favoured.

So the background music increases the sensitivity of different groups. This increased sensitivity or readiness to go active will mean that the pattern sequence (sequence of shift of the yellow patch of activity) will be different when the music is playing from when it is not playing. This is a very important point indeed.

In brain terms we are looking at the effects of 'emotions' or background chemical changes which favour one area of neurones. This means that patterns are more likely to flow in such areas. So the response to exactly the same stimulus will vary according to the chemical background state which itself is determined by emotions. This emotional effect could just as well be neurological as chemical – it makes no difference.

This readiness of a particular group of octopuses to become awakened (go active) can also be achieved in another way. We saw how a second yellow patch created by a separate helicopter light at a distance from the first one would be temporarily suppressed by the stronger pattern. But the readiness of that group to become active would still be enhanced above other octopuses, so the yellow patch of activity would be more likely to shift in that direction. In this way the surface would take account of other inputs which were occurring at the same time. Note that if the two helicopter lights were close together in the first place, the two yellow patches would have been integrated to form one patch.

We can now summarize the readiness of any particular octopus to wake up and go active:

Direct stimulation

Stimulation from other octopuses and degree of connectedness (which depends on past history)

Increased alertness after the boredom phase

Background music

The negative factors of boredom and stink are the same as before.

What is memory in this model? The soreness that is the basis of increased connectedness becomes permanent. In the neurone world this increased connectedness may be achieved by enzyme changes, by laying down new proteins or by actual additional dendrites (tentacles).

We can list the characteristics of this system:

1. Activity of an octopus can stimulate other octopuses into activity if they are connected (activity is shown by the yellow colour change).

2. The total size of the activated group is limited by negative feedback (the pungent smell).

3. A tiring factor or boredom factor means that activity will shift from the stimulated group to the next ready group.

4. Stimulation is on a 'threshold' basis and is non-linear.

5. Any octopuses which are activated at the same time will have an increased connectedness (the soreness effect).

As a result of these simple characteristics the system is capable of the following general behaviour:

1. Unitary attention.

2. Pattern recognition and reconstruction.

3. Integration of different inputs.

4. Creating sequence patterns bringing in past experience.

5. Creating repeating circular patterns.

6. Responding differently to stimulation depending on background activity (or chemical base-line).

All these are powerful effects. They add up to the behaviour of a self-organizing pattern-making and pattern-using system. They add up to the behaviour of perception.

We shall now move away from the system explanation and deal with the behaviour of the system in order to show how these effects have a direct relevance to our understanding of human perception.

HOW PERCEPTION WORKS

I have described a very broad type of self-organizing information system made up of neurones. This system is fully compatible with what we know about the human brain. The system has also been simulated on computer (by M. H. Lee and colleagues) and does behave largely as predicted. So what?

From time to time I get detailed letters from individuals who have a highly idiosyncratic way of looking at the world. There are unlimited ways of describing anything. I could tell you that the cup in front of you is actually made of trillions of little creatures that have suspended their animation in order to form themselves into a cup. The useful question is 'so what?' I do not reply in this manner because it is offensive, but in any description or model we want to know what difference it makes. As the great American pragmatist William James would have said, 'What is its cash value?'

The purpose of science is not to analyse or describe but to make useful models of the world. A model is useful if it allows us to get use out of it. Use is not confined to predictions of behaviour but also interventions. For example the use of the model I have described resulted on one occasion in the saving of $300 million.

The model I have described is very broad. It covers a whole variety of self-organizing systems. We may eventually find that the details are not correct. We may find that we use several brains at once or several independent layers of brain (as I suspect), but this will not alter the broad picture. The key in science is to make a model as broad as possible so that it can cover many different actual systems. At the same time it must not be so broad that we cannot get anything useful from it. As we shall see we can get a great deal of useful information from the behaviour of the described system.

Traditionally we have been obsessed with the 'telephone switch-board' model of mind. In this model a very busy operator keeps plugging in lines to make connections. This is the 'table-top' passive system I have mentioned so often in this book. Seated at a table, the operator (the sense of 'I' or ego) moves things round according to certain rules.

The model I have described is totally different. It is a model of a self-organizing system (the one I put forward in 1969 in *The Mechanism of Mind*). Such a system has a life and dynamism of its own. There is total activity. The arriving information and the nerve networks interact with their own vigour. The 'I', ego or operator is part observer and part an aspect of the action – as we shall see later.

I want to list here some of the things (this list is by no means exhaustive) that will happen in broad systems of this sort. Again I want to emphasize that 'broad' because I am describing a very broad type of system. I shall then describe each type of behaviour in more detail.

PATTERN-MAKING: the brain works by providing an environment in which sequences of activity become established as patterns.

TRIGGER: the brain will reconstruct the whole picture from just part of it or a sequence can be triggered by the initial part.

ASYMMETRY: the sequence patterns are asymmetric and this gives rise to humour and to creativity.

INSIGHT: if we enter the pattern sequence at a slightly different point we may follow a short cut. We can rely on chance to bring this about or do it deliberately.

LEARNING BACKWARDS: there is good reason to believe that learning things backwards is much more effective than learning them forwards.

SEQUENCE: the brain is a history recorder and the patterns are highly dependent on the initial sequence of experience.

CATCHMENT: each pattern has a very wide collection basin so that a variety of inputs will give the same output.

KNIFE-EDGE DISCRIMINATION: the boundary between two catchment basins is very sharp, so very clear distinctions may be made between things which are quite similar – provided the patterns are in place.

PRE-EMPTION: once a pattern exists it is very hard to cut across it to establish a new pattern.

MISMATCH: if what is offered to the brain contradicts what is established as pattern the brain notices this strongly.

READINESS: the patterns in the brain are not solely in an active/inactive state but there is a 'readiness' to go which is dependent on context and emotions.

CONTEXT: the actual patterns that emerge are determined by history, by activity at the moment and also by context which sets the background readiness level of different patterns.

CIRCULARITY: a circularity can be established in which patterns lead back into each other. This is the basis of belief systems.

MAKING SENSE: the brain has a powerful ability to put together and to seek to coalesce into sense whatever is put before it.

ATTENTION: there is unitary attention which may take in the whole field or focus on part of it, ignoring the rest.

RELEVANCE AND MEANING: attention will move to those areas which trigger existing patterns.

NO ZERO-HOLD: the activity in the brain cannot stabilize into a zero-hold which accepts input but does not seek to follow an accepted pattern.

As they are listed here these characteristics of behaviour may seem abstract. But, as we shall see, they have a direct impact on our daily thinking and behaviour.

Sequence Patterns

Could you afford to spend forty-five hours getting dressed every morning? If not, be grateful that the brain sets up sequence patterns.

One day a young man decided to figure out in how many ways he could get dressed using his standard eleven items of clothing. He set up his personal computer to do the work for him. The computer worked for forty-five hours non-stop to show that out of the 39 million possible ways of putting on eleven items of clothing only about five thousand were possible (you could not put your shoes on before your socks etc.). The figure of 39 million is easily obtained because you have eleven choices of the first item and then for each of these ten choices of the next, so you multiply $11 \times 10 \times 9 \times 8 \times 7 \times 6 \times 5 \times 4 \times 3 \times 2$.

When you pour out a glass from a bottle of Saint-Véran you do not have to work out which way up to put the glass. When you drink from it you do not have to work out the best way to hold it or whether to put it to your mouth or your ear. Your patterns may even have told you that Saint-Véran is a white wine from the Burgundy area and a very recently accepted French appellation (or you may be establishing that pattern right now).

The definition of a sequence pattern is very simple. At any moment there is one direction of change which has a much higher probability of occurring than any other. For a railway train going along tracks at any moment the probability (or likelihood) of going forward along the track is rather higher than of going in any other direction. In the brain the change from the present state of activity to the next is more likely to occur in one direction (to one particular next state) than in any other.

The natural and inescapable behaviour of our self-organizing brain model is that it is a pattern-making and pattern-using system. That is its natural activity, it cannot do anything else. Rain falls on a virgin landscape. Eventually the interaction of the rain and the landscape forms streams and rivers. The newly arriving rain now follows these patterns. That is the natural behaviour of the system. A person blind from birth is suddenly made capable of seeing. But that person cannot yet see, for everything is a blur. It takes some time for the brain to set up patterns of seeing.

If the brain were not a pattern-making system we would not be able to read, write or talk. Every activity, like getting dressed in the morning, would be a major time-consuming task. Sport would be impossible – for example, a golfer would have consciously to direct every part of every swing. Consider the millions of people who drive along the roads every day using patterns of perception and reaction and only occasionally having to work things out. There are routine patterns of action, like driving or playing golf. There are routine patterns of perception, which is why we can recognize knives, forks and people. There are routine patterns of meaning, which is why we can listen and read and communicate.

Traditional computers have to struggle quite hard to make and recognize patterns. The brain makes patterns very easily and recognizes them instantly. This is the very nature of the brain and arises directly from the way self-organizing systems work.

Trigger and Reconstruction

In 1988 AT&T announced a major breakthrough: the construction of the first neural chip. This means an electronic chip whose mode of operation is based on the behaviour of nerve networks (rather like the one I have described) rather than traditional computer chips. If a picture is once shown to this chip, in future any part of that picture will call forth the whole picture. There is reconstruction of the whole which is triggered by any part of the whole.

Again this is the natural behaviour of a self-organizing system. Such behaviour follows directly from pattern-making and pattern-using. The beginning of the pattern is triggered and the rest follows or is reconstructed.

At the MGM Grand Hotel in Las Vegas, I once watched a stage magician make a lion disappear a few feet from where I was sitting. It was most impressive. I have the greatest of admiration for stage magicians because of their ability to fool all the people all the time. They do it by consciously using the triggering effect. They set up something to trigger the audience's pattern in a certain direction. Then the magician takes a different direction. One simple example is for the magician to carry out a trick at once but then go through an elaborate ritual of how the trick is about to happen (for example a disappearance).

In July 1988 a group of four robbers walked out of an airport office in New York carrying with them one million dollars. There had been no violence and no threats. The robbers had dressed themselves up in the usual uniform of the courier service which collected money about this time. They presented authentic-looking cards. These things triggered the way they were treated.

The shapes on this page trigger patterns that give words, sense and meaning.

The pressure on a trigger might be the same but what is set off might be a water pistol, a shot-gun at a clay pigeon shoot, an Armalite rifle killing someone or even a missile that might shoot down an airliner.

By and large the triggering system in the brain is immensely useful. If it were not for this triggering we would have to spend a great deal of time being sure about which pattern was required. Instead of this active selection there is automatic triggering. You recognize a friend instantly without having to take out calipers to measure his nose or eye width.

But the triggering can be too quick. A friend of mine stopped to help a woman who had been knocked down by a car which did not stop. As he was bending over her to help her another motorist drove up and immediately assumed that he had hit her in the first place (the injured person and the fact that there was only one car triggered this response). In anger the newcomer knocked my friend unconscious.

Eye-witnesses can be unreliable because the eye is not a camera. The brain reconstructs what the witness thought he or she saw.

Triggers will set off what you think is there rather than what is actually present. So it is easy to trigger stereotypes about people or races or situations. Labels, slogans, images and symbols, whether used in advertising or for political purposes, make full use of this triggering and reconstructing effect.

By far the biggest killer phrase in creativity is the phrase 'this is the same as ...'. This is much worse a response than saying that the idea is absurd, nonsense or impossible. The phrase 'the same as ...' means that the idea is not new and therefore need not be discussed at all. What happens is that some part of the proposed new idea triggers an already known idea in the mind of the listener who refuses to listen any more.

The key question is whether the triggering of patterns can actually change what we see in front of us. It is a matter of the competition between a stored pattern and actuality. There are psychological experiments which suggest that this is possible (as indeed happens with stage magicians). But this is not so important. It is sufficient that the triggered pattern sets off emotions and stereotypes which then directly affect our perception of what is in front of us. This changed perception will determine (as we shall see later) what we pay attention to and what patterns are used. The result is that we really do see something that is different from what another person might see. This applies to physical situations and even more to thinking situations when we are responding to words or print.

I once suggested that habitual criminals might be tattooed for ease of identification. This aroused a reaction of horror. The horror was not on the grounds of unfair or cruel treatment, but the 'tattoo' idea immediately triggered images of the tattooing of inmates of Nazi concentration camps and that was the source of the horror.

The phenomenon of triggering and reconstruction is natural behaviour of any patterning system. On the whole it is immensely useful and life would be impossible without it. Nevertheless triggering is one of the factors that ensures that there cannot be any truth in perception.

Asymmetry of Patterns

Why is humour the most significant characteristic of the human mind? Why have traditional philosophers and others paid so little attention to it?

Humour arises directly from the asymmetry of patterns in a self-organizing system. It is significant because humour is a direct indicator of this type of system. It could not exist in the passive table-top model of information systems. Reason is a relatively cheap phenomenon which can be obtained with boxes, cog-wheels and transistor choices, but humour can happen only in an asymmetric patterning system. The reason traditional philosophers have paid so little attention to it is the best indication that they have been working only with passive table-top information systems.

The asymmetry of patterns also explains why for two thousand and four hundred years, or more, we have been unable to understand creativity or to use it more deliberately. What is asymmetry?

Asymmetry means lack of symmetry. If you wear one black shoe and one brown that is asymmetric – I predict that asymmetry is going to become very important in fashion. Gothic buildings were asymmetric because each side was not the same, as it would be in a classical building. If you invite someone to an elaborate dinner and they invite you back just for a drink that is asymmetric.

If you ask someone to start with the word dog and to link it by means of other words to the word 'knife' you will get (across many people) a different string of words than if you had started with 'knife' and asked a person to link it forward to 'dog'. In other words the path from dog to knife is not the same as from knife to dog. It is in this last sense that patterns are asymmetric. The path from A to B may be long and tedious but the path from B to A is short and direct.

You set off across the city to drive to a friend's house for dinner. You take the way you know, following familiar sections of the road. When you are ready to leave your friend suggests a much quicker way back. You could never have found this way on setting out because you could not have known that an insignificant road you went past was the key road.

Children's books often have a picture of four youngsters fishing. There is a tangle of fishing lines. There is one fish on one hook but nothing on the other hooks. You are asked to find out which person caught the fish. If you start out from each fishing person you have a hard time because there is no way of telling which line is going to end up with the fish. But if you start backwards from the fish you only have to follow the line to the lucky fishing person.

Both the journey across the city and the one fish story are examples of asymmetric tracks. Why is asymmetry so important in a patterning system?

Another evening you set off to drive out to dinner with some friends who live in the countryside. You have clear instructions about how to get to the nearest village. Then you have been told to 'take the third turn on the right after the church'. You try what seems to be the third turn but get nowhere. The problem is that there are roads and small roads and tracks. What should be counted in reaching the 'third turn'? You have to assess each side-turning. This takes a great deal of time.

In a patterning system there is the main track and there are many side-tracks. If the mind had to stop at every side-track to explore its potential, life would be impossibly slow and there would be no point in having a patterning system. In addition there would be a need for a second mind to make these decisions and then a third mind to make its decisions . . . and so on.

The brain is much better organized than that. The natural and intrinsic behaviour of the system I have described ensures that at any point the most probable path forward is enhanced and a less probable side-track (even if only slightly less probable) would be totally suppressed for the moment. So for the moment the side-tracks do not actually exist. We sail along the main track without dithering and with full confidence.

If, however, we 'somehow' jump to the side-track or even start out on the side-track, the path back to the original point is very easy along the side-track. This is classical asymmetry and is much better illustrated with a drawing (see the diagram if you wish).

I want to emphasize again that this behaviour arises directly and naturally from the nature of the system – it is not something that is added on.

If we 'somehow' get across from the main track to the side-track, in 'hindsight' we can see that the track back is obvious. That is the essence of humour. It is the role of the comedian or the punch-line to place us on the back-track. Something which could not be obvious in foresight is obvious in hindsight.

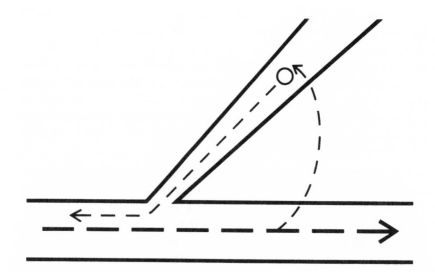

An eighty-five-year-old man dies and goes down to hell. As he is wandering about he comes across a friend of a similar age who is sitting there with a gorgeous young woman sitting on his knee. He greets his friend: 'Are you sure this is hell? – you seem to be having a good time.' 'Oh, it's hell all right. You see I am *her* punishment.'

The connections and the power with which we zoom back down the side-track depend on topicality, ethnic prejudice, comedian's personality and such things, but the mechanics are basic.

Exactly the same process takes place in creativity or what I prefer to call 'lateral thinking'. As I shall explain later the word 'creativity' is much too broad, so I invented the term lateral thinking specifically to cover changes in concept and perception obtained by moving laterally across pattern. Lateral thinking arises directly from a consideration of the mind as a self-organizing patterning system. The word is now in the *Oxford English Dictionary* – although inadequately defined.

In lateral thinking we seek to do exactly what happens in humour. We seek to cross from the main track to the side-track. I have devised specific tools and processes for doing this and shall be describing these shortly. If we succeed in getting across to the side-track, then – in hindsight – we can at once (as in humour) see the value of the new position.

Now we come to a serious dilemma. In fact I would call it one of the most serious dilemmas of our whole thinking culture. It is that every valuable creative idea must always be logical in hindsight. If it were not logical in hindsight, we should never be able to appreciate its value. It would just be a crazy idea suspended without any support. We might catch up with it later or not at all. So we are able to appreciate only those creative ideas which are logical in hindsight. Of course there are creative ideas which most people will be unable to appreciate until they make the necessary paradigm shift (like this book).

We have then always gone forward to claim that if an idea is indeed logical in hindsight it should have been accessible to logic in foresight. Therefore it is enough to seek better logic rather than to teach creativity. This attitude is absolutely correct in a passive table-top system but totally false in a self-organizing system. Unfortunately almost our whole culture is based on passive table-top thinking, which is why we cannot see the absolute logical necessity for creativity.

If we know all this, can we take specific deliberate steps to get across from the main track to the side-track? We can. Many years ago I developed particular thinking tools precisely for this purpose. These tools have been very effective in practice and were, as we have seen, the tools used by Peter Ueberroth to generate new concepts for the 1984 Olympic Games (there are many other examples of use but this one is so clearcut).

To cut across asymmetric tracks we need a combination of two things: provocation and 'movement'. In 1982 IBM researchers stated categorically that in certain types of system (like Boltzmann equations) provocation was an absolute mathematical necessity. This is what I had been advocating as part of the lateral thinking process since the early 1970s.

There may not be a reason for saying something until after it has been said. That is a provocation. Usually there is a reason for saying something before it is said. A provocation is designed to perturb the system and it is the benefits of that perturbation that justify the provocation.

It is easiest to think of a provocation as a stepping-stone. This stepping-stone is not based on experience and lies outside the main track. The provocation serves to get our mind out of the established track. Using the operation of 'movement' we move forward from the provocation to the new track. Once there, if the idea is valuable, we can see the value in hindsight and can forget about how we got there.

In the history of science, provocations have been provided by chance, accident, mistake, confluence of circumstance, madness, bloody-mindedness and many other sources. But we do not have to await such things – we can deliberately act up and use provocations.

I coined the new word 'po' to signal a provocation. For example you might say 'po cars should have square wheels'. Without the po signal such a statement would seem utterly absurd and contrary to all our notions of realistic mechanics. The provocation does, however, lead to a number of useful ideas including that of active suspension. Many many years ago I suggested a suspension system in which the suspension would lift the wheels over bumps like a horse picking up its feet. This concept is now being put into effect by Lotus (now part of GM) and some other manufacturers. The result gives a ride that is far superior to any existing suspension system. I have no way of claiming origination of this idea.

The word 'po' is taken from words like hypothesis, suppose, possible and poetry. In all these cases we use a statement or idea to go forward. Po can also be taken to stand for 'provocative operation'.

Provocation is quite useless unless we learn the operation of 'movement'. Movement is a new operation quite distinct from judgement. In judgement we compare an idea to our existing patterns and reject or criticize the idea if there is any mismatch. In movement we use the idea to move forward – not unlike what we do with poetry.

There are specific and formal ways of setting up provocations. There are deliberate and formal ways of getting 'movement'. These comprise the specific tools of deliberate creative thinking. This is not the place to go into such things in detail.*

A factory placed on a river puts out pollution. People downstream suffer. What can be done? We put in a provocation: 'po the factory is downstream of itself'. This sounds absurd and impossible. But it leads directly to the very logical idea of insisting that the input to the factory must be downstream of its own output. In this way the factory is the first to get a sample of its pollution and is more concerned to clean it up. This idea was suggested many many years ago and is, I am told, incorporated in legislation in some countries.

I have spent some time on these matters for two reasons. The first is to show that our failure to understand the behaviour of self-organizing patterning systems has meant that we have been unable to treat creativity properly. This is a very serious matter and has meant that progress has been much slower than it need have been. The second reason is to show that understanding the nature of self-organizing patterning systems can lead to practical outcomes, for example in the design of specific creative tools that can be used deliberately to generate new ideas. Here we can see the legitimizing of two mental operations: provocation and movement.

The asymmetry of patterns also leads to the phenomenon of insight and a further, very simple, creative tool.

---

* There are other books of mine that focus on practical lateral thinking, such as *Lateral Thinking*, Ward Lock Educational, 1972; Harper and Row. I shall shortly be writing another book to bring these matters up to date.

Insight

Archimedes leaps naked from his bath shouting 'Eureka'. Alexander Fleming suddenly sees the significance of the petri dish contaminated with the penicillin mould. Kekulé suddenly sees the benzene ring as a snake biting its own tail. The moment of insight, the eureka moment and the 'ah-ha' moment have been well documented by historians of creative achievement. Paradigm shifts, though somewhat slower, are also instances of insight. It is not a question of the accumulation of a lot of new evidence. Somehow we get to see the same things differently.

How can insight happen in a patterning system where things must flow along the established pattern? Surely a patterning system is the very opposite of what takes place with insight, in which we suddenly get a new pattern. The paradox is that it is precisely the nature of patterning systems that gives rise to the phenomenon of insight. Again there is a close resemblance to humour.

As we go along the main track we cannot get access to the side-track. But if somehow, on one occasion, we happen to start at some point along, or near, the side-track, in an instant we back-track and see that it makes sense. It may be a chance remark, a new piece of information, something unconnected in the environment which gets us to start at this new point. The proverbial apple falling on Newton's head (apparently untrue) would be just such an example.

Intuition and insight are not the same thing. Insight is a sudden realization like a mathematician or a computer programmer suddenly realizing that something can be done much more simply. Intuition is a gradual building-up of background patterns which often cannot be verbalized or even made conscious. Sometimes a key pattern falls into place and makes this whole network accessible and usable.

We can take this phenomenon of insight and try to bring it about artificially. How can we provide a new entry point? How can we substitute for the chance event or piece of information that provides access to the side-track? The answer is surprisingly easy and gives rise to the creation of what must be the simplest possible lateral thinking technique. This is a technique that is much used by people involved in designing new products or in need of a stream of new ideas. We cannot choose a deliberate new entry point (although even this is a useful process) because it is likely to be chosen by reference to our existing ideas in the matter. So we need a new entry point but cannot choose one. The answer is to obtain one by chance.

For convenience we use a word (preferably a noun) which is a package of functions and associations. We obtain such a word by chance, for instance by opening a dictionary at any page, taking the fifth word down and proceeding to the first noun, then holding that word in juxtaposition to the focus area in which we want a new idea.

For example the focus area is 'cigarette' and the random word was traffic-lights. Very quickly the idea arose of putting a broad red band round cigarettes some distance from the butt end. This would provide a 'danger zone', a 'guilt zone' and a 'decision zone' for smokers. If they stopped before the red band their smoking was somewhat safer, and they were gaining some decision control as well. The band could be placed progressively higher on the cigarette for those who wanted to cut down.

In a passive table-top system this absurdly simple technique would be utter nonsense, for by definition a random word has no connection with the focus area. The same word would do for any subject and any word would do for any subject at all. This must be nonsense in a passive system. But in a self-organizing patterning system the process is perfectly logical. As you come in from the periphery, from any starting-point, you are likely to hit tracks you could never have taken when moving out from the centre. This arises directly from the asymmetry of patterns.

In addition the random word sensitizes certain patterns (the word 'traffic-light' sensitizes such patterns as 'control', 'danger', 'stop') so that the flow of thought can visit certain patterns it might otherwise have passed by. The technique is extremely effective and very easy to use. This is yet another example of the practical value of having a system model from which to work forwards to produce useful ideas. As I have said the random-word technique could never have arisen from the table-top model.

The effectiveness of the random-word technique in no way proves the correctness of the model, because there may be further models which might also show this effect. But the model does have a real value if it can generate practical thinking tools that can then be tried out directly. The purpose of any scientific model is to provide real value and not just another description.

Learning Backwards

If you were teaching someone how to use a wood-turning lathe you might use the following sequence: check the machine, switch it on, position the tool in the jaws, position the wood in the chuck, re-check, switch on the drive, observe and control the process ... switch off the drive, take out the tool, remove the formed wood, switch off the machine. This is the normal time sequence in which the operation would be carried out and it seems sensible to teach first things first.

But this way of teaching may be quite wrong. It may be best to teach the sequence backwards. Perhaps the first thing we ought to teach is how to switch the machine off, then how to remove the formed wood ... and lastly how to switch it on.

The logic of patterning systems suggests that learning backwards might be far more effective. This does not necessarily apply to language, where there is a meaning in one direction but not in the other, but it may also apply here, for example in learning a long poem. Some preliminary work I have done suggests it does.

Imagine we are learning a sequence ABCDE in the normal way. We would learn A and when we have learned this move on to B and then to C. In each case we would be moving from something we knew well to something we were only just learning (building on the base we might call it). Because we are moving into a new area we are likely to make a mistake or take a wrong turning. This is very difficult to unlearn. Now let us look at the reverse direction.

First we would learn E and then we would learn D. This means we are now moving forward from what we are just learning to something we already know well. Therefore the chance of making a wrong turning is very much less. Next we learn C and again move forward with confidence.

The principle is that if you know where you are going, having been there already, it is much better than moving from what is known towards the unknown. I have been told that some choir masters have traditionally used this approach: teaching the last phrase first and then the penultimate and then the one before etc. This way the choristers move forward with full confidence into territory they already know. I also believe that some people are beginning to teach golf this way. You start with the end of the swing and then move back to end up with the beginning of the swing.

A lot more work needs to be done on matters like this. They could make a profound difference to the way we handle education. It is not easy to make the transition from simple sequences over time to matters of differing complexity. In matters of increasing complexity what does working backwards mean? We can conceive this in terms of the specific design of a sequence of concepts.

This is another example of something that is counter-intuitive but arises directly from a consideration of the broad behaviour of self-organizing patterning systems. Again, it could have considerable practical value.

Time Sequence

If you are setting out to work in a new field you should thoroughly research that field. Right? Wrong!

The traditional view is that you should read all you can in order to get the base of existing knowledge and then move forward from this. There is a flaw in this argument and it is a flaw in the scientific method. We do not just get knowledge, we get knowledge packaged up as concepts and perceptions. In the table-top model, knowledge is there like items on a table top. We can play around with the items. In the self-organizing patterning model, knowledge is inextricably packaged as concepts and perceptions. Together these concepts and perceptions give what Thomas Kuhn called paradigms.

Why does big progress often come from the innocents in a field or indeed from a different discipline? The history of the new science of chaos is full of such examples. This is not just a matter of the establishment wishing to defend its own turf. The problem is one of sequence. Patterning machines are really history machines. Patterns are formed directly according to the sequence of experience. The pieces are already joined up, they are not free to be moved around as in the table-top model. This is the very essence of the nature of self-organizing systems.

On a lifetime scale St Ignatius Loyola (give me a youngster until he is seven and I shall set his life), Freud and the Marxists are right. Get in early with the patterns and new patterns will be built from this base. On a research level the history of our experience or research in a field will set our patterns. Sometimes this is good and sometimes bad. Alexander Fleming was able to recognize the significance of penicillium contamination because of his long background in the research for anti-bacterial effects. My own background in medicine (and in particular the integrated systems of ion control, kidney function, circulation control, and respiratory control) was essential to my interest in self-organizing patterning systems. Had I come from a background in philosophy, logic, mathematics or computer science, I would have picked up the idiom of symbol manipulation and would have been in the table-top model.

At other times the experience can be restricting because we are trapped in the existing concepts. Perhaps the ideal would be to read enough to become generally familiar and then to do your own work. You may, however, need to learn the powerful tools and techniques in the area. But even this may be dangerous: if you have a hammer, every problem will be treated as a nail.

We run airlines as we used to run railways because railways came first and we just transferred the railway concepts to airlines. With airlines such concepts (fixed routes, owning hardware) are not only unnecessary but very costly and inefficient.

Even moment to moment patterning systems are extremely sensitive to sequence. Consider the following announcement in an airliner full of passengers on a tarmac. 'This is the captain speaking. I'm afraid I have some bad news for you. You've all heard about congested airspace. I regret to have to tell you there's going to be a five-minute delay.' This is a true experience. Now the first part of the utterances makes passengers expect something awful like a major technical problem. Then the mention of congested airspace removes that worry but suggests a long delay. Air travel is stressful enough to suggest the need for some announcement training. The captain should have begun by saying that there would be a delay of only five minutes.

Always give the good news first.

Catchment

I once had dinner beside the Mississippi river about a hundred miles from the Canadian border. We usually think of that river as a southern matter, but the Mississippi drains a great deal of the USA.

There is an interesting ridge in the west of Switzerland. If you stand on top of that ridge on a rainy day and spit to the east your spit will eventually end up at the mouth of the Danube, carried along with the water flow. But if you spit to the west your spit will end up at the mouth of the Rhine in Holland. There are two points here. One is the sharp divide between two huge collection or catchment basins and the other is the size of these basins.

The Mississippi, the Danube and the Rhine have huge catchment areas and 'catchment areas' are what I want to deal with here.

Imagine a one-inch diameter tube sticking upwards out of the ground. You are trying to drop a small ball-bearing down that tube. You have to get close or aim very well. Now we get a large funnel about one foot in diameter and place the nozzle in the tube. Our task is much easier. We do not have to aim so exactly. Instead of aiming for a hole one inch in diameter we now have a hole twelve inches in diameter. Yet the outcome will be the same.

The funnel is a system which allows a wide variety of inputs to have one output. Now let us take that funnel out of the tube and hold it over a tray of sand. From a wide variety of starting positions the ball will end up in the sand in only one place. If we take the funnel away the ball will land in many different positions on the sand.

What has all this got to do with the patterns in the mind? A great deal: do the patterns have a very broad catchment area (like the funnel and the rivers) or a narrow precise catchment area (like the tube without the funnel)?

If you put a large cornflakes box on the table and then walk round it with a camera, snapping away from all angles, you will get pictures that physically look very different. How is it that the eye has no difficulty in recognizing all these different shapes as the cornflakes box?

For years workers in artificial intelligence would puzzle over this property of mind and eye and would elaborate very complex schemes of scanning and comparison. In a self-organizing patterning system the answer is very easy. The patterns for the cornflakes box (and box-like objects in general) have a very wide catchment area – and they all lead into the same pattern. Again there is nothing special or exotic about this, it is the natural behaviour of the simple patterning system I have described. Such a system could not work otherwise.

For the moment I want to leave out competing patterns and the 'knife-edge' effect and look at the catchment area of one pattern. If this is broad, a variety of things which are related or somewhat similar will end up being seen as the same pattern. From a practical survival point of view this is immensely useful. Instead of having to learn lots of separate patterns we can get by with a few broad patterns. Most things will flow into the catchment area of one or other pattern. Imagine the simplified patterns of a baby and how most things flow into these simple patterns.

How does this happen? Put down a number of circles on a piece of paper. Each circle represents a particular 'state of activity' in the brain system. Each state (all things being equal – later we shall see how they may not be) will tire and be followed by a new state. So we connect that circle to another by a line and put two strokes across that line to indicate that this is the preferred route of change. But if that second state has itself just been active, it may be too tired to respond, so we need a second-choice change. Connect the first circle to any other and put a single stroke through that line. Connect up the circles randomly. Just make sure that each circle has at least two lines going to it: one of these should have two strokes on it (first choice for change) and another line just one stroke (second choice). You may start at any circle. Exit by the preferred route but if you have entered by that route exit by the second choice.

Whatever you do you will always end up with a repeating circle (occasionally two). All other states will feed into this stable state. There is no magic about this. It is the natural behaviour of self-organizing systems as they move from unstable states to stable states. The result is that a wide variety of inputs may all come to stabilize as the same established pattern. That is the wide catchment area.

Initially, for survival, this broad catchment mechanism has great advantages. But later on it comes to have very serious defects indeed. Our civilization is suffering gravely from these defects.

The Innuit (who used to be called by the somewhat derogatory term Eskimo) used to spend a long time huddled together in Igloos in the long winter nights. If you are forced to be in such close quarters human relationships become very important – and very subtle. So, I believe, the Innuit developed a rich language to describe nuances of human relations. They also have about twenty words to describe snow, which is also much part of their lives. In terms of human relations they have more than twenty words along the spectrum ranging from love to hate. For example there is one word to describe the following sentiment: 'I like you very much but I would not want to go seal hunting with you.'

Think of the practicality of that richness of definition. Think of its value in human relations, business relations (I like you very much but do not trust you one inch) and international relations (we are certainly enemies but we are joint trustees of this planet – Howard Baker's phrase – and must make it work).

But we do not have that richness. The English language (like many others) is extraordinarily poor in this respect. We have love, hate, like, dislike, distrust, trust. We have friend and enemy. We have to make do with these crude patterns and so each has a very broad catchment area. The problem is made worse by the phenomenon of centring, which I shall describe shortly.

There is a reason for this poverty of definition in English. English is a richly expressive language and is a process description language. This means that we can adequately describe by means of a combination of words, phrases and adjectives a very sensitive spectrum between hate and love. This is fine for literature and poetry but absolutely useless for perception. Description is one thing but perception is another. Description describes perception that has happened. Perception is when it is happening. We need rich and subtle patterns at that point, not ways of describing nuances of feeling later.

So English speakers are actually cursed by the rich expressiveness of their language — and also the way the language is so proudly defended. The static language of Germany and the richer codes of Japan are crude at first but actually allow a subtler perception. The result may be a greater pragmatism.

The key point here is that descriptive ability is not the same as the instant of perception.

Imagine one landscape with a few very large catchment basins. Everything ends up in those rivers. Imagine another landscape with very many more and smaller catchment basins leading to different rivers. We could call these very large catchment areas concept 'sinks' or 'traps'. An elephant trap is a hole in the ground with sloping walls. The elephant slides down into the trap and cannot get out again.

Our civilized thinking is replete with such broad concept traps as: freedom, justice, democracy, imperialism. It is virtually impossible to think anywhere in the vicinity of these traps, as you will get sucked into accepted patterns which cannot be challenged. If you challenge democracy you must be a 'fascist' (another trap). If you hint at socialism you must be a 'Marxist'. Like English mushroom gatherers we have a limited number of crude concepts. French mushroom gatherers can recognize far more types of mushroom. This has been made necessary by the communication needs of democracy.

Now we come to the phenomenon of 'centring', which goes hand in hand with catchment. This means that, no matter how broad the catchment area, once something is drawn in (like something straying near the gravitational field of a black hole) it will be sucked right into the centre. In other words the patterns will show the purest types without any of the shading or qualifications that might have been there in the first place. So a criminal is a criminal is a criminal.

Of course we know that the purpose of civilization and education is to break down these crude categories into finer and more subtle distinctions. So why does it not work, as the young girl said to her grandmother who was putting on anti-wrinkle cream?

For the explanation we must look into the phrase 'seek to break down the large crude categories into more subtle ones'. The key word is 'breakdown'. We must also, at this point, look back to the Greek thinkers and Aristotle and to the basis of our logic. There are categories and classes and members of a set. But the category is above all. So we have the overall category of criminal and then we seek to break it down. To be sure there is a difference between an insider trader and a mass chain-saw murderer. But not much difference, because even as we hold these concepts in our mind we also hold, in the background, the overall category of criminal.

How else might we have done it? Instead of broad categories which then break down into more specific patterns we could have had a rich differentiation of patterns. We might then have noticed uniformities among these classes. We would not have proceeded to make overarching categories of these uniformities (the very basis of our Greek logic system) but would have treated them purely on a practical basis (all these people have broken legs, we can probably use plaster casts on them all).

I shall return later to the serious problems arising from our category habit which reinforces a bad habit of patterning systems.

I mentioned earlier the danger of the phrase 'the same as ...' in creative work. This is another example of catchment and is also used dismissively to get rid of anything new you do not like. Any reviewer who cannot understand what he or she is reading uses this strategy.

The very word 'creativity' is a huge concept trap in the English language. It covers everything from just making something happen (like creating a mess) to artistic creativity, to mathematical insights, to finger painting by children. That is one of the reasons, among many, why we have done so little about the matter. It was precisely to escape this concept trap that I invented the term 'lateral thinking' to apply very specifically to the changing of concepts and perceptions in a self-organizing patterning system.

We need many, many, many more new words. The outraged defenders of language will call these jargon ('same as ...' phenomenon). They will claim that the existing language is sufficient to describe anything – and so completely miss the point that description and perception are different. The word 'train' is fine. The phrase 'iron rail road' is absurd.

One of the things I have been working on is a new language for thinking that will allow us to perceive a much wider range of concepts, concepts that cannot be perceived in ordinary language because they would be contradictory or because of concept traps. Potentially the language would be much richer than English (for certain purposes only). The work has been done and I am now exploring the best way to introduce it.

With nouns we try to communicate what 'is'. Then there are adjectives which are quite different and set out to communicate what the communicator feels. The adjectives are there to set off the emotions of the listener, in resonance with those of the talker. Adjectives are insidious and highly dangerous because they trigger emotional backgrounds which may be totally unjustified. Any adjective in a critical review is suspect and bad writing. A reviewer at a furniture exhibition writes about a 'pretentious chair'. If the reader cannot see the actual chair he or she can only accept that disparagement.

Just as we have rather crude patterns for nouns, we have even cruder patterns for evaluation and adjectives. We have broad assessments such as good/bad, right/wrong. These have arisen for practical purposes – for bringing up a child, for simplifying education. Without a right/wrong system every student might be at the mercy of any idiosyncratic teacher. Religion needs a way of indicating what is permitted and what is not and accordingly offering reward and punishment. I shall soon come to the problem of knife-edge discrimination of dichotomies like right/wrong. For the moment I just want to dwell on the extraordinary broadness of these patterns.

It could be said that basic action is itself limited to 'do' or 'don't do', so there is every reason for the linking adjectives to be just as basic. It could be said that the chemical balances in the brain that determine our basic emotions are also limited, so it is appropriate to invite them to take part in as simple a manner. All this is to accept and enter the conspiracy of a dichotomy (on or off in an electronic switch).

You can visualize the source of a smell, or a situation with that smell, but not the smell itself. Yet we can recognize and act on a smell. What makes a good cook is the ability to re-taste or re-construct tastes in different parts of the mouth in order to devise a new dish. You cannot visualize adjectives like nice or horrible and yet will emotionally react to them. Again these are broad and unspecified. One of the problems of centring is that when an experience at the periphery falls into the catchment area of a pattern and is then 'centred' as a pure example of that pattern, all the adjectives and emotional baggage get attached to that perception. Suppose you wanted to put someone in a job where she would be happy and really use her skills. We do not have a word for that action. The nearest is the word 'manipulation', which has a whole lot of negative baggage (exploitation, self-interest, pulling the strings, treating people as objects). Much of argument consists of edging the opponent towards a catchment area and then pulling him in, with the result that all the negative baggage of the pattern can be attached.

So up to a point we should be very grateful for the broad catchment areas of patterns, but beyond that point this broadness becomes dangerous and limiting. So are broad catchment areas good or bad? The inability to describe situations where something is good up to a point but bad beyond that is a grave defect in our logical system that I shall come to later. In a table-top system qualities are attached firmly to entities.

Knife-Edge Discrimination

The scene is the 1988 Wimbledon singles tennis final: Boris Becker is playing Stefan Edberg. Edberg is at the net. Becker sends a hard drive towards him, Edberg steps aside and lets it pass. The ball lands a few inches over the baseline. How could Edberg have been able to tell that the ball was going to be out? It was travelling at a high speed and was only a few inches over the line. The answer is that the mind is extremely good at making knife-edge discriminations. Once again this arises simply and directly from the very nature of the sort of self-organizing system I have described.

An anthropologist is fascinated by two villages which are less than half a mile apart but speak dialects that are so different that they are almost different languages. Surely there would be interchange between the villages. Surely they would come to speak a very similar dialect. How could this come about? The answer is simple. There are two river valleys and settlements have formed along the rivers. People on the rivers came from, and communicated with, people down the river. So the dialects for each river settlement were different. Gradually the settlements spread inland away from the river bank until the circles of spread almost overlapped. The two villages half a mile apart were placed on the edges of the circle of spread. In other words the villages were standing back to back, facing in different directions.

We return now to that ridge in the west of Switzerland which is at the border of the two catchment basins of the Rhine and the Danube. In one direction your spit will be carried into the Rhine but if you spit in the other direction your spit will reach the Danube. If you imagine any two catchment basins spreading, there comes a knife-edge point when the two basins come into contact – they cannot overlap. At this knife-edge point a very slight difference will decide whether something goes one way or the other.

Imagine a tall, thin pole almost balanced upright on its point. The slightest movement will make it fall one way or the other. When it comes to rest on the ground the tip of the pole will be very far from where it would have been if the pole had fallen in the other direction.

Self-organizing systems are unstable between stable states (established patterns). They will always end up in one pattern or another. The process gives a very fine discrimination if the catchment basins for the two patterns are adjacent.

The two most class-ridden societies in the world are probably Great Britain and the Soviet Union. In Great Britain classes are based partly on history but also on a series of very complex signals (accent, schooling, clothes, job, confidence etc.). In the Soviet Union the classes are based on level of importance. In assessing the class of the person in front of him a man will make very fine discriminations, consciously and unconsciously ('He is not one of us'; 'She is not important').

This property of mind is very important in a survival sense because it overcomes dithering. Recognition, perception and judgement can be very rapid. As I shall explain presently the mind moves quickly from 'maybe' to complete certainty.

This knife-edge discrimination is used very strongly in the dichotomies that are so important in our traditional table-top logic system. In order to use the powerful principle of contradiction we have to have mutually exclusive categories. These are not easy to find, so we create them. We do this with the word 'not'.

Can you imagine a 'not-orange'. Probably not, but you can say it. You then go on to say that something cannot be an orange and a not-orange at the same time. So if we have 'democracy' anything else will be called 'not democracy'. This sort of thing is uncomfortable for the mind, since there are no natural 'not-orange' patterns.

With chess pieces it becomes much simpler. If you say a 'not-white piece' obviously you can visualize a black piece. So the mind tries to fill the 'not' slot with something tangible. 'Not-democracy' comes to mean 'dictatorship'.

Once dichotomies are established in this way the battle is lost. If you seek to challenge democracy you must be favouring dictatorship (and all the baggage it carries). Yet there are many states other than democracy and dictatorship, some of which I can conceive and some of which I cannot yet conceive.

I intend to explore this serious danger of dichotomies later in much more detail. The danger is that we set up this artificial system for the sake of our box logic and then let it slide into a practical way of looking at the world. This becomes the basis for all sorts of 'us' and 'them' discriminations – and also the impossibility of creating new perceptions that cut across this divide.

In a court case, if a person is not guilty then surely that person must be innocent. What other system could there be? Many court systems, such as the English courts, do work on this crude basis. Some systems allow further categories. In Scottish law there is the verdict of 'not proven', which is by no means the same as 'innocent'. In the US system there is something called 'noli contendere' whereby the defendant does not admit guilt but does not contend the charge. We might even imagine a future system in which we had verdicts of 'highly suspicious grade I' or 'somewhat suspicious grade IV'. I am not, at this point, arguing that this would be a better system – but it would be different.

Scientists are divided into 'lumpers' and 'splitters'. Lumpers progress by pointing out that things which had seemed very different actually belong in the same class or exhibit the same underlying process. Splitters, on the other hand, achieve progress by showing that things which have always been taken as similar or in the same class are actually very different. Both habits depend on observation, hypothesis, what you choose as your basis for discrimination and the knife-edge habit of mind.

It is obvious that broad catchment, centring and knife-edge discrimination can mean that two things that are really very close may get to be regarded as very different. This is the process of 'shift' in perception.

An unpaid volunteer spends her time and her money helping down-and-outs in a city. Surely this is noble, wonderful and Christian. Let us see what happens when the process of shift gets to work. The first catchment is the term 'well-meaning', which is true enough but already carries a slight sneer. The next catchment is 'do-gooder' and here the implication is one of 'self-indulgence' and doing good for your own sake. The next shift is into 'nuisance'. This is how we can set about knocking anything if we so choose, through the process of shift.

Pre-emption

In gold-rush days each miner scurries to stake out his or her own claim. In opal mining in Australia you stake out your claim and then try to resist the temptation to tunnel sideways under your neighbour's claim. If someone has already staked a claim, you cannot stake another claim to that piece of land. You have been pre-empted. If there is a river flowing along your land you cannot cut a drainage channel to go across the river.

If there is already a pattern established it is not possible to establish another pattern in the same area because our mind will always swing back to the first pattern. The phenomenon of 'the same as . . .' is but one example of this. The result is that we are stuck with our patterns, perceptions, concepts and words.

Language is an encyclopaedia of ignorance. Words and concepts became established at a period of relative ignorance – which each period must be, compared to the subsequent period. Once the perceptions and concepts are frozen into the permanence of language, they control and limit our thinking on any subject because we are forced to use those concepts. Should we try to develop new concepts, others would not understand us (after accusing us of jargon) and would, in any case, interpret the new words in terms of existing ones ('same as . . .'). This is clearly the same phenomenon as we met earlier with regard to how much a researcher should read in his or her field and so be forced to follow existing perceptions.

We need a lot of new words to allow us to say – and to perceive – things which we cannot perceive at the moment. Perception needs a framework just as the scientific examination of evidence needs the perceptual framework of a hypothesis. But we also need new words to say afresh things which are now said with concepts that are inadequate or carry a heavy negative baggage. In order to make progress there are a lot of basic concepts that we may need to re-conceptualize.

It is sometimes possible to establish a new pattern as a finer discrimination within an existing pattern: just as the concept of lateral thinking was established within 'creativity'. Patterns can sometimes be changed by adding something to them and eventually shifting their meaning. They can be changed by altering their emotional loading – at least the pattern may stay the same but the effect changes. For example the concept of 'old-fashioned' swings in and out of favour. Sometimes 'old-fashioned' is a sneer meaning left behind or out of date. Sometimes it means a return to true values, true craftsmanship and non-processed cooking.

Patterns rarely die through being attacked, for this just reinforces their use. They die through atrophy and neglect. They can also die or be changed through an alteration in the context. For example the context of the birth control pill changed many perceptions about sexual behaviour. It is sometimes possible to start a totally different pattern and then gradually extend its catchment area until it may take over some catchment from the original pattern you want to change.

But the fundamental difficulty remains. This is the establishment of a new pattern in territory that has been pre-empted for an existing pattern. Try having a conversation with a business executive in which you seek to re-design the concept of 'profit'.

Mismatch

Up to a certain age a child wants a story to be told in exactly the same way. The slightest deviation by the parent is immediately pounced upon. Then an age is reached when the child wants new stories.

One of the basic elements of traditional table-top logic is the principle of contradiction. This is totally artificial, but of value when dealing with static systems and symbol systems. Its relevance to the real world is much less, for something may be or not be depending on how it is looked at and also the circumstance of the moment. In spite of this artificiality there is a strong natural counterpart to contradiction in the human brain. This is mismatch.

In a famous experiment (Bruner) subjects were asked to look rapidly through a pack of cards. Amongst the cards would be some mismatches, for example a black eight of hearts. Apparently there were subjects who felt physically sick at this point.

At first sight there appears to be a contradiction between the concept of mismatch in which something has to be exactly as expected and the concept of broad catchment in which anything roughly within range is accepted into a pattern. In fact there is no contradiction. The broad catchment is before we enter the pattern. A whole range of inputs will eventually stabilize as a particular pattern. But once the pattern is entered or in motion, any slight deviation will instantly be noticed. This is a sort of inbuilt anomaly detection.

Someone tells you that he was on holiday on the east coast of Scotland and enjoyed watching the trout jump up a waterfall.

Instantly you have an urge to tell him that they were not trout but salmon. This is because jumping up waterfalls is a characteristic behaviour of salmon. So it seems to you that he has got the wrong pattern. You may also have special knowledge that trout do not jump up waterfalls. In that case there is also a mismatch within the trout pattern.

In effect there are several types of mismatch. One type is: 'That fits better with another pattern.' A second type is: 'There is nothing in my experience to support what you offer.' A third type is: 'What you suggest is directly counter to my experience.' A fourth type is: 'What you suggest is logically impossible.' The last type has some reference to something else like the laws of physics (for example the suggestion of a perpetual motion machine).

What is the importance of the natural mismatch phenomenon? It is that once the rigid categories, absolutes and dichotomies of our table-top logic are accepted into our perception — through language and in other ways — the vehemence of our natural mismatch system gets applied to this rigid perception with consequences that are at worst disastrous and at best far from flexible. If we were pretty relaxed about mismatches and simply shrugged or said 'So what?' or 'It doesn't really matter if the pattern isn't quite right,' the rigidities would matter much less.

Maybe there is survival value in the mismatch effect. If you switch on a pattern and then follow it, you may need a mechanism for disengagement. If a yellow berry signals 'OK to eat' but then the taste is unusually bitter you need a way of breaking off. That is why rats can be so difficult to poison.

It may be that in system terms mismatch is just instability in the nerve network with inability to settle down to an established pattern.

Readiness

'Readiness' is extremely important and is a key part of the behaviour of the self-organizing nerve network I have described. I have already covered this matter in my description of that network, but it is important enough to repeat here, in a different way.

Imagine a beach with some sunbathing beauties lying half asleep on their towels. A team of good-natured octopuses with very long arms creeps quietly up onto the beach between the bathers. The octopuses gentle tickle some of the bathers, but not strongly enough to make anyone laugh. The tickled bathers are 'ready' to laugh, or more ready than the untickled bathers. One bather is fortunate enough to be tickled by two octopuses at once. That bather bursts out in a shriek of laughter.

In a more exact model the shriek of laughter would actually inhibit all other bathers from laughing. In addition the bather would herself be an octopus who, once awakened, would then set about tickling her neighbours. What I want to focus on is the 'readiness to laugh'. There are degrees of readiness, then suddenly a threshold is reached and laughter rings out.

If you arrive late during the performance of a comedian you often cannot see why people around you are shrieking with laughter. What the comedian is saying is mildly funny but no more. The point is that the readiness to laugh of your neighbours has been built up before you got to the performance.

In the nerve networks of the brain you read 'excitation' or 'activity' for bursting into laughter. A nerve unit is tickled up by inputs from other units. A threshold point is reached whereupon that nerve unit springs into activity. This effect is often called a 'threshold' effect and is characteristic of nerve structures. It is a typical non-linear effect. There is input and more input but nothing happens – then, suddenly, the nerve is fully active. The expression 'threshold' comes directly from a simple analogy. There is flooding in the street outside: heavy rains or faulty drains. The inside of your house is perfectly dry. The water level in the street rises. Still your house is dry. But as soon as the water level reaches the top of your 'threshold' the water floods in and soon your house is as deeply flooded as the street outside.

In computers and electronic machines we are used to looking at either analogue machines or digital systems. That is the dichotomy we know. In analogue systems the signal is proportional to the input, just as a scale indicates your actual weight. In digital machines the signal is treated as a series of on/off signals. It is as if there were a series of switches each of which could only be fully on or fully off. The digital method is much easier to deal with because we can always re-create the exact signal by repeating the on/off sequence. It is as if a photograph was made up of minute boxes which could only be fully black or fully white. If you had the instructions for each box you could always imitate the original photograph exactly.

But the brain system is neither digital nor analogue. It is analogue up to a point and then digital and then analogue again and then digital again. All this is set against a background of chemicals that give gradients and field effects. It is possible that the analogue/digital dichotomy has made it more difficult for electronic engineers to understand the brain system.

To increase the 'readiness' of something (a bather to laugh, a nerve unit to become active) is to sensitize that thing to further inputs. So the various inputs into the mind sensitize various areas. Suddenly an area springs into activity. This area eventually tires and is succeeded by another, depending on input and also connectedness to the first area. So several states follow each other in sequence and eventually settle down into a pattern (which may be represented by a repeating circuit or a temporary stabilization).

That is how the brain puts things together and assesses probability and competing claims. That is how catchment for a pattern takes place. The sensitizing inputs create a whole area of 'maybe' in the brain. Suddenly this springs into 'certainty' and we feel this as a flash of recognition. So the brain is a 'maybe' device that switches into the certainty that we need for action.

Poetry is based directly on this sensitizing effect. Each word, image and metaphor stimulates part of the brain and the over-all effect is a jumble of patterns or even just emotion. In contrast to prose, which seeks to communicate one pattern at a time, there is an overlay of patterns. Prose must make sense. Poetry must produce an effect. Prose is communication. Poetry is sensitizing. Poetry is a squad of tickling octopuses on the beach. Prose is a daisy chain in which each person tickles only the next person. This distinction is rather too sharp, because there are times when prose also seeks an overlay of multiple images. Modern art could be said to be poetry as against the prose of classic art, except that in art there is always an overlay of images just as there is with smell.

Poetry is closer to perceptual logic and prose is closer to table-top logic. In poetry we begin to develop the operation of 'movement' which is so essential in the creativity of lateral thinking. 'Movement' has no place and no logical basis in table-top logic.

If we understand the process of sensitization, we can build from it to develop new grammatical forms. For example, I am suggesting here a 'stratal', which is related to 'strata' and simply means a 'layer structure'. A stratal would consist of four or five lines in parallel about a subject. Each line is complete in itself and does not carry over to the next line. The lines do not have to add up to a conclusion. The stratal is not a definition and does not seek to be comprehensive. It may contain contradictory statements. It does not have to have rhyme or meter like poetry. It is somewhat related to blank verse but has no artistic pretensions. Its purpose is to sensitize the mind – just as poetry does. Here is a stratal on traditional table-top logic:

Boxes on a table with high sides, once in there is no way out.

Messiness of perceptions into the certainty and comfort of truth.

Examined pieces assigned to the boxes with a cleared table.

A belief system with a great value we have outgrown.

How to tell a Frenchman, in English, that he should speak English.

   Here is a stratal on perceptual logic:

A landscape with rain organizing itself into rivers.

A rubber model of the landscape with features inflating and collapsing.

Enough certainly for action but not enough for a prison.

Existing crude and cumbersome concepts frozen into place.

New words and new concepts as tools for new thinking.

   If that sounds too much like bad poetry, that is because it should not be seen as poetry at all. A stratal is a form of perceptual communication. Advertisers have been working in this direction for years.

Context

You have just come towards the end of dinner at the Courtyard Restaurant of the Windsor Arms hotel in Toronto. On the table in front of you there is a rich brown chocolate mousse made with armagnac (perhaps your dining companion ordered it). Let us look at a variety of possible reactions.

'I really like chocolate mousse and I'm going to enjoy eating this.' Perhaps you are still hungry or, even if not very hungry, you will still enjoy eating the mousse.

'I couldn't eat another bite of anything.' You have eaten too much and have no appetite at all for the chocolate mousse.

'I'd love to eat it but I'm on a strict diet and must resist the temptation.' You feel like eating it but there is an over-riding instruction to yourself.

'I'd love to eat it but I've found that chocolate gives me migraines, as it does with some people.' Some prior knowledge affects your reaction to the mousse.

'Since I've had jaundice the sight of that mousse makes me feel sick.' A change in the body chemistry has changed the way you feel about the mousse.

In all these cases the mousse and the setting are exactly the same but the reactions are very different. So here we come to a key point. If the brain is indeed a patterning system and if we are locked into patterns, surely the chocolate mousse must trigger the same pattern and we should behave towards it in exactly the same way every time. Something of this sort has always been the main objection to 'patterning' concepts of mind.

The key factor is the 'context'. A different context will mean that different patterns are followed. But what does 'context' mean in terms of the nerve circuits in the brain? Here we link up with 'readiness' or 'sensitivity', described in the preceding section.

Let us take the example of jaundice, which often kills appetite. There are chemical alterations which affect the hunger mechanism so that this no longer sensitizes other areas. So the mousse is no longer attractive. The same applies if we have overfed. If we are hungry, however, the hunger mechanism sensitizes other areas, so the 'mousse to be enjoyed' pattern is very active. This matter can go further. If we are not very hungry (but not jaundiced or overfed), the sight of the mousse may switch on the hunger mechanism which in turn makes the mousse attractive. Here we see how perception can change an 'emotion' (in the broad chemical sense of that word) which will then affect perception.

So the change in context may be brought about by chemical changes in the brain. That is why people sometimes feel like sex and sometimes do not – and why perception can sometimes change that feeling.

The 'readiness to go' among the different patterns in the brain can also be altered by other inputs into the brain which are there at the same time. Such inputs include the self-instruction of dieting and also knowledge of the migraine connection.

A simple example of self-instruction changing perception is an experiment anyone can do at a sports meeting. First you just look around at the crowd. Then you give yourself the instruction to pick out people who are wearing 'red'. You now look at the crowd again. Suddenly you notice all the people wearing red. You try it again for yellow. The self-instruction has altered the readiness of the mind to notice red or yellow. I shall return to this point when considering the process of attention.

Here we come to an interesting and very important point about free-will. In practice it probably does not matter whether we really do have free-will or only the illusion of it. I have given a person a post-hypnotic suggestion suddenly to put up an umbrella in the middle of a dinner party on hearing a trigger word. The person does this and immediately rationalizes that he was acting freely for a specific reason. Recent experiments have suggested that the brain actually starts carrying out an action even before the person has consciously made the decision to do the action. This makes it seem that 'free-will' is just a description of what is happening anyway.

In some ways this is a very basic and important philosophical point, because much of our civilization is based on the concept of 'free-will'. Religion, reward, punishment, law all depend on this basis.

Imagine that the situation in front of us stimulates the 'I' pattern (which is like any other). Now that pattern, which includes our past experience and knowledge of law, religious precepts etc., then triggers an emotion which in turn alters the way we see things and allows us to make a decision which seems contrary to normal inclinations. So the 'I' factor is actually making the decision. This we call free-will. So patterning systems do not exclude free-will. But discussions of free-will without apprecia- tion of the behaviour of patterning systems are pointless. In short the 'I' is a context factor.

The readiness of any pattern to fire or go active or become the stabilized pattern is determined by a number of factors which together form the context:

Other inputs that are there at the same time or triggered off. These include self-instruction and other external matters (for example a note saying 'this mousse is contaminated').

Immediate history, including what has just happened before, which will affect readiness through the 'tiredness' of circuits and their recovery.

General background or the whole situation, which will affect context even if it has not been noticed at a conscious level.

Emotions, which probably act through a chemical effect but could also have direct nerve links.

Chemical background, which may be either local in the brain or part of a general bodily chemical setting.

The 'connectedness' of the different patterns, which is based on historic association and will determine readiness to 'go next' (this is not so much context as part of the potential pattern available).

Remote history or stored knowledge, which will determine the connectedness mentioned in the previous sentence.

So we can see that there are many factors which determine context. In this way a patterning system can give a very rich response. It is more like an airliner than a train, which must stick to the tracks. The route of the airliner will be determined by the context of air space available, weather conditions, airport conditions etc. In the past it has always been claimed that patterning systems are too restricted and rigid to describe the richness of human experience. This was because philosophers, without any system knowledge, could base their understanding of patterning systems only on the word 'pattern'. Now if philosophers insist on that restricted meaning of pattern, we must design a new word for these self-organizing patterning systems. Again we see the restrictions of language and table-top logic.

There is a story (like most good stories, probably untrue) that in the early days of the computer translation of language a computer was asked to translate into Russian the phrase: 'The spirit is willing, but the flesh is weak.' Without hesitation the computer printed out: 'The vodka is agreeable but the meat is inferior.' The problem of computer translation of language has always been that of context in the very literal meaning of that word. The words around the sense and the title of the piece are all part of the context and have sensitized parts of the brain so that certain patterns are more easily aroused than others. The brain makes an easy and automatic job of context because of the phenomenon of sensitization, which is a normal part of nerve behaviour.

Once again I want to emphasize that the phenomena I have described in this book (such as context) are not special things which the brain has been programmed to carry out but arise directly, simply and inevitably from the natural behaviour of the nerve system I have described.

Many important practical things can be developed from a good understanding of context. Some artists and storytellers use them implicitly. I want, however, to put forward an extremely simple thinking technique based directly on the phenomenon of context.

The 'six thinking hats' system is now being used effectively by many major corporations, including the most valuable corporation (stock market value) in the world, which is Nippon Telephone and Telegraph (NTT) in Japan (350,000 employees).

We set up six artificial contexts for thinking and characterize these as six hats which can be put on or removed, metaphorically. There is the white hat for attention to pure and neutral data. There is the red hat to allow the input of intuition and feeling without any need for justification. There is the black hat of the logical negative, which is caution and points out why something cannot be done. There is the yellow hat of the logical positive, which focuses on the benefits and feasibility. For creative thinking there is the green hat, which calls for new ideas and further alternatives. Finally there is the blue hat for process control, which looks not at the subject but at the thinking about the subject (meta-cognition).

The six hat system works very much like the suggested self-instruction at the sports meeting (look for people wearing red, yellow etc.) which I mentioned earlier in this section. The hats are a ritual which sets the context. In effect they offer an artificial form of emotion.

There are suggestions that the brain chemistry may be slightly different when we think positively from when we think negatively. If this is so, something like the six hat system is a necessity, because if we try to do all types of thinking at once, we can never get the optimal brain chemistry for each type. If there is indeed this chemical change, the hats can serve as intermediaries to set the right chemicals.

What is most important is that this simple system turns out to be highly effective in practice and its use is spreading rapidly to organizations which are tired of the unproductive nature of argument.

From a consideration of 'context', one very important point arises. Traditional table-top logic with its absolutes simply does not allow for context: a thing is a thing is a thing; a criminal is a criminal is a criminal. Whether a theft is committed through desperate need to feed a family, or for kicks, or as a convenient way to make a living, the end result is a simple criminal. In practice we do allow some flexibility in terms of extenuating circumstances and sentencing, but that is really bucking the system. This failure to consider circumstance is a major defect of traditional table-top logic and as a remedy I shall later be suggesting and explaining a new type of logic called 'hodics', which replaces the absolute of 'is' with the flow of 'to'. In this new type of 'water' logic all we can say is: A flows to B in circumstance C.

Circularity

There is a story that in the great days of the Houston boom the chief executive suites were shifted from super penthouse positions to the ground floor. This was because the fire chief insisted on so many fire drills in which executives had to evacuate buildings without using the elevators.

A very talented journalist friend of mine will walk twenty floors up to a New York party because she has a phobia about lifts. She is not afraid of the lift breaking and rushing to the ground but of being trapped. Whenever she looks at a lift she sees only a place in which to be trapped. The chances of being so trapped are probably less than choking on a piece of steak, but perception does not compute statistics. There is a simple circularity about phobias because, if you always avoid the situation you fear, you can never get enough experience of it to show that your fears are groundless. If you never talk to a nasty colleague you may never discover that he is a sweetie at heart.

One farmer (nationality omitted) said to another: 'You see the trails made by those planes high up in the sky. Well, they are trying to make rain. I can prove it. You never see them on cloudy days, do you?' There is a nice circularity to this and, once again, perception is a key element.

Suppose we have a hypothesis that the whole of a person's personality is ultimately determined by that person's love for their mother. If a person in later life shows love for their mother, this supports our view. If the person hates her, we explain this by saying that hate is really another form of love and amounts to the same thing. If the person shows indifference towards her, we interpret this indifference as being love which is deliberately suppressed. With this hypothesis, belief system, or way of looking at the world we may then find that every case we look at confirms our belief. If this belief suggestion appears to resemble the Freudian hypothesis, that is only the effect of the 'same as . . .' phenomenon I have already mentioned many times.

Any scientific hypothesis sets out a scaffold for perception which permits us to seek data which will reinforce that hypothesis. In all these cases we see a broad type of circularity taking effect. The basic principle is that there are perceptions which allow us to see the world in a way which will strengthen those perceptions. Perceptions are a form of 'readiness to perceive' and act through the sensitivity and context mechanisms, so that we are more likely to see something than something else, as in setting the mind to pick out people wearing red clothes at the sports meeting. We shall return to this matter when considering the phenomenon of attention.

A woman executive in a bank does not get promoted to a senior post that she feels she deserves. She claims that it is because of gender discrimination. Because she sees it that way it will be that way to her. The real reason may be that she was not so competent as the person who got the post. Clearly there are times when either of these explanations may be true. But in every case a feminist would be entitled to perceive it as gender discrimination, so the belief would be eternally reinforced.

In Great Britain an Indian developed a rare form of skin condition in which the skin loses all pigment (vitiligo). In effect he became 'white'. This permitted him unusual insights into being both brown and white in one lifetime. His comment was that very often (in the area where he lived) people were so ready to see racial discrimination that ordinary rudeness by a shop assistant would always be interpreted in this way.

Language and perception is a very basic form of circularity. Experience provides us with language which is a referral system for experience. In particular language allows us deliberately to bring to mind experiences which are not available, at the moment. But once we have language we may be able to see the world only in the ways defined, packaged, and boxed by language. That is a danger I have already mentioned – the danger of crude language concepts – and shall return to later.

Circularity is a very basic function of any self-organizing patterning system. A simple illustration of how such a system will settle down into a repeating pattern was given earlier. It may be that what we regard as a 'thought' is always a circularity of this sort – or a thought may be a temporary stability in the flow of activity from one active area to the next (on the basis that the next area is so 'unready' that activity stays longer with the present area).

Concepts may also be based directly on circularities which may include in their circuit the actual language word we use for the concept. In this sense concepts are really 'mini-beliefs'.

As we move up the scale we come to the macro-circularities described in this section. With these, experience triggers a perception which then controls what we see in front of us. We saw that phenomenon with one instance of the chocolate mousse. We are not specifically hungry but the sight of the mousse makes us hungry, so we now see the mousse as desirable.

This circularity is important because it can be seen as the basis of phobias, paranoia and belief systems in general. Paranoia is a fascinating mental illness because it seems to differ from all others. Most mental illness involves a breakdown in meaning and co-ordination. Paranoia goes in the opposite way. There seems to be an excess of meaning. Everything that happens can be fitted, with wonderful logic, into a complete picture, with the sufferer as the centre point. Once that mind-set or belief system is in place, any experience can be interpreted in this light and used to reinforce the belief. The phone rings and it is a wrong number. Obviously, someone is checking up where the person is at that moment. A car is parked across the street all day: it must contain observers. The registration number of the car can be construed as having a special significance. A headline in the newspaper is sending a threatening message.

It is clear that circular belief systems are very easy in the brain and therefore belief is a cheap commodity. People are willing to believe almost anything. Belief is a form of perceptual truth, but it may be far removed from reality. This is not to say that there can be no true belief systems. All those readers who know their belief systems to be true will know that my remarks do not apply to them but only to false belief systems. Beliefs are self-fulfilling systems. Our wonderful development of language allows us to form complex circularities by putting in, as links, abstract ideas which are not part of daily experience.

For centuries one of the much enjoyed philosophical arguments (by those attacking each other) was between those who felt that things existed in their own right and we were only permitted to observe them, and those who believed that things existed only as we observed them. I think one lot were called nominalists and the other lot idealists, but I am uncertain which was which, though I suspect the observer lot were nominalists. As with most philosophical arguments both sides were right. Experience forms perceptions and perceptions (through a name or language) allow us to see things in a particular way. When you look up at the night sky do you see a spot of light or do you see a 'star'?

There are all sorts of auxiliary aids that have been used to reinforce belief systems. For example if you create a class of bad people, enemies, or unbelievers, that must make you 'good' people. Ritual is valuable as a reinforcer because every time it is carried out there is a reinforcement. Indeed the strongest belief systems usually have a lot of ritual. Also ritual discourages straying because there has to be a conscious effort 'not' to carry out the ritual and also there is a guilt point. National flags and symbols are part of this whole apparatus of belief and categorization. Any category is itself a belief system and as we divide 'us' and 'them' we reinforce that system. At the same time as having the categories we look for finer and finer points of knife-edge discrimination.

Later I shall discuss the very valuable contribution of belief systems in setting a structure for evaluation and purpose. At the same time belief systems in their most rigid forms have been the cause of much strife. What I wanted to do in this section is to show that 'circularity' is a very natural and easy phenomenon in self-organizing patterning systems and that what we call 'truth' is often dependent on this circularity.

Making Sense

I was told, in Moscow, that the Red Star of the Soviet army actually came from Trotsky's interest in the Kabala and was based on the pentagram, which is one of the significant symbols. Now the US military establishment is housed in a building shaped in pentagon fashion and is often referred to simply as the 'Pentagon'. Surely there must be some significance in the use by both opposing military establishments of the same 'penta' symbol. Maybe there is and maybe there is not – but the mind has a wonderful urge, and ability, to make sense of things.

When things are presented to it, the mind tries hard to make sense of what is before it. In fact the mind does not try to do anything. What happens is that the various inputs into the self-organizing system create a state of activity which eventually settles down into a stable state. It is the stable state that is the 'sense'.

If, in the scene we are confronting, there is something we recognize, we may ignore the rest and follow only that pattern. This is an aspect of attention I shall come to later. But if there is nothing so obvious or we want to make sense of the whole, we do try to put things together.

In nerve circuit terms the process is one of association. Philosophers and psychologists have long talked about association and usually with good sense. In technical terms, at a micro-level, it means that, if two areas of nerve network are activated together, in future the connectedness of these networks will be higher than otherwise. I predicted this in *The Mechanism of Mind* and now it has been shown to be a physiological fact. This increased connectedness is brought about by a specific enzyme which develops at the contact points to facilitate transmission along that route.

So there are three things that can happen with inputs to the brain. A broad catchment may lead to the emergence of a particular pattern. Some part of the situation may attract attention (and lead to a pattern) and the rest is just ignored. The whole scene may be put together to make sense. As we get older there are more patterns already formed, so the 'learning' or making sense aspect drops away.

Perhaps the simplest example of 'making sense' is cause and effect. If something is always followed by something else we are inclined to say that the first thing has 'caused' the second thing. This type of association is natural and the philosopher Kant was probably right in assuming that the brain has a certain limited number of ways of putting things together. 'Cause and effect' gives a time sequence which can be picked up and repeated in the time sequence of pattern flow in the brain. After a while this natural perception of association across time becomes firmly established as a concept so that whenever something happens we always try to find the cause.

When I practised as a doctor many patients with cancer would try hard to find some event which they believed to have triggered the cancer. It may have been a heavy fall or a period of worry. We now believe that there may be some truth in the notion of mental states lowering immune system efficiency, but what was clear was the need to 'find a cause'.

Cause and effect is a grouping across time. When we group at an instant of time we get recognizable objects, situations, experiences and concepts. Repetition of the same grouping will allow us to isolate these repeated experiences from one-time experiences. If at the same time we are learning a language then the language-described experiences will be favoured. If we take a hallucinogen, like LSD, we may (through discoordination of neural paths) disrupt this packaging so that we now see things not as known objects but as shapes and forms or colour, or in all their 'isness', as some would say. That this may be an interesting experience is possible; that it is an approach to deeper truths is only a matter of belief. Which is the more true: a piano in tune or one out of tune? That analogy could be countered with: which is the best, a piano playing a new tune or one playing an old one?

Imagine you have a number of plastic pieces on a table in front of you and you are asked to put them together in the best way to suggest a human face or a bridge. You will have some success. If you were not given any specific instructions but just asked to put them together to make some picture, you would move the pieces around a bit until a picture suggested itself which you would then try to complete. If you were not happy with it or just naturally creative you might try again and again. It is just possible you might scatter the pieces randomly, then look to see what you had and rationalize that it was indeed a picture (that represents the feet, that the head etc.). Mostly you would move the pieces until some possible picture suggested itself and then go on to form that picture.

The pieces do not need to be concrete. You could have a set of abstract concepts which you are trying to build into a picture. You try them out in different ways and get different pictures. If there are obvious gaps, you might fill them with a newly con-structed concept. This sort of game-playing is more or less what philosophers have been doing over the ages in order to construct a picture of the world. It is what every individual does, day to day, on a less exalted level.

At one point in history Talleyrand (in France) and Metternich (in Austria) were two cunning opponents in the diplomatic games and power struggles which occupied the attention of Europe at that time. When Talleyrand died and the news reached Prince Metternich he was heard to mutter: 'I wonder what he meant by that.' Everything has its significance if we think it has.

People who go to clairvoyants or have their fortunes told often find that they can integrate what they have been told into their lives in such a way that the predictions seem true. This is usually a matter of paying attention to some things and ignoring others, of giv-ing high significance to something that would otherwise have been ignored, of self-fulfilling prophecies (if you are told you are going to meet a significant dark stranger you will treat the next dark stranger with a significance that may indeed lead to true significance). This does not prove that clairvoyants are charlatans, it simply sees that the mind has a wonderful capacity for making sense.

It is the natural tendency of a self-organizing patterning system to reach a stable state that gives rise to this ability to make sense.

Attention

Art is a choreography of attention.

You stand in front of a fine building. It makes sense as a whole. Then your attention flows to the pillars, the placement of the windows, perhaps the architrave, then back to one part of the whole, then to the detail of some scroll work. This is a dance of attention.

Attention is perhaps the most fascinating aspect of the behaviour of perception. As you stand in front of the building you feel you can direct attention to any part you like. You can choose to look at the front door. You can choose to look at the upper left-hand corner. You can choose to look at the proportions of the whole. Such choosing reinforces the notion of 'I' and free-will.

So there is attention flow and attention directing. I want to look at attention directing first. Walk into a room and looking fixedly ahead repeat to yourself: 'Chair, chair, chair.' Unless you consciously resist it, you will find your attention drawn to the chair in the room (if there is one) even though you are not looking at it. This is an exactly parallel process to the self-instruction to find red clothing at the sports meeting. The instruction sensitizes certain circuits and so these patterns become active and we notice or pay attention to these things.

The attention-directing instructions may be even more simple. An explorer returns from a far land and reports on an active volcano and a strange bird that does not fly. What else was there? The sponsoring committee want more than that for their money. So they send the explorer back with some simple attention-directing instructions: look north and note what you see, then east, then south, then west. Equipped with this simple attention-directing framework the explorer returns with a more professional report.

This is exactly the method we use for teaching thinking in schools with the CoRT programme. In the section designed to improve breadth in perception we have a set of simple attention-directing tools. For example there is the PMI. This tool is used for deliberate scanning of the Plus, Minus and Interesting points, so that a thinker can properly evaluate a suggestion instead of just taking an initial emotional view and using thinking only to defend that view. There is the C&S (Consequence and Sequel) for paying attention to the consequences of an action. There is the OPV tool for paying attention to the other people involved and their view. The tools are practised on a variety of different subjects so that skill is built up in the use of the tool which can then be transferred to real-life situations – and is indeed so transferred.

A person stands before a picture and says: 'I like it' or 'I don't like it.' After a course on art appreciation that same person stands before a picture but now has a handful of attention-directing tools: look at the composition; look at the choice of colours; look at the use of light and shade; look at the brushwork; look at the way the clothing is treated; look at the background; look at the background figures. After a time this richer attention scan becomes automatic. In addition there are things that will now be noticed that may indicate a period of painting or a particular painter or a particular period of a particular painting (Picasso late period, Warhol early period).

We cannot see things unless we are prepared to see them. That is why science advances by fits and starts as paradigms change and we are allowed to see things differently (I shall return to this point later). That is why the analysis of data can never produce all the ideas present in that data. That is why analysis is a limited tool, not the complete one we have always believed it to be (I shall also return to this point later). The James Gleick book on Chaos shows how the pioneers in this field went back to look at old data but to look at it with new perceptions and could now see new things.

We come back now to sensitivities in the nerve network and the readiness to go active. Contrast the directing of attention by specific self-instruction (look at the upper right-hand corner) with attention flow. We look at a scene with a mind that has been sensitized by hunger. Immediately our attention is drawn to the food. We look at a scene with a mind sensitized to pick out certain patterns, so we notice them. We look at a scene with a mind sensitized to pick up the slightest hint of insult or discrimination, so we immediately notice this (even if unintended). Sometimes we use the word 'notice' when attention seems to flow to a particular area or when we pick something out.

In reality there is very little difference between directed attention and attention flow. The directions sensitize our minds so attention flows into that area. In the sports meeting example our instruction sensitizes the mind to notice red, so our attention flows to red clothing.

Underlying all this there is one key feature which I have not yet mentioned. This is the 'unitary' nature of attention. It is in the nature of a self-organizing patterning system (at least the one I have described) to have a single area of stabilization. If there are two competing areas at any time, the large one will expand and the lesser one will disappear even if the difference is very slight. This arises directly from the wiring of the system and is not an imposed condition. It leads to one area of attention at a time. It does not exclude the possibility that there are functionally different and parallel brains within our skulls.

Relevance and Meaning

A toilet sign at an airport may have meaning but no relevance if you do not happen to need to go to the toilet. If you need to go to the toilet, the sign has both meaning and relevance. If you were in Japan or Greece and could not even read the lettering, the sign would have relevance but no meaning. So you would never know how relevant it was.

If you collect beetles, Byzantine icons or incunabula, any specimen in your collecting field that you come across has a great deal of relevance. It might be a new item which you do not have in your collection. You may already have one of the items but you will want to compare this new one with your own.

As a visitor to a country you are listening in to an intense sports conversation: about baseball in the USA or cricket in England. Some of the terms used do not make sense to you, for example 'offspin bowling' or 'silly mid-on' in cricket and a 'loaded base' in baseball. You just do not have those recognition patterns available in your brain. Someone will explain the terms to you, but you are likely to forget them very soon. But most of the sports conversation will have meaning, in the conventional sense, though very little relevance. An Englishman may not really care what the St Louis Cardinals are doing in the World Series and an American might not much care whether Gower is to captain England in the first test match.

For there to be meaning there has to be a pattern. For there to be relevance that pattern has to have some importance. What do we mean by importance? Relevance is easy enough if there is some need (full bladder, hunger, or an aroused sex drive). All these will have an input, either chemical or neurological, which will sensitize some parts of the nerve network more than others. But what if the matter is more cerebral, like collecting icons or beetles? We can avoid the problem by just saying that even these things become emotional. There may be a more 'interesting' answer.

The interest may lie in the very word 'interest'. What makes something interesting? The answer to that question is extremely valuable because if you are making films or designing TV programmes or publishing books you need to know what your viewers and readers are going to find interesting.

I believe that we can begin to work out the sheer mechanics of interest. What makes one thing interesting and another thing less interesting? Why are 'games shows' apparently interesting (which suits TV programmers because they are also cheap to produce)? Why has snooker (pool) been such a success in England on BBC-2? Very few of the viewers understood the game and even fewer had ever played it.

There is the interest of a rich-pattern repertoire. If around any subject there is a rich network of patterns, that subject becomes interesting. Any subject can be made interesting in this way. The problem is to build up that rich network, because if we do not have some initial interest in doing this then we never shall. That is supposed to be one of the purposes of education: to build up a critical mass of interest, for example in literature, so that thereafter the interest is self-sustaining. It may be that your father has been very interested in photography or bee-keeping and so the background of patterns is gradually built up at home. There is a hump or investment threshold. Up to that point it may be effort (though not always), but after that the investment pays off in 'interest'.

The whole thing can be argued the other way round. If you happen to like a certain pop star, your interest in that matter may lead you to build up a very detailed knowledge of every aspect of that star's life. The more the detail the more the interest becomes self-sustaining. Both mechanisms are at work. The output is the same: a richness of patterns so that the initially excited pattern does not just die away with the neurological equivalent of 'so what?'.

A second type of interest seems to have different mechanics. You want to know what is going to happen next. With snooker (pool) you see the coloured balls on the nice green background. You see the serious intent of the player (who has been built up by the commentator as a character). It is very obvious what the player is trying to do: get the right ball into the pocket. It is obvious that you are going to have to wait only a few seconds to find out. So you wait those few seconds. And then the next few seconds. And the next. The mechanics of a game show are similar. The background is the prize money and the human interest of the lively participants, who have been carefully screened for the show. In the USA, it is by no means just anyone who can compete on game shows. Then there is the clear direction of expectation: will the questions be answered? Again you have to wait only a few seconds. So you wait. If the expectation is clear and the time is short, the mind needs to remove 'the will she/won't she' uncertainty.

Where the working-out of some suspended question takes a long time, as in a drama, the TV viewer is simply not going to wait around. To keep things going there has to be a lot of moment-to-moment incident (the cheapest form is violence) or an interest in the characters, which is back to the 'investment' type of interest and is difficult to build up. It may, however be built up over time, as in classic soaps such as *Dallas* or *Dynasty*.

I think that very shortly we shall be able to work out the neurological mechanics of interest in a definite way. Here I have only touched on the subject with a mention of two types of interest: rich network interest and expectancy loops.

Zero-Hold

The invention of the 'zero' in mathematics made a fantastic difference. Previously, in both Greek and Roman mathematics, multiplication and division were immensely complicated. The zero was a clever and difficult concept because it was a position without a value.

We badly need the equivalent of a 'zero' in human thinking but we do not have one. We cannot conceive of what we cannot yet conceive. This seems obvious enough. We cannot see what there is to see if we cannot now see it. In practice we find this very difficult to believe and even more difficult to achieve.

Someone comes to you and tells you that there are only two alternatives. Occasionally, when we are dealing with particular closed systems or a constructed system, this is true. Usually it means: 'I can think of only two alternatives, therefore there can't be any more.'

Suppose we were to use the word 'po' as zero-hold. We would then say there are three alternatives: these two and po. The word po would cover all the as yet unconceived alternatives. The size of this po space would indicate our sense of the possible richness of alternatives we had not yet conceived.

In practice we would find this immensely irritating and unworkable. Every defence lawyer would say to the jury: 'Think not only of the explanation for the evidence that I have given to you but think also of the po space. Can you really convict under those circumstances?' The system would be unworkable. We prefer our absolutes and our certainties.

When we look at any situation, the mechanics of attention and the broad catchment areas of patterns mean that we must quickly slide into some established pattern. We lose innocence and freshness. We become unable to put things together in new ways. We are unable to notice things we have not noticed before.

To escape from this easy clutch of patterns we may go to meditation, Zen buddhism or hallucinogen drugs (not the same as mood drugs or pleasure-centre drugs). Usually, as I have mentioned earlier, we do this in a search for 'isness' or what we regard as a deeper reality, because very many belief systems put the truth below surface appearances (why? perhaps only the surface is the truth).

I am not referring to this deeper reality here, I am talking more about neutrality. That is why I call it a zero-hold. We take in the information or perceptions but we refuse to move down the usual patterns.

The patterning nature of the self-organizing system cannot permit this suspension of activity, this void. We cannot instruct the patterns to freeze in time and to stop acting. We can disrupt them so they no longer make the usual sense and this is often the route of drug-taking. We can try to train the mind to develop a deeper and deeper attention to the item itself, so that attention does not slide off into 'meaning'. This is the method of various types of Eastern training. The same holding of attention is used with 'mantra' systems, where attention to the mantra prevents flow down the usual patterns.

What I have in mind is something much simpler, more practical and easier to learn: the use of the word 'po' to signal that something is to be held outside patterns and pattern flows and judgement. Someone tells you that your accountant has defrauded you. You listen and then say 'po'. This means: 'I have taken in what you have told me but I am not switching into an emotional or reaction pattern right away.' In practice it would be no more than a pause.

David Lane at the Hungerford Guidance Centre started teaching the CoRT thinking lessons to youngsters who were too violent to be taught in ordinary schools. He told me that the level of violence dropped dramatically. It seems that the youngsters were impulsive and would snap into action clichés (quickly available patterns) all too fast. Having some thinking structures introduced a 'pause' element. The pause element probably allowed a richer perception, with a different output from before.

We can now go back to relevance and meaning as discussed in the previous section. Something may have meaning but no relevance, like a discussion on a sport in which you have no interest. The zero-hold of 'po' is designed to accept meaning but block relevance. It is as if you are listening to something and understanding what is said but it has no direct relevance to yourself. So in the accountant story it becomes as if you were reading about the robbery in a newspaper.

We need 'po' as a zero-hold to prevent us switching too quickly into the most obvious pattern, to allow attention to take in more data before defining its area of settlement, to allow us to re-create freshness and innocence in areas we know well, and to be able to set up ideas which are deliberately meant to be provocative.

As a signal po is much stronger than 'maybe' or the Japanese device of 'mu'. Po is not 'don't know' but more 'don't yet want to know'.

In previous points of consideration of the behaviour of self-organizing patterning systems I have focused on the natural behaviour of such systems. I have tried to show how such systems would lead our perception and thinking to behave in certain ways. Most of these ways are highly beneficial and life would be impossible without this sort of behaviour. Sometimes system behaviour which has a high survival value may have a negative effect when mere survival is no longer the issue. In this section on po and the zero-hold, I am pointing out a natural deficiency in a patterning system and suggesting a practical way in which we might seek to overcome the deficiency.

For those who like to operate 'the same as . . .' system (seeing anything new only in terms of what is already there) we could liken one use of po to 'hear me out before you jump to a conclusion'.

OUR TRADITIONAL THINKING
HABITS

In the preceding section I attempted to show how the natural, normal and inescapable behaviour of a self-organizing patterning system would affect our perceptual thinking (including such matters as attention). As I have emphasized from time to time, this behaviour in all its described aspects arises directly from the nature of the system. It is not a matter of having a system which has been 'programmed' to behave in this way. The system would be incapable of behaving in any other way.

I would not claim that all self-organizing neurological models would behave in exactly the same way. Nevertheless the principles I have put forward are very broad and do apply to a wide range of systems, not just one particular model.

It may have been apparent that the behaviour of the system bears a close relationship to the usual activity of the mind (humour, attention, insight, recognition etc.).

I have sought to show that the behaviour of the system does give rise to certain perceptual effects. I have not started at the other end – which is the traditional approach. I did not set out to analyse and explain such things as humour and insight. I worked upwards from the intrinsic behaviour of the model to discover behaviour which seems the same as what we call humour, insight, attention etc. That is the purpose of models in science. We set up models to work forwards from them and then to see the relevance of what we find.

I focused on a number of aspects of the behaviour of a self-organizing patterning system such as asymmetry, catchment and 'readiness', and went on to how these gave rise to certain mental behaviour (essentially in the area of perception). In most cases I related this mental behaviour to our common experience of perception. I commented on the value of particular habits of perception and also commented on how these habits could be limiting or harmful.

In the following section I want to start at the opposite end, from our habits, traditions and culture of thinking, and then to see how this compares with what we have learned from the behaviour of self-organizing patterning systems. How valuable, how limiting and how dangerous are our habits of thinking? Are they inevitable or just the result of a particular cultural direction? Were they imposed on our minds as a sort of mental discipline or did they arise naturally from the behaviour of mind combined with the development of language?

Did the Greek philosophers who largely determined the thinking of Western civilization do a good job? Did they do a good job for a time, but we have outgrown the system and should be aware of its limitations? Did the Greek philosophers, like Aristotle, observe the natural behaviour of mind and then set out to sharpen it up with thinking tools and habits (like I myself try to do)? Or did they construct a sort of belief system that they felt was necessary in order to run society and make progress? Why does our thinking seem to be so much more successful when dealing with technical matters than when dealing with human affairs?

Already in this book I have hinted at many of the things which I shall be writing about in the following section, seeking to draw the threads together in order to make a clear case for the deficiencies and faults of our thinking culture.

I do not intend to use one of the faults of logic which I shall later be attacking. I do not intend to claim that all traditional thinking occurs as I shall be describing it. It is enough that 'by and large', 'most' or even just 'a significant amount' takes place as I shall claim. Were I to say 'all' it would add nothing to my case and would open the door to suggestions that there is a particular branch of logic where things are indeed done differently.

I shall try to be fair to our current thinking traditions, because I do believe they have great value and anyway polarized point-making (as contrasted with genuine exploration) is one of the traditional habits I shall be attacking. In any case an improvement in our thinking system is going to take time. In the transition stages we shall need to modify some attitudes and fill in some deficiencies.

The underlying problem is that of deciding whose thinking habits it is proposed to change. Is this book written for a few philosophers, psychologists and system theorists? Is it written for the 'thinking elite', on the basis that the effects (if any) will eventually trickle through by means of education? Or is it written for ordinary people, which definition might fall short of the masses but need not, who do have an interest in how to use that ultimate resource of human thinking to make the world a better place? It is this third group that is of interest to me: because thinking is everyone's business; because in democracies it is everyone's business that everyone else should think better; because the trickle-down process working through education is slow and ineffective; and because the third group buys more books and so motivates the publisher and bookshops to make the books available – without which none of the other purposes will be achieved.

Here is a list of the different aspects of our thinking culture which will be examined in the coming pages:

LANGUAGE: marvellous as a communication system but poor as a thinking system, yet it dominates our thinking.

INTELLIGENCE: highly intelligent people do not necessarily make good thinkers. Thinking is a skill, not intelligence in action.

CRITICAL THINKING: a greatly over-esteemed part of our thinking culture. It is easy and satisfying but produces little.

LAFFER CURVE: a major type of error arising from table-top logic. Something is good so more must, surely, be better.

PROBLEM-SOLVING: part of the maintenance mentality which will get us back to where we were. Progress requires different thinking.

ANALYSIS: a central and valuable part of our thinking system but assumes all situations are closed and cannot produce ideas.

DESCRIPTION: both describes perception and can set perceptions through naming. But has no more validity than any perception.

NATURAL: the view that 'nature' and deep feelings are what really matter and should set our decisions rather than thinking.

MATHEMATICS: the strong certainty of a constructed system, powerful within its area of application, which is limited.

EITHER/OR: the seductive dichotomies which we need and create in order to operate the logical principle of contradiction.

ABSOLUTES: the need for truth and its multiple purposes. The problem is that absolutes must be circumstance-independent.

ARGUMENT AND CLASH: the motivated exploration as a subject. There are better methods of exploration. Clash is not generative.

BELIEF: a making sense of things. The circular system in which belief sets the perceptions that reinforce the belief.

SCIENCE: a methodology for testing beliefs. Driven mainly by the 'cause and effect' idiom. Weak on the perceptual side.

CREATIVITY: strongly neglected because it seems to happen anyway and we have not understood at all what is going on.

HISTORY: almost an obsession, possibly deriving from the period when all future progress could be got by looking backwards.

LOGIC: we use little explicit logic in our everyday thinking because we have fed it into our language habits already.

ART: this is directly concerned with reflecting existing perceptions and changing them, but does not encourage perceptual skills.

Language

As an exercise I sometimes ask youngsters to put down the consequences they foresee if dogs could be taught to talk. They foresee that dogs could then work and might be enslaved by their masters to work for them. They foresee tittle-tattle about the dogs' owners and problems with secrecy, 'doggy rights' movements and a demand for a political vote. One even foresaw a dog going to a doggy restaurant and asking for a 'people bag' to take the remnants home.

In the minds of the youngsters the ability to talk would virtually turn the dogs into a new class of people. There is the underlying assumption that talking without any thinking would be no different from teaching a parrot to talk, so that in posing the question I must have meant more than this – which I did.

There is mathematics, there are computers and there are pictures, but the bulk of our communicated thinking is done with language. I do not believe that language is essential for thinking, though it may be for extended thinking. But in society the communication of thinking is through language. Culturally language has come to dominate our thinking – and this is a grave defect. Language is a communicating system, and not a thinking system. Thinking and communication are quite different, and we run into serious trouble when we confuse the two. I believe it was Wittgenstein who said that the function of philosophers has always been to protect the truth against language.

Language is marvellous as a describing system but that does not mean it is excellent as a thinking or even a perceiving system. When you come across a beautiful stained glass window in a medieval church in France do you look 'at' the window or 'through' the window at the meadow outside? Most people would look at the window rather than through it. One of the basic problems with language is the divide between those who treat words as windows through which we look at the world and those who treat words as important and defined symbols in their own right.

All thinkers have envied the neat constructed systems of mathematics. Take a steel ball two feet above a table. You release the ball. How long does it take the ball to hit the table? A mathematician says: let x represent the height of the ball above the table, y the acceleraton of gravity and v the initial velocity. So v is zero, since the ball starts at rest; x is two feet, since we were told this; and y is an acceleration of thirty-two feet per second every second (we know this to be the acceleration of gravity). We plug all these values into a known formula and get the answer. Why cannot language be like this?

Philosophers have always yearned to treat language as a strong symbolic system where each word has a constructed meaning which allows no deviation. They have often believed they have succeeded. They have often acted as though language was a table-top type of system where the operator sits before a table on which are blocks of unchangeable shape and colour with which the operator then plays.

But if the philosophical language game is going to have any value beyond mere self-indulgence (which is sufficient for many scholars) there must be a point at which the world is translated into the symbols and a point at which the results are translated back into the real world.

It is at this translation point that language runs into the variability of perception and the interactive complexity of the world, which is not easy to chop into the blocks needed for table-top logic. Computer enthusiasts would love to plug in a P for people, and M for money and an H for human happiness and then proceed to work out the ultimate formula for human happiness. Economists, using various linkages, have tried to do the same.

The word 'up' is based on experience, but we could also define it in an unchangeable way: up is up and always will be. But when we get into a space craft with zero gravity and bodies that are floating about in all positions, 'up' no longer has its usual meaning. What is 'up'? We overcome that problem with a simple definition: 'up' is applicable only when we are standing on the earth, in which case it means away from the centre of the earth (or contrary to the force of gravity). Can we then use the word when referring to a graph which is lying horizontal on our desk (as in 'the line then turns up')? By analogy we can.

Definitions depend on other definitions and on frames of reference. Very often we take for granted stable circumstances when we should not. For example before space flight we would have taken for granted that 'up' was always going to be used in a gravity system.

We shall return later to the problems of absolutes, truth and certainty in our thinking habits. For the moment it is enough to point out that attempts to treat language as a rigid constructed system have not been very successful – though we still base most of our behaviour on the belief that we have been successful in this matter.

As a means of description, there can be little doubt that we are much better off for having language. One of the problems with description is that words package the world in a certain way. Thereafter we are inclined to see the world in this way, as I have discussed at length in previous sections on catchment, circularity, readiness, attention etc. This naming and packaging is most valuable, since without it we might not have been able to notice things at all.

Difficulties arise when the words are too big and clumsy and cover too much, or where we do not have words at all. This is not a problem of description but one of perception. Description can always break down a big word into smaller parts or use a qualifying adjective. For example the 'big word' criminal can be broken down into shoplifter, fraud, murderer etc. Nevertheless, because we have the broad category term 'criminal' they will tend to be regarded in a similar way. We perceive them the same even though we are able to describe them as different.

I would like a word to communicate the following idea: 'This matter can be viewed in two exactly opposite ways with equal validity unless particular circumstances are defined.' Now since I can write down that idea it is obvious that language is fully capable of describing it. But describing it in this complex and cumbersome way does not put that concept into general currency. I would prefer to invent a new word, 'janoid' (from the god Janus, who looked both ways at once). In the course of a conversation I could now say 'At this point it is a janoid' and imply the whole idea. In some particular cases the word ('janoid') might come close to 'double-edged', but the meaning is not the same. I could say that the shooting down in 1988 of the Iranian airliner by the USS *Vincennes* was a janoid: a terrible tragedy when looked at in one way and of benefit when looked at in another because by getting sympathy for Iran it may have encouraged that country to accept the UN resolution for a ceasefire.

I would like a much better word for 'the way we look at things'. At the moment I have to use the word 'perception', but that is not really good enough, because it implies visual perception. I did invent the term 'lateral thinking', because creativity is much too broad a word and I also found it inconvenient to keep repeating: 'the type of thinking required to cut across patterns in a self-organizing patterning system'.

It is true that new words do arise as the need for them becomes very strong. For example the word 'gazump' is well established in the property market in the UK (to agree to sell to one buyer and then change your mind and sell to another at a higher price). The words 'astronaut' and 'software' are obvious other examples.

Mostly the new words that arise are for new situations and the need is obvious. With old situations the need will never arise in the same way because we are happy looking at things in the old way. So sometimes the new word needs to come first – ahead of the need – in order to enable us to see things anew. Although deliberately created, the term 'lateral thinking' is now used widely as an ordinary part of the English language.

But those who have not yet realized that description is not the same as perception, fiercely resist the very many new words that are needed if we are to think more effectively. Such people do not see the need for the new words, or claim that the function is already expressed ('same as . . .' phenomenon) or that the matter can be adequately described by a circumlocution. In fact all new words are lumped together as the big word 'jargon', which carries its own negative baggage of deliberate obfuscation.

What about the use of language for persuasion, argument or to prove a point? I think, for reasons I shall give below, that language is highly suspect for this purpose. I feel this even though I am a writer who uses language for these purposes. At the very best language might trigger an insight in the reader.

We use language so very extensively for political purposes and as a general guide to our thinking that we need to be aware of the perceptual deficiencies. For these purposes we pretend to use language for thinking, whereas with art the aim is directly perceptual. I shall come to that later.

One difficulty is that we confuse fluency with substance. Something that is well said seems to have a right to be true. Something that is said clumsily seems as incorrect in substance as in expression. So fluency of style masquerades as integrity of thought. Another difficulty is the partiality of attention which I have mentioned before. No matter how honest we may try to be we cannot put down every detail and every qualification. What gets in tends to support our case. This partial truth can be as dishonest as an outright lie, though it never seems to be. Then there is the problem of loaded words. Here the value is not separate, as with an adjective, but part of the word. So anyone who has been responsible for a death can be called a murderer, so receiving all the baggage associated with that term.

Adjectives are extremely easy to attach to anything. Particularly dangerous are the adjectives that have no basis in fact but express a slight sneer: self-appointed, so-called, pretentious, domineering, pathetic, irrelevant, simplistic, confused, misguided. The more obvious adjectives of acclaim or disgust are less of a problem because they clearly express an emotion, not a line of thought. In general a simple adjective count is a good way of testing the thinking of any piece of writing or a speech.

The problem of 'catchment' and 'shift' is serious, as is the either/or problem of dichotomies. Anyone who criticizes any aspect of democracy must be a fascist; anyone who questions certain of the more excessive capitalist habits must be a Marxist; anyone who advocates more welfare spending is a bleeding-heart liberal. A very simple example of shift is with the term academic. Anyone who has anything serious to say or who can add up more than three figures is clearly different from the ordinary run of writers and so is honoured by being promoted to being an academic. This shift is, however, something less than an honour because the baggage of that title includes: impractical, head in the clouds, utopian, ivory tower etc. On the positive side as soon as there can be a shift into 'family', 'human values', 'ecology', and community, then the argument is won.

The basic game is so easy, so transparent and yet so repeatedly effective. All the habits of perception that I listed in the previous section can be manipulated to present as a logical argument what is no more than a perception from a very particular point of view.

There are those who have already given up and who accept that perception is so dominant over logic in the use of language that we should never pretend to be honest or impartial but should unashamedly take one side or the other and leave it to others to restore the balance.

At best we should accept that thinking expressed through the descriptive medium of language is concerned with perception rather than the certainties of logic. Then we should go on to realize that perception is almost always a narrow one from a particular point of view, not a broad perceptual exploration. The question is whether the writer does have a broader view but wishes to express a narrow partial view or whether the writer can see no more than the narrow view, which is the way perception usually behaves.

Thinking and Intelligence

One of the problems in designing a really smart thinking computer, as distinct from a super-calculator, is that we would probably not believe the conclusions and decisions that the machine eventually puts before us. That computer would have to be smart enough to realize that those around were not so smart and therefore needed all the steps to the conclusion laid out in the open.

In our thinking culture we have always regarded intelligence much as I have here treated the 'smartness' of that new thinking computer. Intelligence has always been enough. If you have a high intelligence, it will all happen in your head. This is an unfortunate fallacy that has had two disastrous consequences in education. The first consequence is that we believe that for those with a high intelligence nothing needs to be done about their thinking. The second consequence is that we believe that for those with a more humble intelligence nothing can be done. Therefore we have not bothered to do anything about teaching thinking until very recently.

Unfortunately many people with a high intelligence actually turn out to be poor thinkers. They get caught in the 'intelligence trap', of which there are many aspects. For example, a highly intelligent person may take up a view on a subject and then defend that view (through choice of premises and perception) very ably. The better someone is able to defend a view the less inclined is that person actually to explore the subject. So the highly intelligent person can get trapped by intelligence, together with our usual sense of logic that you cannot be more right than right, into one point of view. The less intelligent person is less sure of his or her rightness and therefore more free to explore the subject and other points of view.

A highly intelligent person usually grows up with a sense of that intellectual superiority and needs to be seen to be 'right' and 'clever'. Such a person is less willing to risk creative and constructive ideas because such ideas may take a time to show their worth or to get accepted. Highly intelligent people are often attracted to the quick pay-off of negativity. If you attack someone else's ideas or thinking there can be an immediate achievement together with a useful sense of superiority. In intellectual terms (as we shall see later) attack is also cheap and easy because the attacker can always choose the frame of reference.

The intelligent mind works quickly, sometimes too quickly. The highly intelligent person may move from the first few signals to a conclusion that is not as good as that reached by a slower mind which is forced to take in more signals before proceeding to a conclusion. This is an instance of the need for the zero-hold (po), mentioned in the last section.

Money is useful when you want to buy a fast Lamborghini or Ferrari. Genes are said to be useful when you want to be intelligent. But having a fast sports car does not automatically make you a good driver. You may have a powerful car driven badly: someone else may have a more humble car driven well. The horsepower and engineering of the car provide the 'potential'. It is the skill of the driver that puts this potential into operation. In the same way 'intelligence' is the potential of the mind and the way this is put into operation is thinking skill. There may be powerful minds used badly and more humble minds driven well.

One day we shall probably be able to measure intelligence by a simple chemical test (for example the injection of a labelled chemical followed by a brain scan). Intelligence could be acting at several points in the nerve network. Possibly a greater speed of scan is obtained because an area of activity 'tires' more quickly, so the activity flits to the next area sooner than usually. Possibly the negative feedback (inhibition aspect of the model) is stronger, so areas of activity are more sharply defined. There are many points at which the functional efficiency of the model could be improved. Perhaps the enzyme which handles connectedness is more efficient, so associations are made more easily. I do not intend, at this point, to make a choice.

In the past we have placed a lot of emphasis on traditional IQ tests because we always like the security of measurement even if the substance of what we are measuring is suspect. On the whole IQ tests do correlate reasonably well with performance in schools for the simple reason that school thinking is very like the thinking required in IQ tests (reactive and analytical). IQ tests are, however, a poor predictor of success in after-life, where a different sort of thinking is required. To be sure there are some professions where the entry gates are an extension of the school system and here the IQ test would also be a good predictor. Howard Gardener at Harvard and others have begun to question the notion of a single intelligence and write about musical intelligence, athletic intelligence, artistic intelligence, in order to emphasize different areas of gifted ability.

I have often defined thinking as 'the operating skill with which intelligence acts upon experience'. We need to develop thinking skills with which to make full use of the potential offered by experience. That is why I have been so involved in the direct teaching of thinking in school. In practical experience we have found that gifted students (top intelligence brackets) need to develop thinking skills as much as anyone else – to some extent even more, in order to overcome the natural arrogance of their known intelligence.

Highly intelligent youngsters often seem to prefer 'reactive' thinking. They are good at solving puzzles when all the pieces are put out before them on the table. They seem much less happy with 'pro-active' thinking in which they have to collect and assess what factors need to be considered in coming to a conclusion, less happy with the perspective, balance and practicality of solutions.

Obviously we can define the word 'intelligence' to mean everything that is good and wonderful in thinking. Therefore, by definition, anything which falls short of this cannot be called intelligent. This is a hindsight definition of a result and is therefore quite useless in describing a process. This particular use of 'intelligent' is rather more appropriate as an adjective to describe 'excellent thinking'. Then the question becomes: why does the possession of intelligence sometimes result in less than intelligent behaviour?

The more sensible use of the word 'intelligence' is as a process of mental ability, quickness of mind and the ability to do well in intelligence tests. This is now a process, not a description of a result.

It could be that the very chemical balances that make for intelligence (enzymes, neuro-transmitters etc.) also lead to caution and timidity and types of personality which inhibit the successful application of that intelligence. It could be that the excellence of intelligence is more directed towards reactive thinking and puzzle-solving than at broad pro-active thinking where factors like guessing and prioritizing must come in. It could be that intelligence alone without specific skills of thinking is not enough. It could be that the very excellence of intelligence is itself counter-productive. A tall man may be advantaged at times (looking over the heads of a crowd) but disadvantaged at other times (digging a foxhole). The sharper the knife the more useful for its purpose but the more dangerous. So it may be that the sheer excellence of intelligence allows us to play the perceptual game very well indeed. Since this game is very defective, we shall be playing a defective game well and the outcome will be a disadvantage.

The natural behaviour of perception is to form strong patterns, to recognize them quickly and to use them without deviation. As I have emphasized repeatedly, this process has initial survival value but thereafter packages the world in much too limited and rigid a fashion. A brain that by virtue of its chemistry can play this game superbly well will end up with poor perception (in terms of breadth, exploration, seeing things in different ways).

I have set out to show that perception is very different from table-top logic. I have not pretended that perception is a wonderful system. Far from it – for example there is no such thing as perceptual truth. But by understanding perception we can become aware of its faults and limitations and also design tools to enable us to get more out of the system.

At school the more intelligent children learn to play the conformist game: how to pass exams, how to please the teacher, how to do only as much work as necessary. Creativity tends to be left to the rebels who cannot play the right game or do not want to (because they will not excel at it). If, however, we can understand the game of creativity (as with lateral thinking), we may get the strange paradox that the conformists can now become more creative than the rebels, because they will now be better at the new game.

So we must break away from the tradition that intelligence is enough.

Critical Thinking

Anyone who makes errors of logic in his or her thinking is regarded as a poor thinker: faults of perception are hardly ever noticed and, even when they are noticed, they are much more tolerated. So if we set out to remove these errors of logic, surely we shall have a good thinker? This has always been one of our most basic cultural beliefs and an implicitly fundamental concern of education and, more recently, an explicit concern.

A bad car driver makes faults in driving. If we remove those faults surely we shall have an excellent driver. Unfortunately this is not so. The simplest way to remove all faults in driving is to keep the car in the garage. Simply removing faults in thinking does not provide the generative, constructive and creative aspects of thinking. Removing faults is certainly worth doing, but it is only a part of the process – probably no more than a third of thinking, or less. Yet we have always esteemed critical thinking very highly and we sometimes regard it as the summit of thinking performance. This high esteem is based on a whole number of questionable assumptions.

There is the Socratic dialogue method as reported by Plato. For various reasons arising from the Renaissance we have venerated this rather inefficient model. (I shall explain my choice of the term 'inefficient' when I come to deal with 'argument' in a later section of this book.) Medieval theologians had to place a very high value on critical thinking because they had to deal with the ever more subtle creativity of the heretics (like the Donatists, who tended to tie St Augustine in dialectic knots). The Church, having preserved civilization through the Dark Ages, set the tone for schools and universities and culture in general.

Critical thinking does seem a superior sort of thinking because it seems as though the critic is actually going beyond the scope of what is being criticized in order to criticize it. That is only rarely a true assumption because, most often, the critic will seize on some little aspect that he or she understands and tackle only that.

Critical thinking seems a full accomplishment: there is a purpose, a line of thought, and an achievement. With most of creative and constructive thinking the achievement is not complete until the idea has been put into action and shown to work.

Finally there is the underlying assumption that we shall get better and better ideas by criticizing the ones that exist or are offered. Surely, if you point out the faults in an idea, a modification can correct those faults, with a better idea as a result.

This last assumption is based on the very serious assumption that better ideas will be obtained in an evolutionary process. This assumption is serious because it underlines virtually the whole way we go about seeking better ideas in society and even in science. For reasons I shall explain later, I believe this assumption to be quite false. But if we do have this evolutionary model, clearly we see critical thinking as providing the evolutionary pressures which will determine (on a classic Darwinian basis) which ideas deserve to survive and which to die. It is obvious, however, that criticism can only be directed from within the existing paradigm, so there is ever increasing resistance to paradigm shifts.

We also esteem critical thinking because we believe it to be a difficult sort of thinking. Critical thinking puts a thinker ahead of those who just accept what they are offered or are too easily persuaded. In fact it is a very cheap and easy sort of thinking. Clearly there is a spectrum of critical thinking which runs from picking out the flaws in an elaborate mathematical treatise to disliking a picture at the local amateur artists' exhibition. Most of the activity tends to lie at the easy and cheap end.

Critical thinking is easy because the critic can focus on any aspect he or she likes and ignore the rest. Matters can be taken totally out of context. The critic can set up his or her own arbitrary frame of reference and make judgements on that basis. A good critic may condemn a meal in a restaurant as being too plain and boring to justify the price (by choosing a more elaborate frame of reference). If, however, the meal had indeed been elaborate it could have been criticized as over-rich, a confusion of taste, pretentious. This sort of stuff is so very easy.

If we were to remove the concept of 'consistency' from the expected virtues of politicians, much political commentary would cease overnight. A lot of political criticism is on the basis that a politician is not consistent with his own ideas, or what he said two years ago, or his party line, or his electoral promises. A politician might reply, with reason, that he or she had had a change of mind, or that changed circumstances require a change of opinion. Commentators are unhappy with that because it removes one of the main frames of criticism. Such commentators would claim that the politician had been elected on a certain basis and must stick to that. In some cases this is undoubtedly true, but in many cases changing a view is a sign of the intelligent political behaviour for which most people vote.

'Consistency' is, of course, the key word in critical thinking. Is something internally consistent – the favourite line of criticism of anyone who does not know the subject (as with a bureaucrat)? Is it consistent with what is generally held or with science as we now know it? Is it consistent with principles that we know to be true or absolute (or need to treat as such)? Is it consistent with my experience and perceptions? Is it consistent with the way I want to look at the matter? All of these come down to: is it consistent with my pattern of perception?

So the process of judgement may be thorough but the basis for the judgement is a perception held generally or personally. Constructed systems are an exception to this, as I have suggested very much earlier. What is a true constructed system and what we claim to be a constructed system is another matter.

It is sometimes claimed that critical thinking operates on two levels. The first is the assessment of what is offered in terms of its reliability or 'truth grade'. 'My grandmother had a friend in Egypt whose servant died of an infected mosquito bite, so all insect bites are dangerous' offers a conclusion that is only slightly supported. The second level of critical thinking is to attack the nature of the idea rather than its base or source. It is the latter that has concerned me more in this section, for the first level is simply the application of prudence to the scattiness of perception.

How do we get to criticize something that is beyond criticism in its adequacy? How do we get to change something that we cannot criticize? This is a major flaw in the system. How do we overcome complacency? Within the framework we have accepted, within the limits of our imagination, within the closed system of our analysis, it seems that what we now have cannot be faulted. So how do we begin to change it for something better?

If, for improvement, we rely on the correction of faults, we can get no improvement if we can perceive no faults. And often we cannot perceive faults unless we can already perceive the possibility of something better. The Japanese search for quality in manufacturing is unending (once they were turned on to this game) because, no matter how good something is, there is always the possibility of doing it better. But the Western habit of critical thinking means that first we must find faults and then seek to put them right, so anything without faults is impossible to improve.

So we can see that critical thinking as a major element of our thinking tradition has quite severe limitations and even when it is working well must in the end depend on perceptions which we prefer to treat as absolutes.

Laffer Curves

Taxes raise money, so more taxes will raise more money. Efficiency in industry is good, so more efficiency is better. Law is good, so more law is better.

The Laffer curve is probably the simplest and clearest example of the deficiencies of traditional table-top logic. It is named after an economist who claimed that there comes a point beyond which increased taxation will actually reduce the revenues obtained. Beyond that point the motivation to work is lessened and people spend a lot of time and ingenuity sheltering their income from taxes in various ways. Beyond that point businesses choose to do something because it is 'tax efficient' rather than for productive commercial reasons. Over the last few years many countries, including the Reagan presidency and the Thatcher government, have reduced taxes. It seems that the tax yield is indeed increasing – though this is difficult to separate out from other things going on at the same time. So up to the peak point more taxes raise more revenue, but beyond this point more taxes lead to reduced revenue. This process drawn on a graph gives the Laffer curve, looking like a simple mountain peak.

Efficiency in industry is necessary for competitive purposes. The efficient producer is the low-cost producer. The efficient producer has better profits to re-invest. The efficient producer keeps shareholders happier. So all excess fat must be squeezed out of an operation. Every bit of capital must earn a good rate of return. All plant must be fully in use. Business methods get better and better. Some years ago 50,000 new railcars a year were required in the USA. Today the figure is down to 12,000. This is not because there is less rail traffic but because each car is now in use for ten months instead of just two months. Computer tracking has worked this miracle. Surely such efficiency is a wonderful thing and more of it must be better.

This is true – up to a point. Beyond that point more efficiency means 'brittleness' and loss of flexibility.

You can tune your efficiency to present conditions, but if conditions change there is no longer any fat, there is no longer any cushion, there is no longer any leeway. So the efficient organization can collapse very suddenly. You get rid of all the divisions that are not showing a good enough return (your share price goes up) but then a major competitor emerges in your remaining field, and suddenly you are in trouble.

In business the new word is 'flexibility'. Instead of becoming more and more efficient at making bicycles you have a flexible factory. If bicycles are selling you make bicycles, if health equipment is selling you switch to making health equipment. In electricity generating plants you build in a multi-fuel capacity. If oil is expensive you switch to coal, if gas is cheap you switch to gas.

Law is necessary to make a society work. Yet an absurd position can be reached when obstetricians stop doing their job of delivering babies because the malpractice insurance costs and liability make it too expensive a business. The height of such absurdity has been reached in the USA, where legal considerations are a major concern for business. The Texaco/Penzoil dispute is just one example. I was once told by a major European corporation that in Europe a certain division shared a lawyer with another division. In the USA the equivalent division had fifty full-time lawyers. Lawyers have to earn a living and if you can get more profit out of a lawsuit than out of industrial production then that is the way the rules of the game are written. I shall be returning to this point later under the concept of 'ludecy' (playing the game for its own sake).

In table-top logic the different pieces lie before you on the table. A blue piece is a blue piece and does not suddenly become red. The attachment of a value to a subject is permanent. Something lies in one category group or it does not. There is no mechanism for the item suddenly to jump out of that category group to join another. The logic system would be unworkable if there were not this permanence. If we had to 'depend' on circumstance at every point we would no longer have classic logic but the type of water logic that I have mentioned and shall be describing later.

Most traditional philosophers have been aware of this major defect in the category system. The difficulty is that the change point (the peak on the Laffer curve) is not easily defined in concrete terms. No salt on food is bad, some salt is good, more salt is bad, but the points of change may vary from individual to individual. Philosophers have sought to overcome this problem in rather a feeble way: they have advocated 'moderation in all things' and the 'golden mean'. But this is paternal admonition and not logic.

It is reasonably obvious that no food is bad, some food is good and too much food is bad again. The American concern with obesity is witness to the practicality of this logic. Tall is good, but very tall is not better – unless you want to be a basket-ball player. Such matters are not too difficult to decide on a basis of 'sufficiency' or 'keeping within a normal range'. Some defence spending is good but at what point does defence spending become 'bad' or a waste of resources?

The whole purpose of the design of table-top logic was to free us from having to make these difficult decisions. We were supposed just to identify a matter as belonging to some category and then the decision would be made for us.

Truth is good, justice is good, ecology is good, family relationships are good, community is good. Could we conceive of a point at which too much of any of these things becomes bad? Probably not, and if we could perceive of such a point we would never admit it because opponents would too easily claim that such a point had been reached. We attach permanent value labels precisely because we do not want to make multiple difficult decisions.

The value label is part of our perceptual pattern in these cases. You might pick up a strange-shaped piece of wood and say to yourself: 'Is this of any use to me?' But as soon as the words justice or ecology or efficiency or law enter a discussion you know automatically that these are 'good things'.

Quite a lot of the problems in society arise from our inability to see that the Laffer curve (I prefer to call it the 'salt curve') applies to many things. Knowledge is good, so more knowledge must be better. As we have seen this is not necessarily so, because it can stifle originality in research. Criticism is good, so more criticism must be better. There comes a point when self-indulgent negativity becomes an end in itself. Democracy is good, can too much democracy be bad?

I am not writing about absurd excesses, because it is easy to show that an excess of anything is likely to be harmful, but about those situations where the switch in value occurs within a normal range, as with putting salt on food.

Problem-Solving

There is one simple saying that, by itself, almost destroyed America's basic industry: 'If it's not broken, don't fix it.' Why did this simple – and apparently sensible – dictum have such a disastrous effect? The industrial idiom in America was: 'Let's keep on doing what we're doing and if something goes wrong (breaks) then let's fix it and continue. That's what we're about.' This is the 'maintenance' concept of business and for many years it was dominant and sufficient.

Then competition started coming along: from Japan, from the other Pacific tigers, from West Germany. Now competitors knew that they could not compete just by doing the same things. So they had to look for improvement. This meant seeking to do things better, not just fixing problems and continuing as is. So they looked at points which were not problems: could we improve the design at this point; could we make this cheaper; how can we make this more reliable?

'If it's not broken, don't fix it' is the exact opposite of competition. The saying assumes a static world where what you are now doing will always be sufficient. It is the opposite of progress in any field. This lesson has now been learned in the industrial field but not yet in the fields of education, politics, economics or international relations. We do tend to have a 'problem-solving' mentality. We assume that what we are doing is fine and if there is a deviation from this norm we must fix this deviation as we fix a flat tyre. There is a disastrous habit in American psychology and education of regarding all thinking as 'problem-solving'. Educators now talk about introducing problem-solving into schools because they are much too embarrassed to talk about introducing 'thinking skills' (because this is what education was supposed to be about all along).

There is no doubt that 'problem-solving' is an important part of applied thinking and that we can use the term as a 'big word' to include all purposeful thinking: we want to get somewhere, how do we get there, let's solve the problem. But as with all 'big words' (catchment difficulty) we very soon restrict our vision to the pure example of a problem: something is wrong, let's fix it. This excludes opportunity thinking, initiative thinking, enterprise, improvement, and all those types of thinking in which we set out to think about things which are not wrong.

Problem-solving and critical thinking are part of the same cultural background: let's put faults right, let's pick out the faults. We fail to realize that they are maintenance procedures. They assume that what we have is a perfect system or, if not, one that will progress in that direction by steady evolution. All thinkers have to do is to keep the vehicle on the road and repair those parts that break down. The notion of progress through changes in perception, paradigm shifts and deliberate design does not come into it at all.

When we do set out to solve problems we use a very traditional method. We analyse the situation. Then we seek to 'remove the cause' of the problem. Removing the cause will often solve the problem: if you have a nail intruding into your shoe you remove the nail; if too easy credit gives rise to inflation you raise interest rates; if contaminated water spreads cholera you change the water supply or boil it; if an 'o' ring leaks on a rocket you re-design it to eliminate the 'o' ring. But not all problems can be solved by removing the cause. You may never find it. You may find it but are quite unable to remove it (earthquakes or climatic droughts), or there may be a complexity of causes which cannot be removed (sectarian violence).

'Remove the cause' is only one of the problem-solving idioms, but much of our effort is locked up in this simple approach because of its cultural background in logic and even the concept of 'sin'. The primitive notion of 'cause and effect' means that for any problem there must be a cause – so remove the cause.

What other approaches might there be? There is 'design'. In

design we say: 'Here's the situation. How can we move forward?'
If you want to build a new town on a swamp you might say:
'Let's remove the cause of the swamp.' But if you want to build a
new town in the desert you do not set out to remove all the sand
but instead you say: 'This is a desert. How do we design houses
that can stand on the sand?' So with a problem like the sectarian
problems in Northern Ireland you might try to remove the causes,
but this is difficult since they go way back into history and
culture – or you might try to design forward from the given situation.

Another approach, which overlaps with design, is to alter the
system. In a complex interactive system we can alter linkages or
relationships: cutting some, introducing others, altering the parameters of the relationship. Often, if you change the rules of the
game, human nature and greed will operate the new system very
well. When US insurance companies wanted to reduce escalating
hospital costs they introduced Diagnosis Related Groupings
(DRG) which guaranteed a flat-fee payment to hospitals for each
diagnostic grouping. Hospitals found they could now make more
money by sending patients out earlier rather than by keeping
them longer (the possibility of malpractice suing is some protection against a patient being discharged too soon).

But our traditions of thinking have always preferred analysis
to design. Surely if we analyse something better we must find the
cause and then we can remove it. This idiom is not incorrect but
of limited application. Yet we continue to teach only analysis and
not design. This is because analysis seems to require only logic
(which is a fallacy, since it really also needs creative perception)
whereas design requires creativity, which we have not known
how to handle.

At this point some traditional philosophers might take refuge
in word-play. 'Everything must have a cause. A problem must
have a cause. If the problem has been solved, then by definition
the cause has been removed. How you have removed the cause
does not matter – it is still removal of the cause.' This sort of
descriptive hindsight has held up intellectual development. The
situation is exactly the same as we saw in the use of the word

'intelligence'. 'All behaviour which is good, effective and valuable is intelligent behaviour and therefore an intelligent person cannot be capable of inefficient thinking. If a person is a poor thinker, by definition he or she is not intelligent.' 'There cannot be any faults in logic because, by definition, logic is free of faults, otherwise it is not true logic.' This sort of thing comes up again and again and it is mere descriptive word-play.

There are probably multiple causes for the traditional British hooligan behaviour at football matches and elsewhere. These causes possibly include weakened family ties and discipline, fashion and peer pressure, boredom, a pop culture of free expression, alienation from the complexity of society, youthful aggression with no outlet, violence on TV etc., etc. You can try to remove all those causes or you can try to design steps forward.

So the traditions of problem-solving and removal of causes are valid as far as they go but they are only part of the thinking required. As with so much of our traditional thinking, it is all right up to a point but inadequate beyond that point. Yet we are so complacent about the excellence of what we have.

Every male in America, unless he has a moustache or is of American Indian ancestry, shaves his upper lip every day. How often does someone who is using a traditional wet razor stop to consider whether instead of moving the razor it might be easier to keep the razor still and to move the head instead. In fact it is rather better. But no one does try it because there is 'no problem to fix'. Progress does not come just by fixing problems.

Analysis

There is a story about a supermarket operator in New Jersey who found that his wastage (losses from theft) amounted to a staggering twenty per cent. He set about a thorough programme of investigation. All the figures were examined carefully. Each check-out operator was watched intently to see that all purchases were correctly recorded. Detectives mingled with shoppers to observe any large-scale shoplifting. Nothing could be found. The system was operating without any fraud. But the losses continued. One day the owner visited the supermarket. He had an uneasy feeling that things were not quite right. But he could not put his finger on what was wrong – just a general sense of unease. Suddenly it hit him. He had installed just four check-out points but now there were five. The staff had got together and installed a fifth check-out point from which they took all the proceeds. So at every point the system was working perfectly – but it was not the same system.

Analysis likes to work with closed systems. How many systems are really closed? Where do we draw the line? It is easy in hindsight to say that the analysis of the supermarket fraud should have checked the number of check-out points – everything is easy in hindsight.

In an early book I put forward some mechanical problems involving making a bridge with knives balanced on top of bottles. In one problem I said that 'four' knives could be used. The solution actually required the use of only three knives. So I got lots of very irate letters complaining that if only three knives were needed I should not have made four available. This is a reflection of closed system analysis and school textbooks: use all the information given.

This closed system analysis is like the puzzle-solving aptitude of gifted students. If all the pieces are there, they are good at puzzle-solving.

In our tradition of analysis we behave in much the same way. Draw the line to enclose what is relevant: how much of the world are we going to include in our system? Then we analyse the factors and the inter-relationships.

In the past, people queueing at various service counters (bank, post office, airline check-in) would get stuck behind someone who seemed to have a lot of complicated business. So the new concept of a one-point queue was introduced. There was a single queue. When you got to the head of it you went to whichever counter was free. This was a great improvement (at least psychologically) because you could not get stuck behind someone who took up a lot of time. Now there are various very sophisticated operations research procedures to analyse the mathematics of queueing. They will give suggestions for optimal queueing strategies in terms of the number of points needed etc., but where are the next ideas to come from?

Imagine an extra queueing window (service point) above which there is a sign reading: '$5 for service at this window.' Anyone in the queue who feels that his or her time is worth $5 would go to that window. The choice is there to take or not take: you can now put a price on your impatience. If too many people make the choice the price is raised to $10 or more. Now this idea is unlikely to come from an operations research analysis of queueing.

So the first problem with analysis is: do we really have a closed system? The second is: where do we draw the line to get a closed system? Obviously the answers to these questions depend very heavily on perception. We may include things we perceive might be relevant – but we need that perception first.

Analysis is a traditional and powerful tool of thinking for many valuable reasons. We may not be able to recognize the complex whole, so we break it down into recognizable patterns and then we know what to do. In order to understand the system involved we analyse something into the parts and their relationships. That is the very essence of applied mathematics. If we seek to understand a phenomenon, we analyse the situation to get our explanation.

A growing objection to this traditional process of analysis is that, in a complex system, when you have the parts you no longer have the whole. And the whole cannot be reconstituted from the parts. For example in medicine there is a feeling that the mental attitude of the patient might effect recovery but will not show up on a bacterial slide or a measurement of antibody levels. Even in mathematics there is a move towards more holistic ways of looking at things. Does meteorology depend on a series of pinpoint measurements or an overall view of patterns and processes?

It is very likely that our analytical and atomic view of economics has held back progress in this field.

I want to move on to what, I think, is an even more serious defect of analysis. We have grown up with the tradition that if you want to know what is happening and if you want new ideas you should analyse the data available, or collect more data through experiments or surveys. This is the very basis of science and of market research. Computers have enabled us to collect and sort data in a remarkably efficient way. So we have been able to pursue this data analysis tradition with much greater effectiveness. We believe, or many believe, that the analysis of data is enough and is the basis of rational behaviour. There is, unfortunately, a serious flaw in this tradition.

The flaw is that we can never really analyse data. At best we can check out a hypothesis we have or see whether any of our limited repertoire of relationships can be found in the data. In short, we have to have the perceptual framework first. Most often we use very simplistic perceptual frameworks like 'correlation' or 'cause and effect', 'time courses', 'decay times'.

In my early days in medical research I did some investigations on circulation through the lungs. In a normal flow model you measure the pressure drop between two points and then measure the flow. This will give a measure of 'resistance'. On this basis the figures never seemed to work out. Then I applied a 'waterfall' model. In a waterfall the height of the fall will have no effect at all on the flow above the fall.

In developing the new area of 'chaos' investigation mathematicians have gone back to old data and applied the new conceptual model. So data analysis will confirm or reject a hypothesis and will allow us a choice between well-known models of relationships but will not itself generate new concepts. It is only recently in economics that new types of relationships (non-linear, threshold, waterfall etc., etc.) are being tried out. If data analysis could have directly given these new ideas, they would have become visible a long time ago and would have replaced the primitive linkages with which economists have been working. I shall return to this point when discussing the scientific method. The point is an important one that depends directly on perceptual organization: we can see only what we are prepared to see.

As computers become more and more able to do the data analysis for us, so we should develop more and more conceptual models for the computer to try out. We can now do computer experiments. Early data showed that people who wore seat belts were much less likely to be killed in road accidents. This seems to show that wearing seat belts will increase survival chances. Further analysis showed that the relationship (though valid) was not quite as simple. The cautious drivers wore seat belts and drove carefully, so their accidents were small ones. The reckless drivers did not wear seat belts and also had bigger accidents. Bigger accidents were more likely to kill people. But you have to think of this possibility in order to look for it.

Why can we not simply analyse data with all possible combinations? Combinations of what? Even if we could isolate the factors they would already be perceptual assumptions. Even for these isolated factors the number of possible organizations would be colossal, because the mathematics of combination gives large figures. There are 362,880 ways of putting the numbers 1 to 9 into a nine point grid (9 × 8 × 7 etc.).

Hindsight will, of course, make it seem obvious. Once we have the answer all we need to say is: if you had looked for this and that; if you had defined the problem this way; if you had measured the right thing. As I have written repeatedly in this book, such hindsight justification means little (every valuable creative idea will always be logical in hindsight). Hindsight is valid in a table-top model but meaningless in a patterning system. Once you know which road leads to the answer it is easier to choose the road that leads to the answer.

One of the major Greek contributions to thinking was the concept of 'why?'. Before the introduction of this concept thinkers used to be happy enough to say 'this is so' and to leave it at that. The concept of 'why' leads to the rich mental activity of analysis and searches for explanation. The next step follows: if we can understand things, and pick out the fundamentals, perhaps we can change them. It is therefore easy to see why such classical thinking is still held in reverence. It leads to the scientific method even though the Greeks themselves preferred to think in terms of table-top systems and constructed systems rather than experiment.

The concept of 'why' is a very basic part of our intellectual tradition and I have chosen to consider it in this section on analysis because much of our analysis is for this purpose of answering the question 'why': why is inflation rising; why does the AIDS virus lie dormant for so long; why was there a five per cent swing in the votes; why is there a trade deficit?

I have already mentioned the perceptual and conceptual contribution to analytical search for explanations: we need to pay as much attention to our perceptual repertoire as to the data. I want now to look in the opposite direction. Explanation looks backwards and design looks forward.

We have been obsessed with analysis but paid very little attention to design. To be sure we have designed temples, textiles, furniture and space rockets, but design has always been considered a sort of craftsman's activity compared to the intellectual excellence of analysis. Partly this is the result of our search for truth, which (possibly mistakenly) we believe to be more likely to come from analysis than from design. Possibly it is another aspect of the influence of theological reasoning on our education. Mainly it is the result of our erroneous belief that if analysis lays bare the components and systems then design is a very simple matter of putting these elements together in order to achieve some purpose.

The traditional concept is that 'knowledge is all' and, once you have knowledge, things like taking action and design are minor intellectual operations. So education and universities are concerned with the knowledge aspect. The skills of making things happen are relegated to technical colleges and business schools, which are held to be of considerably lesser intellectual value. While it may be true (and I do not necessarily agree) that the design of a wheelbarrow or a radar system is intellectually easier than the analysis of nineteenth-century political development, the actual process of design is much more difficult and every bit as important as analysis.

The two things that have held back our understanding of the importance of design are: a belief that an analysis of data will give us all the ideas we need (not true in a self-organizing perceptual system); and a belief that evolution will give us all the progress we need (also not true in a self-organizing system).

The opposite of 'why' is 'po'. With po we look forward to what might be – to what might come about as a result of changing perceptions and designing new concepts. What might be is only partly based on what is. There may even need to be an escape from what is, from the existing perceptions and paradigms.

Aristotle said that all new knowledge comes from existing knowledge. There may be some truth in this if we accept that we cannot see new knowledge except through existing perceptions. It might, however, be equally true to say that much new knowledge is prevented by old knowledge. This is because the existing perceptions must be unpicked in order that we may see things differently.

Description

There is the story about the man who finds himself in a hotel elevator with a good-looking young woman. He asks her if she would go to bed with him for $10,000. She says that she would. He thinks for a while then asks: 'What about $50?' 'What do you think I am?' the woman replies indignantly. 'We had already established that,' said the man, 'now we are just haggling about the price.' The man was clear that the descriptive category had been established and this was 'tart'. The woman felt that there was a big distinction between a 'cheap tart' and an 'opportunist'.

A glass falls off a tray and smashes to the ground. We understand that because it is a matter of gravity. The descriptive word 'gravity' is no more than a convenient way of saying: when you release things without any support they fall to the ground. Not many people who happily explain things as gravity know the Newtonian laws of gravity or the Einstein modifications. Not many even know that the acceleration of gravity is 32 feet per second. Even the most advanced physicists do not yet know if there are gravity waves or gravitron particles. So description is somewhat short of full explanation and yet provides a useful convenience.

For a long time science was no more than classifications (even in mathematics) and today there are still many areas where this is the case. Before we hasten to condemn this as primitive we need to see the effect of this on perception and on action. Fine discriminations allow us to see things differently. Before medical testing became sophisticated a doctor would distinguish between a haemolytic jaundice (destruction of red blood cells) and an obstructive jaundice (obstruction of the bile duct) because in the former both urine and stools were pale. Surgery was indicated in the latter but useless in the former. So a discrimination led to appropriate action.

At several places in this book I have made a plea for much finer discrimination in perception because without such finer perceptions we must remain in very broad patterns with their attached values. Someone may well ask for the difference between advocating finer discriminations and the classic category system. At times there is an overlap and at times a huge difference.

With the jaundice example if the doctor had said: 'These both belong to the general category of jaundice and operation is the treatment for jaundice,' the operation would have been carried out on many patients with haemolytic jaundice and would not have helped them at all (apart from being dangerous). To say that both obstructive and haemolytic patients belong to the 'jaundice' category on the basis of the physical appearance of yellow skin and eyes adds nothing in this case. It is also true that both types of jaundice may show certain similar features and side-effects, and here it is useful to know of these shared attributes. But shared attributes can be treated as such – not as membership of a category. That is the key difference.

Old folk remedies, some of which have validity, were based on trial and error. To make that effective there had to be discrimination: this root will work in such cases but not in others.

Of course, too fine discrimination may prevent us from seeing underlying similarities and here we come to the 'lumpers' and 'splitter' attitudes I have already mentioned. (Lumpers see similarities, splitters see differences.)

So when we need to escape the crudeness of broad levelling we need richer naming habits. But when we need to establish underlying uniformities we may need to look behind the naming. If we were to give different names to a glass in your hand, a glass falling through the air and a glass hitting the ground, we might have a hard time realizing that these were all part of the same process. This is a problem physicists suspect they have in particle physics. A one-year-old salmon returning to its home river is called a grilse. The English won't eat them because they think they are different from salmon. The French do eat them because they know it is just a name for a young salmon.

Naming is the simplest form of description. What happens when we move to the next level in which we use description (usually language but not always) to make models of the world? A very great deal of our intellectual effort and tradition is at this level. So much of our thinking culture is based on language and description that we need to be aware of the limits of the system. I have already considered 'language' as such in a previous section.

Someone describes a walking stick as being made up of two parts: the curved handle and the rest. Someone else describes it as having three parts: the handle, the ferrule and the linking bit in between. There is a huge flexibility of description based on tradition, available perceptual patterns, basis for analysis, history (if the walking stick had been assembled from different pieces these might form the basis for description).

Description is perception expressed through available vocabulary and according to rules of grammar. Description has all the virtues and faults of perception – including the impossibility of truth. The simple statement 'I saw a red apple on the plate' should really be 'under those circumstances and at that moment I had an experience which is most satisfactorily described as seeing a red apple on the plate'. It might have been a hologram, an illusion or a model apple.

It is when we treat description as an actual model of the situation that we run into trouble. A description in language is not a model and can only breed other descriptions. A true model should embody other processes (mathematical, chemical, neurological) and it is from the behaviour of these that we make predictions. In a description model there is no generative energy: there are no surprises.

Descriptions can trigger insights, as can random words, or poetry or chance happenings. Descriptions can change perception by showing the possibilities of new perceptions and letting these acquire value through usage. They can shift values through authority, leading fashions, reinforcing emerging trends or direct emotional propaganda (use of adjectives, partial perception and all the other mechanisms). They cannot really provide explanations or 'truth' but may establish a belief type of truth by suggesting the appropriate circular perceptions (for example: lack of concern for conservation will ultimately be disastrous so conservation is a good thing so anyone who disagrees is motivated by selfishness or greed so . . .).

There is, of course, nothing to stop the most weird and fanciful descriptions. You may choose to describe the walking stick as being made up of precisely one hundred segments with thirty in the handle and fifty in the middle and the rest in the bottom end. You may choose to describe the sun as being drawn through the sky in a chariot with precisely four named horses. You may choose to describe a cow as an incarnation of a deity. You may choose to describe any American overseas activity as imperialism. The borderline between perception, description and belief is clearly non-existent.

Description is not difficult. As a result civilization is constantly bemused by dances of description which put forward cohesiveness as a claim to truth.

Description has a great value so long as we regard it as perception rather than the logic of a constructed system. If we regard it as perception, it has the arbitrariness of perception, the fallibility of perception and the circumstance dependence of perception.

When is one description better than another? When it offers fun, spiritual value or a practical outcome? If a belief in UFOs is more fun, accept it on that basis but do not try suddenly to switch to a more practical basis. If one description offers a higher spiritual value than another, accept it on that level but do not seek a right to force the consequent values on others who have not made your choice. If there is a practical value, seek to build forward from that value.

Where a description becomes a belief or a hypothesis there are other factors which I shall cover in later sections.

The main problem with description is our urge to treat it as truth rather than just a perception.

As I have written elsewhere in this book, the fact that we can describe something in a particular way does not mean that we can see it that way. Here I seem to be indicating the exact opposite. The point is that description has no more validity than perception, since it is based on multiple perceptions. When we 'see' something we use the directly available, simple perceptions – not the complicated description we may construct later. I can describe a wheel as 'the locus of a point moving at a fixed distance round the centre of the axis' but when I see a wheel, I see a wheel, not that description.

Natural

If you have a beautiful spirit, by all means liberate it in poetry, song and compassion. If you have an ugly spirit please keep it constrained.

It is part of our thinking culture that natural and free are good and that unnatural and constrained are bad. We have natural/unnatural as one of the sharp dichotomies. I shall be describing dichotomies later as a fundamental aspect of our thinking habits.

Nature is good, so natural is good, so unnatural is bad. Yet nature can be very cruel in parts and totally selfish.

We apply paint to a surface. The paint is artificial, so if we strip away the paint the real surface is underneath. Paint-stripping to find the real wood surface underneath has been much in vogue for years.

Pretence, artificiality and convention can become excessive and stifling, so let us get rid of all artificiality. Pop songs echo the culture: be free, let it all hang out. Ever since Freud there has been a geological streak in psycho-therapy. Dig deep. Dig beneath the surface trash and you will find the real person, the true person.

Suppose this is all wrong. Suppose the surface is the true person and as you dig deeper you find basic and uninteresting trash. If you dismantle a house you have an uninteresting pile of bricks. Suppose each person is an impresario of his or her own presentation to the world. Suppose what we construct out of our experience and our chemical personality is the real value and to strip this away reveals only the scaffolding of the scenery. The

Confucians were not particularly concerned with the Western notion of soul. If you got your behaviour towards others, and your work, right, then society would let you look after your soul – in any case right thinking was likely to follow right action. Perhaps we should teach people better impresario skills and seek to make the best of bad productions rather than digging so deep.

The above comments are meant in a provocative manner to show what happens when we challenge a natural assumption (that assumption being that natural must be better).

Our natural mathematical ability would have got us nowhere without the development of notation and methods. Natural man may be selfish, aggressive and blood-thirsty or natural man may be sweet and at peace. Nature provides both models and human experience can support either.

Manners are a lubricant designed by civilization for the inter-action of people where emotional warmth and spiritual solidarity cannot be relied upon. It might be fine if we all treated each other like loving brothers and sisters, but the emphasis is on 'loving' because many brothers and sisters fight and hate each other. So this sentiment is like saying: everything would be fine if everything was fine.

This fashionable search for the natural is wonderful in some areas such as food and nature but dangerous as a blanket perception.

Youngsters have found that logic has little value because you can argue equally well on any side of a question provided you choose your values and perceptions. They also see their appar-ently 'logical' elders behaving in unattractive ways. They know that emotions cannot be swayed by logic. So they turn away from logic towards raw emotions and feelings. Surely these are the only real and true guides for action?

Here there is a total failure to distinguish between logic and perception. This failure is encouraged by education, which has, itself, never made that distinction.

All emotions are based on perception. You hate someone because that person triggers a stereotype or you have perceived that person to act in a distasteful way. A change in perception can mean a change in emotions. One day a youngster in an institution for young offenders was standing behind a warden and about to hit him on the head with a hammer – because he hated the man. Then the boy thought back to his CoRT thinking lessons (in particular the lesson consequences), so he shrugged, put down the hammer and walked away. His perception of the man had not changed but his perception of his action had changed.

Two students are having a playground fight. A mediator suggests a simple perceptual exercise: look at each other's point of view (called OPV in the CoRT lessons). The dispute dissolves.

Logic freezes things into stereotypes and categories. Perceptions are variable, depend on circumstances and can be changed.

Mathematics

All thinkers have always been in awe and envy of the power and purity of mathematics. As a constructed system it has its own real truths. It is the nearest approach to table-top logic and yet there is a great deal of perceptual skill required in the interaction of a mathematician with a range of possibilities and directions.

When we consider the immense power of mathematics in the technical field (nuclear energy, flight faster than the speed of sound, electron microscopy, visits to the moon) it is remarkable to see how little effect mathematics has had on human behaviour. In an indirect sense the technological changes, such as computers and nuclear weapons, have had a great effect, but in the direct sense the only effects may be the statistical methods that give validity to sociological studies and opinion polls, and the simple counting of votes at an election. That is probably an exaggeration, but the difference is clear enough.

The range of mathematics is limited – not in an absolute sense, because there will be devised techniques which continually extend this range, but in a practical sense. Until the recent development of chaos theory, mathematics could deal only with linear systems and a few special cases of non-linear systems. Chaos work has extended the non-linear range a bit. Computers and iterative processes will extend the range further. The opportunity offered by computers for doing mathematical experiments (setting something up, letting it run, watching the results) is a powerful mathematical development even though the purer mathematicians seemed to have disdained computers at first.

On one occasion when I had been asked to address the Mathematical Society at Cambridge University (for which meeting I was told they had the largest attendance on record) I got talking to some students who were all researching some very specialized aspect of mathematics. Indeed, one student told me that perhaps only six people in the whole world would understand what he was working on.

Once the game of mathematics is afoot, it is possible to play it in all directions – some of them very specialized indeed. Specialization also means compartmentalization, with a growing impossibility of being able to look across all fields. That is a fault of the energy of mathematics.

I was once accused of being a mathematician 'unencumbered by mathematics'. There is one truth in this, since I am concerned with the inter-relationships in a complex system and behaviour in a particular type of space which is defined in terms of the behaviour of nerve networks. Just as Euclid looked at the behaviour of lines in two-dimensional space, so am I looking at the behaviour of 'activity' in self-organizing patterning space. Just as a theoretical physicist makes a conceptual model that must both fit reality and also offer practical outcomes, so do I try to fit our neurological knowledge and devise practical outcomes.

Outside statistics, mathematics is not so comfortable dealing with fuzzy areas, ambiguities, complex interactive systems and instabilities – though progress is being made in all these areas.

One of the key limitations in mathematics is not a fault of mathematics but a fault of translation. How do we translate such items as 'justice' and 'happiness' into the symbols or forms suitable for mathematical treatment? How do we define shifting relationships with the precision required? Absolute precision is not required because mathematics can deal with envelopes of probability, but there does need to be some consensus.

Perhaps, eventually, we shall have to get rid of our ordinary language, based as it is on the variability of perception, in order to deal with fundamentals. Instead of using words like 'happiness' we shall measure the blood level of certain chemicals. Would we also be able to measure decisions as the time profile of other chemicals? Even if we could do all this the interactive complexity of the whole system would make the task daunting.

The great French mathematician René Descartes (from whose name we get Cartesian co-ordinates) was once told the story of how Archimedes was said to have set fire to invading Roman warships by concentrating upon them the rays of the sun. Being a mathematician Descartes worked out that this manoeuvre would have required a concave mirror with a very large diameter. Since this was clearly beyond the technical skills of the day the story must be yet another myth believed by non-mathematicians. Some fifty years later a fellow Frenchman actually carried out the experiment and showed that it could be done, using the Greek shields of the day, which were flat pieces of metal. The point was that the 'mirror' could be made up of separate flat pieces and did not have to be continuous – each soldier simply used his shield to reflect the rays on to the same spot. So the mathematics of Descartes were correct but the starting assumptions were not.

In 1941 a mathematician called Campbell set out to prove that for a rocket to reach the moon it would have to weigh about one million tonnes at the start. The mathematics were correct but the technology of rocket fuels and the concept of staging enabled rockets weighing far less to get to the moon.

For many years various people claimed to have proved that man-powered flight was an impossibility because the human body could not produce enough horse-power to take aloft a plane which would be strong enough to support the human weight. Eventually my friend Paul McCready did it and won the Kramer prize. Since he showed that it was possible various other people have also done it. What had changed were some basic concepts of flight and the availability of materials which were stronger and lighter.

All three of these stories show that the mathematics may be sound but that the starting assumptions, concepts and knowledge may not be.

Economists delight in building complex models with multiple

linkages to simulate economic activity. These econometric models are believed to be valuable in predicting, for example, what would happen if interest rates were to be raised by one per cent. The weakness is that the models can take in only our present assumptions and perceptions. In the past a rise in interest rates may have dissuaded people from borrowing money to buy houses. Today, with people's increasing financial sophistication and the wide availability of money advice columns, a rise in interest rates might signal a fear of inflation, and in such circumstances people may want, even more, to put their money into inflation-proof houses. So the old model, which is a summary of history, becomes valueless.

Today, economic behaviour is about seventy per cent psychological and perceptual and only about thirty per cent mathematical and rational.

So without impugning the excellence of mathematics we have to acknowledge that mathematics has had little direct effect on human affairs because the area of mathematics is limited and because of the difficulties of translating human affairs with certainty into forms suitable for mathematical treatment.

Either/Or

Right/wrong

True/false

Guilty/innocent

Us/them

Friend/enemy

Principles/unprinciples

Tyranny/freedom

Democracy/dictatorship

Justice/injustice

Natural/unnatural

Civilized/barbaric

Capitalist/Marxist

We can see in the above list of dichotomies much of the power source of our ordinary thinking. With dichotomies we come to the great joy and ingenuity of table-top logic. With dichotomies traditional logic comes closer to the constructed system that it desires. There may be something that exists in experience and for that we have perception and language. But the 'opposite' of that thing is a deliberate 'construction' and means only the opposite.

Unfortunately, as I suggested earlier in this book, the mind cannot easily hold an abstract opposite but quickly locates this in experience. So the un-white chess piece is recognized as the black chess piece.

The principle of contradiction can really apply only if the two proposed categories are truly mutually exclusive. In practice this is very difficult to find, so we deliberately set up such mutually exclusive categories – and these are our treasured dichotomies. Without them the principle of contradiction and the certainty of our logic are greatly weakened.

Someone hands you a piece of paper bearing a fine grid – as in a school exercise book. The person tells you that he is thinking of just one of the small squares. He wants you to locate that square by asking questions which will only get a 'yes' or 'no' answer. So you divide the sheet in half with a line and call one half A and the other half B. You ask: 'Is the desired box in A?' If the answer is 'no' then the box must be in B – there is nowhere else it could be. So you now forget about A and proceed to divide B into half, lettering each half as before. Again you ask the question. In the end you must come to the chosen box. The point about this simple strategy is that at every moment the desired box must lie in A or not-A (which is B). There is nowhere else. Nor can the box lie in both A and B.

It is precisely the simplicity and the certainty of this logic that we aim for in our dichotomy design. If something is not true, surely it must be false. If something is not false, surely it must be true. The polarization is a sharp one that allows no middle ground. Yet something may be partly true and partly false. The partial perception ('economical with the truth') so beloved by perception and by the press gives something which is undoubtedly true in itself but false in conveying the wrong impression. What about 'illusion'? This is something we may hold to be true but others can see to be false.

If someone is not guilty, that person must be innocent – and so we run our legal system. As I mentioned earlier the Scottish courts also allow another verdict of 'not proven', which very sensibly indicates that the suspicion has not been allayed – merely not proven.

The sharp polarizations of our dichotomy habit give a fixity and rigidity to our perception of the world. If someone does not belong to 'us', that person is one of 'them'. This makes no allowance for neutrals or people who sympathize with both sides. Even Christ wanted this type of polarization: 'He who is not with me is against me.'

If the dichotomy is democracy/dictatorship, any criticism of democracy automatically means an incipient love of dictatorship – which is nonsense. Take the dichotomy principled/unprincipled. The term 'unprincipled' carries a great deal of terrible baggage (sly, unreliable, opportunistic, corrupt). So a mind which would like to build on the flexible virtues of pragmatism is not so allowed. For pragmatism is also the opposite of principled and therefore must be equated with the bad things of 'unprincipled'.

Every day the leading executives in the Japanese motor industry meet for lunch in their special club. They discuss problems common to the whole motor industry. But as soon as lunch is over and they step over the threshold of the club, out into the street, they are bitter enemies seeking to kill each other's business by marketing, technical changes, pricing policy etc. For the Japanese, who do not have the tradition of Western logic, there is no contradiction at all between 'friend' and 'enemy'. They find it easy to conceive of someone as a friend–enemy or enemy–friend. Why not?

More or less the same attitude applies to our dichotomy of right/wrong. In Japan something can be right and wrong at the same time. Something may be right in itself but wrong under the circumstances. Instead of right/wrong there is the concept of 'fit': does this fit the circumstances, including manners, culture, pragmatism etc.? There is a fine sense of 'fit' ranging from a poor fit to a very exact fit.

In sectarian violence it is easy for one side to see the opponents as thugs or criminals and for the other side to see them as martyrs or heroes. We find it impossible to hold a 'thug/hero' category in our minds. Yet it is obvious to anyone that these people are not the same as ordinary criminals and to treat them as the same is to prolong the polarization.

In practice we often create a concept by focusing on the opposite of something else. We do not really have a strong concept of 'freedom' but we do have a strong and concrete concept of tyranny (arrests, regulation, arbitrariness, permissions etc.). So we define freedom as an opposite of tyranny. This is all right as far as it goes but unfortunately it does not tell us much about freedom. What are the responsibilities? What is licence? If I define sour as the opposite of sweet, I do not learn much about the actual qualities of sour but will simply call all non-sweet things 'sour'.

So dichotomies impose a false and sharp (knife-edge discrimination) polarization on the world and allow no middle ground or spectrum. The 'catchment' and 'centring' properties of patterns ensure that things that are really only very slightly different are forced far apart by the polarizations. It becomes impossible to step across the boundary without at once being seen as directly in the enemy camp. It is not difficult to see how this tradition in thinking has led to persecutions, wars, conflicts etc. When we add this to our beliefs in dialectic, argument and evolutionary clash we end up with a thinking system that is almost designed to create problems.

Since the mind finds it difficult to hold opposites in an abstract sense we soon attach that 'opposite' label to some other experience: a 'not-friend' becomes an 'enemy', with all the fierce baggage attached.

The dichotomy habit has been essential for our traditional table-top logic (in order to operate the principle of contradiction) and imposes a rigid falsity on perception in the search for a constructed certainty.

Absolutes

We apparently need and crave absolutes, certainty and truth. There is the truth for which we have an emotional need, the truth we need as a destination for effort, the practical truth we need to run society, the truth we need to operate logic, the truth we need to define a universe, an inner truth which is sometimes claimed.

The Islamic warrior who goes fearlessly into battle needs to feel with certainty that death on the battlefield means instant entry into paradise. The Christian martyrs had the same certainty. People who devote their lives to the service of God and religion need a faith and certainty in what they are doing. Reward in heaven is not the only reason: the life-style does become satisfying in itself (values, mission, achievement). Religion gives meaning and purpose to life and provides instant values and decision frames. It provides a stable meta-system when the day-to-day vagaries of earthly life provide only confusion. It is the most powerful concept for escaping from short-term gratification values in order to build a longer-term benefit.

There are times when the absolutes of religion clash with the pragmatism of needs. The position of the Catholic Church on birth control is such an example. Many Catholic women do use birth control methods, and surveys show that in the third world the majority of women would like to limit their child-bearing. In certain areas the world may be heading towards over-population. But the Church holds to the absolute principle that any method designed specifically to thwart the natural consequence of sexual intercourse is not permitted. The Church fully knows the difficulties this creates for its members, but absolute principles cannot be adjusted. Indeed this inability to adjust principles in a pragmatic fashion is a confirmation to many that the Church is based on truth, not expediency.

As I suggested earlier, the belief system is a powerful source of truth and absolutes. The mind does have an ease of switching into beliefs, and the vehemence with which a belief is held is more a reflection of the circular behaviour of mind than of the truth of that belief. Nevertheless the likelihood that any number of beliefs are false can never exclude the possibility of a true belief. Proving that hundreds of supposedly Dali pictures are fakes does not prove that Dali never painted.

The practical problem arises mainly when there is an attempt to force a particular belief system on those who have a different system. It is this aggressive nature of 'truth' which has caused so much trouble in history. How necessary is it to convince yourself by proving to others that you have the truth?

Truth as destination is a very powerful motivator. We may never claim to have reached the truth but we journey in that direction. That is the prime motivation behind science and mathematics. We have the compass heading and we journey in that direction just as a boat may journey north but never get to the North Pole. In a way truth as destination seems the opposite of the established, practical certainty of religious beliefs. Yet most religions emphasize the journey towards enlightenment (Buddhism, Hinduism) or self-improvement (Catholic, Protestant, Islam). So the established truths are guidelines in this journey.

Truth is a powerful motivator and, in theory, prevents complacency and arrogance. Anyone in science, however, knows very well that someone claiming to be on a slightly higher step in this journey will show a considerable disdain for those on supposedly lower steps.

We need the notion of absolutes and truth in order to run society in a practical way. Even if we do have some doubts about such absolutes we want to believe in them because we foresee that a society without such a sense of absolutes could be a mess. For example, we do want laws based on absolute principles and held as absolute. Otherwise who is going to decide from moment to moment? We are scared that, without absolutes, decisions will be made on a power basis or on the basis of greed or sectional interests (all this does, of course, happen in democracies but it takes a longer time). Our belief in justice is based on underlying absolutes and the translation of these absolutes into laws which can be improved by due process.

Although we believe in the absolutes we operate them in a more pragmatic way. People must be free to choose what they want (even if someone 'superior' thinks it is bad for them) but we draw the line at drugs. The total death rate from drugs (direct deaths) in the USA is about ten thousand a year. The death rate from smoking-related diseases is said to be 320 thousand. Yet on a historic and pragmatic basis it is difficult to take stronger action.

The discrepancy between the belief in absolutes and the ability to operate them is common to any absolute system – not all religious believers are saints in behaviour.

Our traditional table-top logic system can only work with absolutes and certainties which we claim to find or set out to construct. We establish categories with sharp exclusions and inclusions. We need to use words like 'all', 'every' and 'none' in order to get logical progression. The system would collapse through weakness if we started to say 'some', 'by and large' or 'maybe'. We would find ourselves moving from certainty to enriched guesses. So we have taken the normal output of perception, with all its fallibility, and shaped it into the tight boxes of language. We have developed the principle of identity, 'is', and the principle of contradiction, and the created dichotomies. If the resulting view of the world is somewhat forced there is, nevertheless, the sort of judgement and certainty we need for action.

Euclid's geometry is always held up as a rigorous system of deductive reasoning. From a few basic axioms can be built up a complex behaviour of lines and surfaces. Yet Euclid's geometry applies only on a plane surface. For example parallel lines on a sphere do meet (longitude lines on an earth globe meet at the poles) and the angles of a triangle add up to more than 180 degrees (any two longitude lines hit the equator at 90 degrees each, yet meet to complete the triangle at the pole). So the logic of

Euclid depends on an absolute definition of the 'universe' in which the system is acting. From this definition of the universe comes the absolute axioms which cannot themselves be proved in the system (Godel's contribution).

It is also in this sense of defining the universe of human thought and behaviour that we need absolutes. For example our concept of 'free-will' is such an absolute, for without it systems of religion and law would fall apart, as would our systems of choice and government. Over the last few decades there has been an increasing movement to try to define the universe in terms of absolute human rights and values which would cut across all belief and behaviour systems. In the sense of defining a universe, absolutes are absolutely necessary. If we drop them, the universe changes.

Finally we come to the notion of Platonic absolutes, which civilization has found convenient as a justification for the arrogance of some of its behaviour. The notion is that there are absolute ideas and that when we see particular objects these are just reflections of those absolutes. In neurological terms, experience will build up certain general patterns which will then be used to enable us to perceive objects that partake of this general pattern. The basic principle is that perception will determine future perception. There probably is a certain amount of intrinsic behaviour in the mind (like 'cause and effect' and Kant's notions of categorical imperatives) which is determined by neurological behaviour, but the rest comes from experience at some point. The obvious appeal of believing in Platonic absolutes is that we can then treat language as a constructed system. Where language does not reflect reality we simply turn the problem the other way round and say that reality is a poor reflection of the absolutes, therefore we are seeing reality badly. This is what reality should be – now go out and see it that way. If you cannot, you have failed. But reality as it should be, is intact.

How do these various uses of absolutes and truths interact with what we are beginning to know about the behaviour of perception? The perceptual circulatory of belief systems shows us how easily beliefs can be established, how difficult it is to alter them (certainly not through logic) and how difficult it may be to distinguish true from false (since this is not a relevant dimension in perception).

With regard to truth as a destination we need to be aware that our apparent steps towards the truth need not always be forward. We may have to step back from some certainties in order to change the paradigm before we can move forward again.

With regard to the pragmatic need for absolutes in order to run society, we may take the purpose of this intention and seek, through design, to achieve these purposes in better ways. This is a step further away from the divine right of kings.

As for the absolutes we think we need to run our traditional table-top logic system, we must attend to the many points I have made throughout this book on this very matter. In particular we must be wary of the false dichotomies.

With regard to the absolutes that we need to define any universe, we must be cautious in not choosing to pin down the universe we now know in such a way as to prevent future changes. If we set our current paradigm in concrete, we shall allow ourselves to work only within this paradigm (universe) for ever more.

With regard to the absolutes of Platonic claim, we should throw them out because from them arises the habit of treating language as a constructed system and seeing the world through such language, so forcing our perceptions into what we think we should see.

In one of my books (*The Happiness Purpose*) I suggested that between the absolutes of the West (good for technical progress) and the sense of illusion in the East, we should place something which I called a 'proto-truth'. A proto-truth is a truth which we hold to be absolute so long as we are trying to change it. This bears some resemblance to what a hypothesis in science should be, but often is not. This gives us the security and base of truth without its cage.

The main problem of absolutes is that they claim to be circumstance-independent. Yet we know that perception is totally circumstance-dependent. Is it possible to construct an approach to logic that takes into account this circumstance-dependency? I believe it is possible to move in this direction and will later in the book introduce the concept of 'hodics' (from the Greek for road). In hodics the central word is not 'is' but 'to'.

Argument and Clash

We love argument and we have been told to love argument. Our political system, our legal system and our scientific system are all based directly on it. From where did this love of argument come and how is it sustained? How is it that such a very inefficient system should so have captivated our intellectual energies?

The kindest thing that can be said about argument is that it is a motivated exploration of a subject. I want to focus on 'motivated' and then on 'exploration'.

Without argument we would have a one-sided view based on the self-interest of the party putting forward that view. This is exactly the same, or worse, than the partial views put forward by the press. So there is a need to obtain a richer exploration. This is done by giving someone the specific role of taking an opposing view.

In the courts of the Inquisition it was felt to be unfair to condemn a heretic without having someone motivated to challenge the prosecutors. So someone was specifically appointed as a 'devil's advocate' to carry out that role. It might also be said, somewhat cynically, that the Church would not have been able to show the power of its logic unless there was some learned person to attack.

In a court of law the role of attack is given to the prosecutor and that of defence to the defending lawyer. Both are motivated (professional pride, fees, reputation) to do a good job. The same is true with political parties. So there is a motivation to explore which might not have been there otherwise.

If we now turn to the concept of 'exploration' we may find that the motivation may actually inhibit exploration. If a significant point occurs to a defence lawyer, but is against the interest of his client, is that lawyer likely to put forward the point? If a political opposition party can see the real merit of what is put forward by the government, is the opposition likely to acknowledge and build on that merit? The truth is that the very roles that were put there for the 'motivation' aspect may interfere with the genuine 'exploration' of the subject. Once people have been put into the roles of 'attack' and 'defend', they play those roles – at the expense of exploration. We then have to accept that 'attack and defence' is itself the best form of exploration – which it is not.

The unkindest thing that can be said about argument is that it occupies a great deal of time and gives to moderately intelligent people a sense of useful intellectual activity. Argument does seem an attractive intellectual exercise because it is almost always possible to say something. In an earlier section I indicated that critical thinking was one of the easiest types of mental activity (choosing perceptions, values, frames of reference, point of attack etc.). So we like argument because we become intellectually busy.

The dialogue habits of Socrates as reported by Plato were probably a big step forward in the discussions of those wealthier Greeks who did not have to work because that was done by their slaves and womenfolk. Arguments were more fun and more focused than rambling discussion. Eventually argument became a hobby and a skill, and people (the sophists) were actually paid to go to the different courts and teach argument, exactly as I am now sometimes paid by corporations to go and teach lateral thinking to their executives.

In the early Renaissance this rigorous habit of argument was eagerly picked up by the theologians and particularly the scholastic philosophers (like St Thomas Aquinas), who were delighted to discover in Aristotle, Plato, Socrates and the others a powerful and rigorous way of proving that heretics were wrong. All they had to do was to persuade the heretics to play the same game. The heretics were happy to do this because they believed that they could use the same game to upset the Church. This they very nearly did on several occasions – except that the masters of the Church would – at the last moment – pull a trump card out of their sleeves, as St Augustine did with 'divine grace'.

Now the arguing theologians were actually on even more solid grounds than the Greeks, because the language and concepts of theology are much nearer to a 'constructed system'. The concepts of 'God', 'perfection', 'free-will' could all be defined precisely and did not have to correspond to reality. When Socrates was arguing the nature of courage there had to be constant references to real-life situations and actual feelings of courage. So through Church influence on universities, seminaries and schools, the habit and validity of argument became central to Western thinking and were eventually institutionalized in the legal and political systems.

Interestingly the non-Church thinkers, the humanists, also found the argument mode to be vastly superior to anything else around. So the Church in its attacks on heretics and the humanists in their doubts about the Church both used the same method.

Let us look at some of the purposes of argument other than motivation, the occupation of time and the sense of intellectual business it gives to those involved. Argument can serve to point out errors of fact. For example the number of people killed worldwide each year in road accidents is not 90,000 but 200,000. It can serve to point out internal logical faults or inconsistencies. Certain conclusions do not necessarily follow. Certain things are true only in special circumstances. Argument can encourage exploration of a subject by shifting attention from one point to another. It can destroy a case by showing that one aspect is incorrect therefore the whole structure is wrong (or the person putting forward the argument is a fool). It can present a different set of values. It can present different experience, so that the claimed consequence of an action can be compared with other possible consequences (at the onset of inflation will people spend more or save more?).

At its best argument might achieve many of these purposes. At its worst and more usual expression, argument concentrates on proving the opposing case to be false and the people putting it forward to be both stupid and motivated by self-interest. Even in science it is extremely rare for major progress to be achieved by argument. The reason is that those arguing must be within the same frame of reference or paradigm. If not, then neither side will understand the other, so the established side will treat the other side as merely crazy. So paradigms are very unlikely ever to be changed by argument. Argument will tidy up things within existing paradigms but not change them.

For the same reason perceptions and beliefs will not be changed by argument, for the starting frames are simply different. A person looking through a rose-tinted window cannot be convinced by another person looking through plain glass that the world is not rosy.

So argument, at best, is limited in value. The defects are, however, considerable.

There is the adversarial posture and the role-playing (so destructive for example in divorce proceedings). There is polarization and a win/lose substitution for exploration. Almost the entire time is taken up on attack and defence rather than on the creative construction of alternatives. Win/lose implies staying within the starting positions while creative design involves designing new positions that can offer real values to both sides (I have discussed some of these points at length in an earlier book of mine, *Conflicts*). This creation of new values is often referred to as win/win rather than win/lose.

If we had to move away from argument what could we put in its place? The answer is 'exploration'.

In many countries the new family courts are beginning to work on this basis: the situation is to be explored. The Dutch legal system has never had a jury but just three assessors who are there to explore the case. There are powerful techniques of constructive exploration. The CoRT thinking programme which I designed for schools and which is now widely in use is based on perceptual exploration – giving various 'compass points' as directions in which to explore. If we set our mind to developing and practising constructive exploration techniques we would become very good at these.

But there are different values and different points of view and different perceptions. How can an exploration system encompass these?

Countries like Japan, which have never had the Western background of argument, have developed their own system. In Japan information and values are not put forward as ideas for argument but as inputs. Gradually all these inputs coalesce into a decision or outcome. Western businessmen have often complained to me that at a meeting the Japanese will at first seem to hold back and not offer anything. The Westerner with his argument habits does not have anything into which to get his teeth. But the Japanese are not holding back. They simply do not have a position or an idea at this stage – these things emerge only very much later.

Different points of view, different values and different proposals can all be laid down on the table alongside each other. Then they can be compared or even combined. When you are planning a road trip you use a map to see the alternative routes to your destination. The routes are all there on the map. One route is better in summer. Another route is better outside peak hours. Another route is more scenic. In the end you travel along one route, or a combination.

This laying down and examination of alternatives in parallel is very different from the style of argument in which you must show the other side to be 'wrong' in order that you can be 'right'. This fundamental argument attitude is based on religious disputations, the guilt and innocence of law courts, and the absolutes of table-top logic in which two opposing views cannot both be right (principle of contradiction).

It is not difficult to see how the habits of argument arose and why we so mistakenly value it. In fact society often gets a double dose of the argument habit. This is because it is usually lawyers who go into politics and bring their argumentative habits to congress or parliament, which are already set up on an argument basis.

Argument is not exactly the same as 'clash', which is another of our thinking habits. There are many cultures which have a tradition of opposing elements. In Hinduism there is Vishna for creation and Shiva for destruction. In Chinese culture there is the Yin and Yang contribution. In the Christian tradition (influenced by Manichaeism) there is the clash of good and evil. In Marxism there is the basic struggle of capital against labour and the philosophy of dialectical materialism. There is Hegelian conflict and Darwinian evolution. There is the thesis, antithesis and synthesis of Greek thought. We give a sort of mystical meaning to this sense of clash. Perhaps it reflects the early human experiences with tribal fights and later 'glorious' wars.

But what is supposed to happen with 'clash'? To be sure the new attack may overcome the old order and replace it – that is revolution or simply war (depending on who is involved). From the chaos that follows the clash a new order may spring, phoenix-like. This is much of a hope and less of a reality. The strong motivation to get rid of the old conjures up dreams of a wonderful new, but does nothing to substantiate such dreams – so one power group moves into the vacuum and takes over. The result is a revolution which other people have fought for you. Sometimes there is a synthesis of the two. This very rarely happens because each party is firmly in its us/them position and any temporary co-operation is ended as soon as one side or the other sees a way to get complete control. Yet we persist in this notion of clash as a basis of progress.

In my visits to Russia I became convinced that glasnost and perestroika were sincere and powerful movements. I was, however, concerned that the tradition of dialectic materialism would insist that progress could come only from destruction of the old. Clearly there are a lot of things which do have to be removed before progress can get very far. But this is only half the process. The other half needs to come from deliberate constructive and creative design. Patching up the faults in an old car does not itself design a new car. The habit of dialectic could mean that perestroika would end up as an orgy of self-destructive criticism, with those doing the criticizing feeling that that was the only contribution required.

In perceptual terms clash may be a method for obtaining focus, direction and motivation. Yet it has no creative or constructive elements. The notion of creative tension is a philosophical abstraction which has no reality in a patterning system (being derived from mechanical systems).

We can see how many different things have come together to give us our basic habits of argument and clash. There is traditional logic and truth and contradiction. There is a Greek habit of discourse eagerly accepted by medieval theologians to serve their purposes. There is the institutionalization of argument in law, politics and science.

On the clash side there is the cultural tradition of clash as a basis of nature and possibly the real-life experience of clash as a political fact. There is the incorporation of this into certain philosophical systems as justification for revolution.

Above all we continue in these less than efficient habits because those involved like this way of proceeding and will not put their minds to designing (or accepting) more efficient methods.

Belief

A woman is wheeling along a pram in which are her two children aged three and five years. An acquaintance comes up to her and looks at the children:

'Aren't they beautiful children?' gushes the acquaintance.

'Oh, never mind them,' replies the mother, 'you should see their photographs – now those are really beautiful.'

I sometimes use this story when addressing a conference. People always laugh at the absurdity of the photograph being more important than the real thing. So I go on to explain my point. Maybe the photographs are more important than the children. When you see the photographs you see beauty and the photograph will be the same for ever (a reasonable number of years). The children will grow and change. When you look at the children you may see a smiling child or a dribbling child or a fractious child but the photograph always shows beauty. Perhaps the purpose of the children is only to create beautiful photographs.

This seems a perverse and outrageous point of view, but it is not. Perhaps the purpose of life is to create beautiful and enduring myths and it is these we are meant to enjoy. Day-to-day reality is there only to fuel the myths. It is true that myths and beliefs are easy and often false and impossible to substantiate. Yet they may be the true reality for a perceptual system. Myths provide beauty, purpose, value, comfort, security and emotional fuel. It is also true that beliefs can stand in the way of progress and have, in the past, been responsible for very much suffering – and passive acceptance of what might have been changed.

I have dealt with belief at so many different points in this book

that I do not wish to repeat all I have written, so I shall summarize it very simply.

A belief is a perceptual framework which leads us to see the
world in a way which reinforces that framework. This circularity
is a very natural function of a self-organizing patterning system,
so beliefs are very easy to form. In a sense 'belief' is the truth of a
perceptual system. When you burn your finger at a fire only once
in your lifetime, you are operating a belief system. Your fear of
fire is not built up by induction based on repeated experience.
Your initial trauma creates a belief that prevents you from ever
contradicting that belief, so the circularity is established.

Science

'He did it.'
 'No, she did it.'
 'It was him.'
 'I know who did it but I'm not telling.'

A flower bowl in a kindergarten has been knocked over and smashed. The children are seeking to confuse the teacher as to how it happened. The teacher may want to find out who did it (probably not).

That has been the essence of science. Something happens and using our reliable 'cause and effect' idiom we know there must be a cause somewhere. We set out to find the cause. In the kindergarten story the teacher may have a suspicion as to who did it: in science this suspicion would be the hypothesis. Science sets out to identify and isolate the cause. Isolating the cause has a number of useful effects. It helps you to understand the processes going on in nature, which can then be investigated in their own right. You can remove the cause.

At several points in this book I have commented on the ease of beliefs in a self-organizing patterning system. This easy belief system allows us to make sense of the world even when we do not have much data – as with a growing child. Nowhere is this belief system seen to be more at work than in beliefs about the causes of illness.

The term malaria comes from the region of Rome. The illness we now call malaria simply means the 'bad air' ('mal' 'aria') because it was believed that the bad air from the swamps caused malaria. It was scientific investigation that subsequently narrowed down to the bad air, to the mosquitoes that were in the air, and finally to the parasite within the mosquito.

Within medicine itself there have been powerful dominating beliefs which we now believe to be false. There was the fashion of blood-letting, in which for any illness the patient would be relieved of a quantity of blood. Often this was done to such excess (more is better) that the patient nearly died as a result of the treatment. It may be that in the future we shall rehabilitate blood-letting when we discover that the process stimulates the marrow to produce not only red blood cells but also the vital white blood cells which are the body's defence. It may be that blood-letting also stimulates the adrenal system to produce cortisone or the brain to produce those hormones which stimulate most other things.

Aspirin (from willow bark) and the powerful digitalis for the treatment of heart failure (from foxgloves) were folk remedies that moved from folk belief to medically accepted belief even though the mechanisms are still imperfectly understood. Edward Jenner's use of cow-pox (vaccinia) as a protection against the dreaded small-pox was based on acute observation and eventually served to abolish this disease from the face of the earth.

Science has so ably proved its power and contribution that it must seem beyond criticism. Yet there are some comments that can be made.

The origins of science as the opposite of myths and folk beliefs has led it to eschew all those things in which a rational link of actions cannot be imagined. For example the Chinese habit of acupuncture seems utter nonsense and yet the chemical naloxone, which blocks endorphins, will also block acupuncture – suggesting that there is a rational basis in the possible production of endorphins in the brain. More recently science has begun investigating some of these folklore remedies. That most are nonsense does not prove that all are nonsense.

The basic idiom of 'cause and effect' followed by the isolation and identification of the cause has been powerful. But it is an idiom that does not work so well in complex interactive systems where a whole web of factors are involved. Breaking down things into parts may miss factors that arise on a more holistic basis.

There are many scientists who believe that the mere analysis of data will produce ideas. This is not so, for reasons I have already discussed. We can only look at data in terms of the concepts we already possess, such as simple correlation. In general, scientific training puts far too little emphasis on the generation of hypotheses. Science would probably have progressed very much faster if we had trained scientists to be more imaginative, more creative and more prolific in their ability to generate hypotheses. A hypothesis is not only a framework through which we look at data but also a scaffold which allows us to build data into a structure. Science is not just analysis but also creativity – in hypothesis creation and experimental design.

The notion of the single most reasonable hypothesis which we then set about trying to refute (the Karl Popper view of science) is defective on perceptual grounds. Once we have the most reasonable hypothesis we can see the data only through that hypothesis. At the very least we need another hypothesis (no matter how crazy and unjustifiable) in order to get a differently angled view on the data. The single hypothesis tradition is why we sometimes look back at old data and see how a new finding could have come about long ago – except that the view was blocked by the old hypothesis.

The difficulty of changing paradigms was ably discussed by Thomas Kuhn in 1962. Scientists get stuck in one way of looking at things. They resist and dismiss efforts to change that view until at last, much later, the evidence is overwhelming. Scientists have never learned to dance but prefer to shuffle round the floor with small steps forward all the time. Yet perceptual organization requires steps backwards as well as forwards – as in dancing.

There are times, especially in sociology, when what we regard as proof is really no more than lack of imagination – in providing an alternative explanation. This seems to open the door to all manner of weird beliefs, but in closing that door we must not also shut out the possibility of explanations we cannot yet imagine.

Science usually deals with simplifications, approximations and more or less linear systems. In non-linear and complex interactive systems science is much less at ease. The ability of computers to handle better these types of system should be of help.

In science we measure what we can measure and ignore what we cannot. We can set up and self-validate an IQ test but we have no way of measuring how well a youngster plays the piano. We have no tests of complex performance. So we ignore performance and base our educational assessment on standard questionnaires.

Most of these faults arise from a belief that science is more scientific and logical than it really is. In fact there is a great deal of creativity, imagination and poetry in science. This is because science is as much perceptual as analytic. It is only now – and in certain areas like mathematics and physics – that this is being realized.

Where we can use our existing tools of science (identification of cause) we do very well indeed. We are now at the point of needing to develop further idioms – and this may be happening.

Creativity

Culturally we have done astonishingly little about creativity even though we acknowledge that much of progress has depended on it. There are a number of reasons for this striking failure.

Our basic belief in table-top logic, science and mathematics has convinced us that all progress will happen in steady rational steps, where each step is soundly based on the previous one. The history of science, for example, has shown that this is simply not true at all. So why do we believe this myth?

Every valuable creative idea must be logical in hindsight (otherwise we would never appreciate its value). So once the creative idea has come about we insist that it could indeed have come from step-wise logic. All valuable ideas that come about as a result of insight, chance or mistake must always be presented in the scientific literature as if they had come about by a process of careful step-wise logic, otherwise the paper would never be published. The invention of the triode valve (the foundation of all electronics) by Lee de Forest came about as a result of a totally erroneous idea (he believed that an electric discharge had caused a gas flame to sputter). Yet, in hindsight, the idea was presented as step-wise logic. So we deny creativity and insist that we would eventually have reached the idea through proper logic, or that better logic could have got there anyway.

We have noted that geniuses will keep on coming through whether we encourage them or not. We know that we are unlikely to produce geniuses by direct effort. So we make no effort in the direction of creativity but are just content to let it happen – as a sort of random mutation.

The real reason why we have done so very little about creativity is very simple. We have not understood it at all. We have not understood the process of ideation. We have not understood creativity because it is impossible to do so in terms of the passive information universe, in terms of table-top logic. This is the wrong universe. It is only when we make the jump – which we have not yet done – to the universe of self-organizing patterning systems (with such features as asymmetry) that creativity becomes simple and clear. No matter how hard we try in the wrong universe, we shall not understand creativity.

As we have seen, in a self-organizing patterning system provocation is absolutely logical. Playing and playing around is a form of provocation, yet we have never given it the status it deserves. Those creative ideas which come about by chance, accident or mistake (antibiotics, cortisone, Pasteur's immunization by weakened agent, nylon, X-rays, photographic film etc., etc.) are really coming about by provocation. Chance has provided what we can learn to do deliberately once we understand the system. A provocation is something that does not arise from our present framework. By definition, there is no logical basis for a provocation until after it has been effective.

The use of the broad term 'creativity' has impeded our understanding of creativity because we have sought for uniformities of behaviour across very different fields (Beethoven writing a symphony, Picasso painting a picture, Clerk Maxwell theorizing about electro-magnetism). Hindsight description of behaviour is not of much value in identifying a process. That is why it was necessary to invent the concept of lateral thinking to describe specific behaviour in a self-organizing patterning system.

Then there was the notion that people are naturally creative but are inhibited by the logic of our culture, the fear of looking stupid, and the habit of instant judgement, so that removing the inhibitions should make us more creative. We would be released to be our natural creative selves. This was the background to the 'brainstorming' method developed by Alex Osborne for use in advertising. In some ways this method has helped to get attention for creativity. In some ways it has done a great deal of harm by suggesting that creativity is just a matter of release and lack of inhibitions. This has some value in the advertising world but much less elsewhere.

The release of inhibitions will produce some increase in creativity but not very much. Creativity (in the sense of lateral thinking for changing perceptions and concepts) is not a natural process. The natural process of the brain is to form patterns and to use them, not to seek to cut across patterns. So we need to do much more than just be 'uninhibited'.

There is also the black-box approach to creativity. In this approach we throw up our hands and say it is all a matter of intuition, sub-conscious, emotions and genius. This is just a more elaborate way of saying: it happens but we can do nothing about it.

A simple understanding of the organizing nature of concepts and perceptions will show that progress cannot happen in steady logical steps. It will also show how we can increase the flow of new ideas through the deliberate use of such processes as provocation and random entry. There is no mystery about this at all – just an escape from the table-top universe of passive information systems.

History

We are not going to run out of history. We create more and more history every day and can look with more and more depth into the history we already have (by research, archaeology, magnetic dating etc.). We can comment on the many commentators who comment on history. Culturally we are so obsessed with history that at times there does seem to be a 'culture of corpses'.

History is satisfying because it is there and we can get our teeth into it. The uncertainty of an experiment, or mathematics that won't work out, or the cussedness of living people, don't come into it. If you set out to do historical research you are guaranteed a reasonable outcome (choose a niche). History is non-technical so those research-minded people who do not like maths or science (in which there is now so much maths) have an area for research.

There are, however, much more basic reasons for an attitude that is sometimes extreme enough to suggest that civilization is culture and culture is history. In essence we are positioned by our ancestors – as in those everlasting Spanish grandee names that give an instant genealogy.

There was a time when we could get all progress forward – in science, in mathematics, in philosophy, in literature and in every conceivable field – by looking backwards. That time was the Renaissance. We could best move forward by looking back to the civilized thinking of the Greeks and the administration of Rome and the literature of both. The Arabs contributed as well in science and maths (notation and the zero).

So there was this extraordinary period when we really could

go forward by looking entirely backwards. This was when scholarship and research earned their place and when discourse, learning and universities were becoming established. Before that it was the Dark Ages and the dictate of the Church. So this habit of history, which was so very valuable at the time, became firmly established as a central part of our thinking tradition. Once established it has been ably defended on the various grounds I shall attempt to discuss.

It is said that if we do not know history we are compelled to repeat its mistakes. There is truth in this but also a danger. The world has been changing very rapidly. It took weeks to communicate from England to India in the days of the British Empire; today it takes seconds. Wars were fought by armies in faraway places; now wars may be fought by missiles in your backyard. Modern democracy and modern media mean that people will not so easily be aroused to glorious crusades. Maybe the lessons of history are inappropriate or even misleading.

The answer to the above objection is that history is not about events but about people – and basic human nature does not change. History is the only laboratory in which we can look at 'people in action'. So the lessons we can learn (from Chamberlain and Munich, that 'appeasement' does not work) will be valid as long as human nature is the same. Human nature may be the same, but the way it is used may be different. The Vietnam war did not succeed because television beamed the reality of war directly into every American living room and because pressure on Congress prevented the 'full war' that military strategy would have required.

In the Falklands war and the Grenada invasion the media were kept at arm's length because of the Vietnam experience. So this was a useful lesson learned from very recent history, but lessons learned from more remote history might have been inappropriate. For example, in the past a population might have been aroused to warlike indignation over the bullying of a smaller nation by a large one or by insults to some citizens of that country. Today such indignation would stop far short of war. Human nature may not have changed, but the aspect of human nature that understands the horror of war over-rides the aspect that follows moral indignation or patriotism.

So the lessons of history may be helpful or a trap.

There is a much less mentioned aspect of history that could have a value. If one party in a dispute signals that it is a student of history, this may also signal the way the situation is being perceived and the steps that may be taken. In a subtle way this is a threat of action. If both parties are students of history, the game of 'chess' may be played out by historical reference alone.

If we buy only antique furniture, who will design tomorrow's antiques? If we mostly look backwards, who will be looking forwards? There is no question of the unbalance of intellectual resources in favour of looking backwards rather than forwards. No matter how valuable the idea put forward, any scientific paper has credibility only if it looks backwards and locates the new idea in that perspective of history which we call scholarship. The word 'scholar' implies a student of what has been rather than a designer of what might be. History has its place as does salt on food – and too much can inhibit progress (another example of the Laffer curve).

Logic

There is the problem of the prisoner who knows that one warder always tells the truth and the other warder always lies. The prisoner does not know which is which and does not know which of two exits leads to freedom. For some reason the prisoner can only ask one question. So what does she do? This is a simple problem in logic. The answer is that the prisoner asks either of the warders which route the other warder would recommend. Then the prisoner takes the route which would not have been recommended. This is a nice exercise in logic with a neat and perfect answer.

We use extremely little explicit logic in ordinary life. Most thinking at ordinary level, government level and commentary level is based on perception, language and information. At most there is one logic step: if this then that. Apart from technical matters, like comparing mortgage offers, most thinking takes place in the perceptual stage. How much do we take in? How do we look at things? This perception is based on habits of perception and what we hear, what we read and how we express ourselves. Language therefore comes into it a great deal, packaging perceptions and allowing us to see only what we are prepared to see.

We do not need to use much explicit logic because we have already built the logic into our language. Killing is 'bad' unless justified by war or self-defence. The word 'murder' already has the lack of justification built into it so there is no need at all for judgement. With investment decisions we follow what is recommended and what our friends are doing and then rationalize it with the rationalizations provided. Since everyone does this the behaviour is self-fulfilling and the stock price rises for a while.

When eventually the market gets a severe correction we rationalize that as well. This rationalization is based on information – not on all available information but a selection that fits what we are inclined to do anyway.

Does this mean that the rigidities, categories, dichotomies, contradictions and polarizations of table-top logic are not that important in real life? All these things have now been built into perception and language and style of thinking:

If I can defend my point of view, I am right, so why listen to any alternatives?

With the onset of inflation people will either spend more or save more – there is no other possibility.

Freedom means being free to make your own choices so if people want to smoke they must be free to make that choice.

Marxism is an avowed enemy of capitalism so all Marxists are enemies. We should not trade with enemies.

The Japanese market is not as open to imports as is the US market, therefore we must have some protection against Japanese imports.

There are only two senior female executives in this large organization, therefore there must be discrimination against women.

If the majority feel that way, it must be right. That is the meaning of democracy.

In all the above cases we would like to murmur: 'It is not as simple as that'; 'There are in-between positions'; 'Not in all circumstances'; 'There are other explanations.' Such objections directly attack the fixity and exclusion habits of traditional table-top logic. They signal the partiality of perception; the circumstance dependence of perception; the broad catchment of perceptual patterns; the need to consider alternatives.

I am concerned here with the logic of ordinary life, not logic as an abstract philosophical exercise. It is no use pointing out that these are examples of bad logic and that if everyone used excellent logic all would be well. This is just a hindsight hope. The very structure of table-top logic does not allow the flexibility of perception. There is too much rightness, certainty and definition of categories. It is easy to say that if a person had used a category other than 'enemy' the outcome would have been different – but why should a person have chosen another category when 'enemy' seemed appropriate?

The simplest practical approach is to say: 'We are not using (table-top) logic even though we pretend to be. We are using perception. So let us be aware of the partiality, variability, and circumstance dependence of perception.' This means that we can express a perception but be conscious that it is a perception without those claims to righteousness which spring from logical certainty. We can be willing to find alternative perceptions and to look at the perceptions of others. We can accept that our perception is valid under some circumstances but not under others.

Logic can be used to reinforce perceptions (and prejudices) but logic and argument will not change perceptions. If the military keep quiet about UFOs it is not because they do not exist but because this information must be kept suppressed. Creating alternative perceptions can be more successful: 'There are people who genuinely believe they are seeing something when they are not, as in post-hypnotic hallucinations, so these people who see UFOs are not lying'; 'The mind can be tricked into seeing things which are not there as in magic show illusions; perhaps some of these UFOs happen this way'; 'There are people who strongly believe in fairies and ghosts'; 'Keep an open mind until you see one yourself.' Each of these points would be elaborated more fully and simply laid down alongside the existing perception, without directly challenging it.

If I had to put my finger on the most harmful aspect of everyday 'implicit' logic it would be the habit of dichotomies (either/or) and their use in judgement. In this matter the knife-edge discrimination behaviour of patterning systems is woefully abused so that things which are really quite similar are treated as totally separate (obviously in racism). As I have written before the dichotomy habit arises from the need for: categories, identity and the principle of contradiction. These three things are the essence of table-top logic.

Art

Cartoons may be the highest form of art. This statement is obviously an absurdity, a provocation or a special perception that needs justifying.

There is the aesthetic aspect of art (music, dance, architecture, abstract painting) and the emotional aspect of art (drama, novels, old master paintings, poetry) and then there is the perceptual aspect (cartoons, sculpture). Of course, all these aspects overlap and any work of art can involve any combination – I have merely indicated which ones are the more pure examples of the aesthetic, emotional and perceptual aspect.

A cartoon picks out the essence and can force us to recognize that essence. A cartoon drives perception by leading it very strongly. People come to look more like their caricatures more than the caricatures ever looked like the people. This highlighting is a strong perceptual process. We are forced to focus upon something and thereby become conscious of that thing. Rachel Carson's book *Silent Spring* has been credited with starting the concern for ecology. This focusing and highlighting process is one way in which art can change perceptions.

Culturally we have left perception to the world of art (not just high art but art in its broadest sense). We have believed that perception with all its variability had no place in religion, logic, mathematics or science and could therefore safely be left to art. Does art change perceptions or reinforce the ones that already exist in society? Is art a mirror or a diagnostic kit? There is no doubt that most literature reflects the inner human condition and also the values of the times. Even a book like *Gone with the Wind* reflects the position of blacks in society and perceptions of this position. School textbooks reflected the gender stereotypes of society. If art is going to be a mirror in which people can recognize the human condition, that mirror must indeed reflect what is there.

It is true that reflection, focusing, highlighting (as in Charles Dickens) can itself lead to a change in perceptions. So can the putting of unfashionable opinions into the mouths of certain characters. Once a trend has started, art can very quickly accelerate that trend. In literature all the 'dishonesty' of language (partial observation, exaggeration, adjectives, sneers, shifts, baggage) can be used to ride the trend. It is remarkable how rapidly the general attitude to race and ecology in the USA has changed within a relatively short time.

The mechanisms of propaganda are just as powerful, perceptually, in whatever direction they are used, even though we call one direction 'truth'. Not so long ago a non-smoker would almost apologize for this idiosyncrasy. Today a smoker feels like a pariah. There is the joke about the man who used to go into a drug-store and ask for some cigarettes, and then – in a whisper – asks for some condoms. Today the same person goes into the drug-store and asks for condoms and then – in a whisper – asks for cigarettes.

Perceptions can indeed be changed by art. Feelings towards war have been changed from the glorious (also encouraged in its day by art) to the brutal by literature, film and television.

So we could say that art serves all three purposes: to reflect the perceptions that exist; to accelerate a change in perceptions; and occasionally to initiate a change in perceptions. Art does all this with assurance, dogma, righteousness, emotional intensity, blinkered vision and every trick of propaganda. Art is, and probably has to be, extremely intolerant. So we have all the arrogance of logic and belief systems in action once again. But we do not mind if all this is heading in the right direction (never mind how 'right' is determined). There may not be a mass following at the beginning, but if there is at the end then that must be 'right'.

There is a slight problem in that art (in its very broad sense) must be interesting, emotionally involving and attractive, otherwise no one will listen and there will be channel switching. Now this rather important consideration will come to affect the 'mirror' quality of art. Writers do not want to write about ordinary people (like the boring 'tractor' literature of early Soviet art) but about people with hyper-complex neuroses. Painters have to have styles that can be written and talked about, as Tom Wolfe pointed out so long ago. Television has to be full of violence and deaths because this is the most reliable form of dramatic punctuation.

If we maintain that art does channel and set perceptions, will these perceptions driven by commercial reality (Rambo and others) also set perceptions? Or are perceptions only set by 'good art' and we can dismiss the rest as rubbish without any effect?

Is it enough to say that society can happily leave perceptions to the 'art' side while logic, science and mathematics get on with all the other aspects? While accepting the valuable role of art in improving perceptions, my answer would be a definite 'no'. This is because art may change perceptions but does nothing to encourage valuable perceptual habits. The righteousness and certainty I have mentioned already are the opposite of the subjective nature of perceptions or the possibility of looking at things in different ways. We may rely on art for perceptual enrichment but not for perceptual skills. It is for this reason that I believe we need to teach perceptual skills (essentially breadth and change) directly in school.

I do not want to deny the value of art, any more than the value of science and mathematics, but I do want to point out that from the 'perceptual' point of view there are serious deficiencies in some of our accepted habits and methods.

THINKING IN SOCIETY AND ITS INSTITUTIONS

Society is not made up just of thinking individuals. There are structures and institutions and mechanisms within which – or between which – individuals think. In some cases these structures have arisen directly from our traditional culture of thinking, for example the argument habit of democracy. In other cases the structures themselves generate a type of thinking, as in bureaucracy. In yet other cases a particular subject preserves a habit of thinking, like the obsession with history in universities.

In the following pages I set out to look at some of the structures which arise from, and also preserve, our traditional thinking habits. In some cases I shall be looking directly at an institution, in others at a type of thinking that arises from the nature of the institutions.

Any institution is a structure for making things happen and also for preventing things from happening. I am therefore focusing on 'change' as a basic theme. Almost by definition progress is due to change. This could be change that is so gradual that it is never noticed. It could be change by adjustment and adaptation and response to pressures. Or it could be the extreme change that comes with new concepts, changes of paradigm and perceiving things differently. How do our established institutions cope with the process of change? How do they set out consciously to deal with change and how does the very nature of their structure permit change?

The list of structures is by no means comprehensive and I may well have omitted important structures which should have been included. I have just wanted to show that we can move from the nature of a nerve system to the nature of perception to the nature of traditional thinking habits to the structure of society. In the coming pages I shall be covering the following aspects of the matter:

CHANGE: our basic belief in an evolutionary model. We muddle along and adapt to pressures, crises and innovations as they arise.

THE NEXT STEP: the next step we take is based on where we are and how we got there rather than on where we want to be.

FULL UP: there is no vacuum, there are no gaps. Time, space and resources are all committed.

EDUCATION: a locked-in system that is largely unaware of the need for thinking in society or of the type of thinking.

LUDECY: a new word to describe the playing of a game according to the way the rules are written. Not a matter of selfishness.

SHORT-TERM: much of our thinking has to be short-term (business, politics) because the rules are written that way.

DEMOCRACY: a system designed to get consensus for action but now much more effective in preventing things from happening.

PRAGMATISM: if behaviour is not driven by principles that are fixed and absolute, what is the alternative?

BUREAUCRACY: an organization put together for a purpose but coming to survive for its own sake.

COMPARTMENTS: one trend towards increased specialization and compartments and the other trend towards unifying understandings.

UNIVERSITIES: an educational, cultural and research role strongly based in history and dominating the use of intellectual resources.

COMMUNICATION: the limitations of language and the imperatives of the media and yet a great power to change sentiment.

PACKAGING: our growing skill at perceptual packaging may pose a problem in the future.

Change

The smartest people tend to stay in the ghetto because they can make the system work. It was Bernard Shaw who said that progress was always due to unreasonable people because reasonable people wanted to use the system as it was, not change it.

Like an oscillating spring that is slowing down to a steady state we believe that most of our concepts and institutions are pretty nigh perfect. There needs to be some problem-solving here and there and some adjustments to meet changing circumstances. We do not conceive of, or wish for, any major changes. Where there is not yet democracy or justice we hope that such places will eventually acquire those habits.

The underlying idiom of change is gradual evolution. Different pressures (ecological, economic) and needs (rise in living standards, racial equality) will mould our development, pushing now this way and now that. The pressures will lead by the political process or, more likely, be exerted on it through popular changes in sentiment.

Technical changes will come from corporations, universities and technical institutes which are motivated in that direction. Changes in popular sentiment will occasionally be led by individuals (like Ralph Nader) but more often will arise as an imperceptible trend that accelerates into a powerful fashion.

The system will always be defended by those countless people who have enough intellect to defend but not quite enough to innovate. There are always many who believe that any change, by definition, will threaten the security of their position. Furthermore, since we cannot fully see the consequence of a change before it has happened, it is better to avoid the risk.

There will be major crises which will force change just as the oil price rise forced oil economy and the high yen forced the Japanese to stimulate home demand. Politically, change forced by a crisis is much more acceptable because it is obvious that something must be done – and surviving a crisis is achievement enough.

Some ideas will start and get nowhere, like simplified English spelling. Some ideas will start and progress and then die away. Some ideas will take hold, like conservation. This is the way of evolution. Evolutionary pressures will be supplied by critical thinking, by the sheer inertia of most systems and by general complacency.

Is there anything wrong with this comfortable evolutionary model?

Imagine a game in which someone hands you cardboard shapes, one at a time. Your task is to make the best possible use of the shapes which you have received. By 'best possible use' is meant a simple coherent shape which might be described over the telephone. So you put the first pieces together to get a rectangle. Then you add the next piece to get a longer rectangle. Next you try to add the two new pieces, but the result is not a simple shape. In order to proceed you have to go back and undo the rectangle and make a square. Now you can add the new pieces to make a bigger square.

The game is simple but the principle is important. At each moment we do the most sensible thing. We seek to combine what is new with what we have already. In such a system it is almost inevitable that we shall reach a position in which we have to go back – to undo something that was the best choice in its time – in order to go forward. This is because the direction of organization depends on what we had, not on what might come next. For example, our democratic habits are based on what we had (village hall meetings), not on what the technology of communication might make possible.

This principle does not apply just to artificial games with

cardboard pieces but to any broad system with two characteristics: input over time and the need to make the best use of what
is available.

The problem is that we cannot just build from where we are
but may need to go back to undo certain things in order to move
forward. In many cases we cannot put the pieces together in a
new way until we have freed the pieces from their old configura-
tion which does not apply. Reasoning like this has always been
the justification for revolution – sweep away the old before we
can construct the new. The trouble with revolution is that it
tends simply to substitute one rigid system for another, for
though the pieces may be dislocated there is not time for them to
be put together in a better way.

The second problem with the evolutionary model is that, whereas in the animal world the animals can do little to control their
environment so that species that are not well adapted die out, in
the human world a system can so control the environment as to
ensure its own survival. This is usually the way dictatorships
survive. It is also the reason why Marxism may be acceptable as
a political system but not as a government, because once in
power Marxism removes the possibility of future change. All
political systems have the same ambitions – it is just that some
are more effective and more ruthless in fulfilling these ambitions.

This control of the environment to ensure survival of the
existing system is exactly the same as the belief process. As we
have seen, in this process the belief sets up the perceptions
which ensure that what we see supports the belief. The democratic system sets up a free press which is usually capitalistic
because 'interest' is more saleable than 'ideology'. The totalitarian
system sets up a press controlled by licence, the availability of
newsprint and the threat of job loss.

The belief system lock-in is itself the same as the paradigm system
so often discussed in science. A paradigm is a particular intellectual
model by which we look at the world. New ideas will be dismissed if
they do not fit the model, until the evidence of the need for a change
is so overwhelming that a paradigm shift has to take place.

We can believe that the normal process of argument and disagreement in society can bring about major changes, but the experience of science has shown that this is not the case. Argument and disagreement take place within the existing framework and produce minor modifications but no shift of paradigm as such. You cannot hold any sort of debate if one party is talking English and the other party French. Similarly if each party is coming from a different paradigm no discussion is possible – the person offering the new paradigm is simply dismissed as 'crazy' (as Christ was by most of his contemporaries).

All the comments made earlier in this book about the natural behaviour of self-organizing patterning systems in the brain apply equally to society, which is also a self-organizing system. Instead of patterns we have concepts, institutions and procedures. Because of our contentment with the evolutionary model (and the belief that the only alternative is the revolutionary model) we have never really understood the processes of ideation, change or design.

We fear designed utopias because they are unrealistic, untested, depend on absurd expectations of human behaviour – and are impossible to switch into. We fear design in general because we know that it can go wrong, whereas evolution, by definition, is always right. We fly in designed aeroplanes, but we do not have sociological equivalents of 'wind tunnels' in which to test ideas before flying them. So we are content to let the pressures do the designing for us and to call it evolution.

If forty-two per cent of the electorate has total control of the government for fifteen years (through the Thatcher government in the UK) that is acceptable because that is the way the system works, because Mrs Thatcher happens to be an outstanding person and because any government in power must take into account the views of the entire electorate in order to get back into power. Yet the system is not beyond improvement. Suppose the two leading candidates both got into parliament but that their voting power reflected their electoral support: 38 per cent of the votes means .38 of a vote. Of course, the resulting parliament would be much too large, but there is a principle there.

Even if systems are unlikely to change, there is often a conscious need for new ideas in specific areas: third-world debt, health-care costs, welfare, administration of the law, rising crime, drug problem. Where are the new ideas going to come from in these matters? In the usual way: from the collection of information, the analysis of information and the application of basic principles. Yet these areas are crying out for new ideas in the same way as the 1984 Olympics cried out for the new ideas that were eventually to be generated by the deliberate application of lateral thinking. But we do not understand deliberate ideation and have no place for it. The best we can do is to say ideas will happen and we should keep our eyes open for them. We could do much better than that once we realized that the analysis of information is unlikely, by itself, to produce new ideas.

Economics could do with some radical new thinking. We have become very skilled at juggling the existing pieces faster and faster. Adjustments to the interest rate have to cope with inflation, exchange rate, productive investment, housing and other things. Several of these are contradictory in behaviour. Perhaps electronics will allow us to move from 'water' economics (flow according to gradients) to 'snow' economics (flow according to temperature). Nor have we fully understood the long-term implications of 'financial soup', which is the result when telecommunications removed barriers of time and distance and deregulation removes other barriers.

Any corporation that had the same attitude to change that society as a whole has would be out of business in two years. Muddle along and muddle through may protect us from excesses and disasters but it also prevents us from using to full effect the resources that are readily available.

It is to be hoped that a better understanding of the thinking required for change and a specific allocation of focus and resource to this area might lead to some improvement.

The Next Step

Take a pencil and try to copy the outline of a moderately complex shape with a continuous line. Repeat the process using a series of dots rather than a continuous line. In most cases the second method gives a much better representation. The reason is that the position of the next dot you put down can be easily adjusted to fit the shape you are copying better. A line has a momentum. A line cannot suddenly jig to one side – but a dot can.

In most situations the next step is largely determined by where we are at the moment and not by where we should be or where we want to go. The step is determined by where we are, by where we have just come from, and also by history that is more remote. We are propelled forward by our history rather than drawn forward by our vision. We inch forward. Transitional steps are much more important than final destinations, no matter how excellent these may be. Changes in education must fit the teachers, the test system and current demands on education. Changes in the law courts must be based on present structure and roles.

There is supposed to have been an Irish farmer who was asked for directions to a certain place. After musing for a few moments he said: 'If I was wanting to get there, I wouldn't have started from here.' There is an excellence to that logic even if the comment was not very helpful (although the driver could have taken instructions to get to the 'better' starting-point and then have proceeded from that point).

Then there is the 'edge effect'. This means that the route is clear and the destination is highly desirable, but if you cannot take the very first step the rest is impossible. All US foreign policy initiatives in the Middle East must face the first step: how will this be taken by Israel? (and the supporting lobby in the USA). In a new industrial development the 'environmental impact analysis' is the necessary first step.

Architects build a new building from scratch even though constrained by the site, the money available and the client's taste. It is often easier and cheaper to build a new building than to attempt to remodel an old one.

Mostly in society there is no choice. We have to take the next step from the position at the moment. We may feel that universities are no longer the best mechanism for intellectual progress, but we are stuck with them and cannot close them down in order to design anew.

Slowly a corporation becomes fat and complacent. Inch by inch, moment by moment, the future is built on the existing baseline. It is only a dynamic new executive, a management buy-out, a take-over or merger that provides the opportunity for radical restructuring. Divisions can be sold off, middle management layers can be slashed, unprofitable projects can be terminated, new people can be taken on. Mikhail Gorbachev in the Soviet Union is exactly in the position of a new executive who has been given the task of radically changing a very large corporation that has hitherto just inched forward along a track determined solely by where it came from and the next easy step.

At every moment a flow of water will find the easiest direction. Water cannot flow uphill in the knowledge that this will soon lead to a greater downhill. Water cannot jump over the bank of a river because it knows the plains are there to be flooded. In a similar way, in various matters we pursue what is easy, relevant and rewarded at the moment. Mathematics moved steadily away from non-linear systems because there were other easier areas to attend to. We put a lot of intellectual effort into history because it is an easier option than many others.

As we proceed along the path, each step being the most reasonable from the position we are in, we may find we drift very far from the purpose of our activity. So bureaucracies grow step by step until the purpose for which they were set up becomes poorly served. Layers of over-ride systems that were supposed to hone decisions now make it almost impossible to get a decision at all.

In our thinking we find ourselves looking harder and harder in the same direction because that is where our expertise and intellectual investment has been. It becomes difficult to move away in a fresh direction. People are employed by the institutions that exist, not by the institutions that should exist.

I do not want to suggest that this is a process of drift, because it is not. Each step may be very purposeful, but the direction of the step is determined almost entirely by the present situation, not by vision.

Full Up

Plato came out very strongly against any innovation in education. If you knew, by your own definition, that you were not only right but, 'absolutely right', any innovation could only be a step backwards.

In practice the difficulty with innovation in education is not this feeling of being absolutely right (though it certainly exists) but the fact that the curriculum is full up. There are no empty spaces, there is no vacuum. So anything new that comes in must be at the expense of something already there which has to go out. Why should something go out? Because it is bad or inefficient. That is not often the case. Most things are there because they have a value or, at least, a lot of people believe they have a value.

Every piece of information that is taught is valuable. The more information you have the more valuable every additional piece becomes, because it builds upon and adds to whatever is there already. It would be possible to fill every second of the curriculum with yet more information and still require thirty years of schooling to teach only part of the information available. Unless we are going to reach a god-like state of complete information which renders thinking unnecessary, there does come a point at which it is more worthwhile to teach operational thinking skills (not just critical ones) in order to apply the information we have. At that point we have to make the decision to give up some of the information time, valuable as it is, in order to devote time to the direct teaching of thinking as a skill. Some of the more enlightened countries and school districts are starting to do this.

This example from education illustrates a prime problem with new thinking. Even if something new does not require a disruption of the old, there is no space. People, time and resources are fully stretched – in many cases there is actually a cutting-back in resources.

The paradox is that as we advance into the future the need for change gets greater and greater (to cope with changes in population, pollution etc. and to make full use of our new technologies) but the possibility of change gets less and less because everything is already committed.

A wise general does not commit all his troops but keeps a strategic reserve which can be used as the need and opportunity arise. Society does not do this, because we believe that we have all the bases covered and that progress will come about through evolution, the clash of opinions and the occasional lone innovator.

In addition to allocating funds to research, most successful corporations also allocate funds to new business divisions or venture groups. Like the strategic reserves of a general, these groups are outside the day-to-day combat and are looking for new opportunities.

Democracy could not easily tolerate this principle of strategic reserve, for the unallocated resources would be the target of every department or issue that felt it was under-funded. Emergency funds do exist, but not space and resources for change.

The same thing applies on the thinking level. A person who knows all the answers, has an opinion on everything, has a certainty backed up by rational argument, has very little possibility of further progress. Such a person is unlikely to walk away from a discussion with anything more than a reaffirmation of how right he or she has been all along.

Education

It has been said that the main function of education is expensive baby-sitting and the jobs that provides. There is nothing wrong with that.

'The passing on of cultural values'; 'spiritual development'; 'the teaching of essential skills for living in the world'; 'vocational training'; 'the opening up of potential'; 'encouraging a love of knowledge'; 'producing useful members of society' are the phrases used to describe the aims of education. Yet most things are there because they are there and as a matter of faith.

If we leave out vocational training (for specific professions), there is very little proof that history, geography, science, poetry, literature etc. really make much difference. We take it as an act of faith that they are a necessary part of the 'culture' we wish in our citizens. With matters like reading, writing and mathematics, we take it for granted that these basic skills are so evidently useful that there can be no questioning them.

Yet when it comes to the teaching of thinking skills we demand proof that it is necessary. The question should be put the other way around: how can any education system that sets out to teach the basic skills needed in society (particularly in a democracy) justify the leaving-out of the most basic of all human skills: thinking? The answer would come back quickly: since thinking is indeed the most basic of all human skills, surely education must already be teaching it; surely thinking is being used in the learning of any subject matter?

At the age of sixty a two-finger typist will still be typing with two fingers. This is not due to lack of typing practice – what has been practised is 'two-finger typing'. The fact that thinking is being used does not mean that thinking skills are being taught. This teaching must be done in a much more explicit way, with a defined place on the curriculum, so that students, teachers and parents know that thinking skills as such are being developed. The notion of infusing it into other subject areas may be more convenient (because there are no gaps in the curriculum) but will never achieve the same effect.

The trouble with education is that it is a self-fulfilling system: it sets its own objectives and then proceeds towards them. People in education can conceive of thinking only as 'analysis' and 'critical thinking'. This is because the idiom of education is that material is put in front of the students, who are asked to react to that material. But the rest of life is not all like that. In the real world people have to pull together the factors needed to think about anything; they have to assess priorities; generate alternatives; make decisions; take initiatives. All this is part of what I have called 'operacy'.

Education has been too exclusively concerned with 'reactive' thinking. My work in the business world has shown me the limitations of assuming that reactive thinking is enough. Unfortunately most of those making decisions in education have only the inbred needs of education in front of them. Sometimes there is an astonishing circularity. The tasks in IQ tests are there to test the fundamentals of thinking. So let us teach students how to carry out these IQ test tasks (pick the odd man out etc.). Now let us use these IQ tests to validate what we are doing.

In my experience with the CoRT thinking programme one of the most valuable results has been a change in the student's self-image from 'I am intelligent' to 'I am a thinker'. This is a much more constructive image. It is no longer a matter of 'I am right' but 'I can think about this'. Thinking is also seen as a skill that can be improved by attention and practice – as is the case with tennis, skiing or any sport.

Education is all about information and right and wrong answers as determined by the text. So analysis, critical thinking and logical deduction have been emphasized. Yet the most important part of thinking, the perceptual, is neglected. It is felt that this is sufficiently handled by matters like literature. For reasons I have spelled out earlier in this book, this is a misunderstanding of perception. Literature offers perception – but not perceptual skills.

Education has suffered from the various phenomena I have listed in this section: a belief in change through evolution; the next-step difficulty; the 'full-up' problem.

What might education consist of? There would be a basic skills element. This would include thinking (not just critical but productive), reading and writing, basic mathematics skills (as used in ordinary life), computer fluency, social and communication skills. Then there would be material which showed how the present-day world really worked: business, politics, basic sociology etc. The cultural background level (and possibly the preceding level) would be handled in a way different from today. Matters like history, geography, drama, technology, would be handled by means of well-made video material.

Science would be restructured and dealt with on all three levels: basic skills (methods); the present world; cultural background.

If we are going to look for change in thinking in society we shall have to look to education to carry out its most fundamental task which is to teach thinking skills. This is more important than anything else. Education is remarkably reluctant to do this mainly because people in education are locked into a system which has an extremely limited view of what thinking is about, and because they have to fulfil inappropriate criteria.

The day will come soon when parents will simply demand that schools do a much better job of teaching thinking skills. In a poll carried out by George Gallup many years ago, over sixty per cent of parents declared themselves unhappy with the 'thinking' taught at schools.

Ludecy

Take an intelligent person. Teach that person the rules of a particular game. Then ask him or her to play the game badly. That would be absurd behaviour. The intelligent person will want to play the game fully and according to the way the rules are written. I invented the word 'ludecy' (from the Latin 'ludo' meaning 'I play') to cover the playing of a game according to the way the rules are written.

The stock market is meant to reflect the values of the corporations listed. But a more direct influence on the market price is the tendency of people to buy and sell. So if you attend to and anticipate this tendency of your colleagues you will successfully play the market. After a while it becomes a game in itself and the underlying corporate values fade into the background, even though they are periodically brought forward to rationalize some behaviour that has really been based on other factors. This process is inevitable, because after a while we anticipate the anticipation of an increase in value and then someone anticipates our anticipation of the anticipation.

An inside player knows that sustained rises do not occur very often but money is to be made on fluctuations. All that is required is for some synchronizing signal (it is unimportant if this has validity) to get enough people to act together. Then the price rises and more people buy. By the time the outsiders are beginning to buy, you, as an insider, sell and take a profit. History has shown that the outside rings are quite happy to be milked in this way because they remember the occasional sustained rises when they did seem to make a lot of money for a time. Synchronizing signals used to include Henry Kaufman's views on interest rates and certain market newsletters.

A lawyer makes money by playing the legal game the way the rules are written. This includes divorce settlements, malpractice claims, product liability, corporate takeovers etc. The fact that malpractice settlements hugely raise premiums for doctors (who pass these on to patients) and also make necessary batteries of every conceivable test (also at the expense of the patient) is no business of the lawyer. That large liability claims eventually mean that certain types of activity (like kindergartens) can get no insurance at all is again no business of the lawyers. If the rules are written so that the lawyer gets a percentage of the settlement, the lawyer is going to go for a large settlement. If you play the game, you play it.

Real-estate agents want property prices to be as high as possible because their commission is a percentage of the price. That sky-high prices may make life impossible for first-time buyers is no business of the estate agent.

Education itself also shows ludecy in action. Education sets up standards and tests and then judges its performance in terms of these standards and tests. If these do not yet cover what really needs to be taught that is just too bad because the needs of the test must come first.

If a television producer knows that violence will make a programme watched, then violence goes into that programme. The game the producer is playing is simple: the programme must be watched. If a high level of violence has a harmful effect on society that is someone else's business.

A good politician knows the game of getting elected and knows the media game: how to get noticed but never to commit gaffes, for a single gaffe can destroy a political career. Being good at playing the game of getting elected is not the same as being good in government.

All these may seem to be examples of greed and self-interest. They are not. Greed and self-interest could be more easily controlled by social and peer-group pressure. They are all examples of 'ludecy'. If the rules are written that way, you would be foolish not to follow them. If you hold back, others will not. If as a lawyer you do not go for a high settlement, clients will go elsewhere. If as a real-estate agent you do not suggest a high price the vendor will go to an agent who does. If as a market investor you invest only on real value, not on market trends, you may get left behind.

Interestingly the 'game' of religion is particularly successful in overcoming immediate greed and selfishness. Religion provides a game that is different from immediate self-interest. In as much as people play this game (ludecy), greed and self-interest can be overcome for the sake of future gain, social approval and self-esteem.

Ludecy is a real dilemma because you cannot blame intelligent people for playing the game the way the rules are written.

Short-Term Thinking

In the USA there are quarterly stock analysts' reports. If the stock of your corporation is marked down, people sell and it declines further. So your corporation becomes a target for take-over. In Japan the shareholder is considered last (first the company, then the workers, then the consumers, then the banks and finally the shareholders), so the thinking can be much more long-term. In the USA executives move often between corporations. On joining a corporation an executive must show action. Soon the executive moves on and the results of the action may now come through. The lack of job mobility in Japan means that an executive is around to see the results of an action. The US executive must look for quick returns and actions that will enhance the stock price immediately. Longer-term investments are much more difficult.

I once interviewed a number of senior politicians and senators in Washington. For politicians they had a reasonable time frame: about six months to a year. Then I interviewed some leading journalists and was astonished to find that the time frame was about one day. What was happening today had to be seen as the most important thing. After all, the future could arrive only day by day. This attitude is very reasonable and is another example of ludecy. If you sit down to write a story, as journalists must, you cannot say that not much is happening or what is happening is just a storm in a teacup. You have to show that what is happening today is of the utmost significance – and carry the reader with you.

In Australia the parliament is elected every three years. At best this meant one year of settling in, one year of actual government and one year preparing for the next election. Politicians necessarily have short-term horizons because of the need to get re-elected. Doing something unpopular because you know that in the long term it will be beneficial does not make sense: you may not be around in the long term, and everyone may have forgotten your contribution. Fortunately this problem is sometimes solved by 'bandwagons'. For example, ecology is essentially long-term thinking. No politicians could have risked balancing the interests of ecology against immediate industrial development. But once ecology becomes a fashion, a bandwagon or a 'good thing', it makes short-term sense to vote for ecology.

There is an obvious overlap between short-term thinking and ludecy. If the rules of the game require short-term thinking, ludecy will ensure short-term thinking.

Democracy

In theory society has very little protection against a politician who does not want to be re-elected. In practice there are the politician's vanity and party pressure which serve as a protection against that politician doing too much long-term thinking. The politician wants to go out in a blaze of glory. The party wants to win the seat next time round.

Supposedly democracy has four bases. First, the selection of someone you trust and whom you believe to represent your views and values. Second, the threat that if the representative does not serve your purposes that representative may not get elected next time round. Third, the notion that argument and discussion will thoroughly explore needs, possibilities and solutions. Fourth, the acceptance that a simple head count will be the decision device.

In practice the severe inequities of the selection process are made tolerable only by the party system and the fact that you prefer 'your party' man to the 'other party' man even though both are far from ideal. The control over behaviour once the politician is in power is greatly enhanced by media comment. It is not even necessary for the politician to do something stupid, it is enough to do anything which can be construed as stupid by the media (local and national). Argument and dicussion probably have little value at this point in history, since the issues are so clearly pointed out everywhere in the media. But horse-trading in committee sessions and compromises are part of the necessary negotiation. The head count is crude and simplistic but an arithmetic that we can trust.

Obviously the most powerful force in the whole design is the fear of losing favour, exacerbated, as I have suggested, by media scrutiny. It is much easier to make enemies than to make friends. If you neglect a friend he or she is unlikely to cross to the other side. The friend stays on your side but is resentful or is a friend at a distance. A newly created enemy is, however, instantly lost. So as a politician you do not do things which upset people. A five per cent swing in the electorate may have you thrown out in the next election. So you do not do or say anything that might offend even five per cent of the electorate even if the rest of the electorate want it done or said.

Democracy is an excellent way of ensuring that nothing much gets done. There are always interests that might get trampled upon. Any initiative (unless a response to a crisis) is always wide open to attack. Nor is there any reason for supposing that the changes that are needed are going to be instantly acceptable within the current framework.

Individuals with leadership and vision do occasionally get into power. Popular sentiment may create pressures for change that politicians dare not resist. There are crises which have to be coped with. So changes do take place. They take place in spite of the democratic process and not because of it. This may be a reasonable arrangement, provided there is a lot of energy for change coming from somewhere.

Perhaps one day we shall divide democracy into a jury function and a leadership function. The jury function will represent the values and preferences of the electorate and will judge what is put forward by the leadership function. The leadership function will be people elected on the basis of skills and qualifications to put forward the constructive ideas and changes that might not arise from a purely representative body.

In most countries there is already a convergence of political views. Labour governments in Australia and a socialist president in France behave very much as conservatives. Eventually it will be seen that there are sensible things to be done whichever party happens to be in power. There may be slight differences in the allocation of resources to different areas (health, education, defence etc.), but the policy differences that are always exaggerated by journalists to keep alive some interest in politics will be seen to be phoney.

Pragmatism

In Amsterdam there is a famous street in which the ladies of the night sit in well-lighted windows and wait for clients. I am told that prostitution is illegal in Holland, but the tax authorities charge the women an imputed income tax based on estimates of earnings.

Pragmatism has a bad name because it seems to be the opposite of 'principled', and that is 'unprincipled', so we have the dichotomy problem I explored earlier in this book. Pragmatism does not need to mean the absence of principles but can mean the flexible application of principles. Pragmatism can also mean a refusal to be driven into impractical action by rigid principles.

Although every government or institution is far more pragmatic than that body would ever admit, we do not like the concept of pragmatism. On the one hand it implies wishy-washy behaviour, anything goes and anarchy. On the other hand it implies bending the rules, self-interest and corruption.

There are a number of possible approaches to this dilemma. One approach is greatly to increase the number of available principles. If we have a richer range of principles, we may find that one principle comes to over-ride another. For example one basic principle may drive us to war but another principle of 'prudent action' may prevent that war. The principle of the freedom of expression (lack of censorship) could be over-ridden by a certain cost of expression (say a tax of £5,000 per corpse in a TV programme). There is already in existence a principle of responsibility which might do the job if skilfully used.

The principle of justice might insist that a burglar convicted of a crime should be given a sentence comparable to another burglar convicted of a similar crime. A new principle might add in the prevalence of the crime. If statistics showed that this month (or year) there were many more burglaries than last month (or year), the sentence might be much increased. This may seem odd, but should law be a contract with a criminal to deliver a certain sentence in exchange for the delivery of a certain crime?

It might be pragmatic to give long-term prisoners a reasonable pension on leaving prison so that they did not have to return to their old ways. Statistically the likelihood of recidivism is very high. Our normal principle would recoil in horror from this rewarding of sin. What is the principle to be? Is it to be the punishment of the crime, or the reduction of crime in society?

Should we have loose principles which we adhere to rigidly or rigid principles which we adhere to loosely? 'Respect for others' is a loose principle but it could be applied rigidly. Honesty is a rigid principle but we apply it loosely, in particular with the partial perception of politics and the press.

There is another important point. Should our thinking be driven by our principles or should it be compatible with them? The two are quite different because the perception is different. When we start off with the principle we can perceive the situation only through that principle. When we return to the principle after doing our thinking we have had a chance to get a much broader perception.

Should we be pragmatic enough to be pragmatic and yet to declare that we are following principles?

Law is a matter of principles. Where the law is codified (as in France) interpretations help to decide the application of the principles. With organic law that moves forward according to new cases and new principles (as in the UK and the USA) there are bodies like the US Supreme Court to decide on the principles: is the death sentence 'cruel and unusual punishment'? Some principles are free-floating but others apply only to very particular circumstances. The definition of insanity in a criminal case is apparently free-floating (an insane person is not responsible for his or her actions) but in practice comes down to a detailed analysis of circumstances (is brainwashing or hypnosis a form of insanity?).

Principles need feeding. They exist only as we talk about them, believe them, use them and make decisions (even unpopular ones) with them. Against the rigidity and convenience of principles, pragmatism seems to have nothing to offer. We can, however, introduce the concept of 'fit', which is highly circumstance-dependent. An action 'fits' the circumstance or does not.

It is wrong to kill innocent people. An insane person is innocent in so far as he or she is not responsible for his or her actions. If an insane person was threatening the lives of others (with a bomb on a plane) would there be justification in killing that person? The answer would be the same as with self-defence, which is itself a pragmatic over-ride of a basic principle.

The key point is that if we define pragmatism as action that 'fits' the circumstance, then generally accepted principles are also part of the circumstance. It is not a matter of circumstance or principle but of circumstance including principles.

Although philosophers like William James and John Dewey were great American protagonists of pragmatism, we have not really explored its practical application for fear of what it might lead to and for fear of losing our valuable sense of righteousness.

Bureaucracy

A bureaucracy comes about when a body of people who have come together for a purpose change that purpose to the perpetuation of the body.

Bureaucracy is a classic case of ludecy. Very soon the game which everyone is playing is surviving and thriving in the bureaucracy: this may involve risk avoidance, buck-passing, political infighting, channel creation etc. This is no different and no worse than the ludecy practised in any other profession.

The purpose of a bureaucracy is to avoid mistakes. The good work of a bureaucracy is taken for granted and seldom noticed. Mistakes are points for attack. A mistake hangs around a bureaucrat's neck for the rest of his or her career. There is no escape as in the world of private enterprise, where one failure can be succeeded by a success. There are many who have lost and made fortunes with cyclic regularity.

Suppose the bureaucrat has a good idea, is this not commendable? It will be asked why the idea was so long in coming forth. Possibly a great deal of money could have been saved had it been implemented sooner. Suppose it would not have been possible without the latest computer technology, surely that is praiseworthy? Not necessarily. In some countries the originator of the idea will indeed be acknowledged as an 'ideas man' but passed over for promotion to head of the department, which needs a sound man (who will never make a mistake by never having ideas).

I once suggested that any bureaucrat who could genuinely abolish his or her own job should receive full salary until retiring age. This seems absurd, but it is not. The salary would have been paid if the job had not been abolished. But if the person now gets a salary for doing nothing, all the support and make-work costs are saved. That person would also be free to take and abolish another job.

Bureaucracy was never designed as a change mechanism but to implement things as they are. Unfortunately change often has to go through bureaucracies. Foundations quickly become bureaucracies. Instead of being the venture capitalists that provide seed money for non-commercial innovation in society, they end up with the risk attitude of bankers – concerned with the same low-risk projects as every other foundation. This has certainly been my experience with them.

Many of the potential change mechanisms of society are in the hands of bureaucrats. There is no natural law that says that people who enter and remain in bureaucracies are of less talent than those who do not. Maybe they have been intelligent enough to choose a low-stress life-style. Nevertheless people with vision and enterprise are likely to get frustrated in a bureaucracy and also likely to engender antagonisms that get them ejected. So where change requires visions and enterprise but must also pass through a bureaucracy the outcome is rather likely to be negative. If we put together the ludecy of politicians and the ludecy of bureaucrats the hope for change or innovative thinking is slight.

I once suggested to the Russians that they should set up an Academy of Change with the specific purpose of seeing what would happen if bureaucrats were pointed, formally, in this direction. I would also suggest a minister or a secretary of state for ideas, as some way of focusing attention on this need.

Compartments

One day schizophrenia may be classified as a particular type of enzyme disorder.

In the early days of science and medicine there were multiple classifications because description was all we could manage. As we began to understand basic underlying mechanisms the classifications broke down because we could see that conditions originally classified as very different were just different manifestations of the same thing.

James Gleick in his excellent book *Chaos* describes how this new science or area of interest had to cut across many existing compartments: meteorology, physics, fluid engineering, computer science, mathematics (and many compartments within mathematics). The first work was done by Edward Lorenz, a meteorologist.

So there are two opposite trends. One trend is increasing specialization and compartmentalization. With increasing knowledge and much better investigative methods, an individual has to focus on some tiny aspect of a subject and pursue that aspect with the specialized tools now available. Usually specialists in one compartment cannot even communicate with those in an adjacent compartment. The language is different, the concepts are different, the mathematics is different and the concerns are different. All this is inevitable and it is no one's fault.

The other trend is that as we get to know more and dig deeper we begin to find that processes and systems of organization cut across many fields. At other times in order to understand what is happening in a field there is a need to borrow concepts and techniques from another field. In the future philosophers may need to be neurologists. Already we have seen how computer scientists have had to borrow from neurology to design neural network systems.

New research projects often involve a deliberate inter-disciplinary team (mathematicians, physicists, biologists, computer scientists, materials physicists etc.). Just as the old classifications disappeared when we dug below the surface to understand basic mechanisms, so the distinction between subjects may also disappear. Clearly there are distinctions of scale. A particle physicist is not working on the same scale as an economist. Yet an economist may need to know a lot about chaos theory and non-linear systems. An economist may even need to know about the neural basis of mind in order to understand the behaviour of perception and choice which together so affect economic behaviour.

Yet funding and organization are based on traditional compartment lines. Indeed if a project seems to cross a compartment boundary the funding source may dry up, since the matter has now become the business of another agency. Administrative neatness will always be a long way behind what is actually happening.

Specialists within a traditional field are easy to appoint. Specialists in a new field cannot be appointed until the field is established. Cross-disciplinary generalists are not easy to appoint because in any field they will be inferior to a specialist in that field.

In the future we shall probably have to re-think this whole area of specialization and compartmentalization if the potential of technology is going to be fully used. We shall need to create cross-compartment specializations and interface languages so that knowledge can flow. We may also have to establish 'thinking' about all these things as a discipline in its own right.

Universities

As the name implies, universities try to do too much. There was a time when the whole sum of human knowledge could be encompassed at a university. That time has long gone.

Universities are there to encourage scholarship, research and education. There is the university as the home of a scholar who is investigating some very specialized part of civilization so that the findings may be woven into the general tapestry of our culture. Such scholars might not find a home anywhere else.

This culture exploration aspect of universities may mean that a great amount of resources are tied up in departments of history, language/literature and philosophy. The obsession with history I have noted in earlier pages. Its bias is historic, deriving from that time when history could teach us a great deal (the Renaissance). History departments are productive, attract students and are large enough to defend their status. History is perhaps the easiest area in which to achieve that scholarship which is so highly prized. Indeed, the very word scholarship is almost synonymous with historic awareness and perspective. For those members of society who do not want to be technologists the departments of history and language/literature provide a 'general' background.

In the USA more and more students are going into law and business administration because they see this as a suitable background for business activities in later life.

In mathematics, science, medicine and various areas of technology the university training is more or less vocational. Since society needs such people, this training has to be done somewhere. Some countries, such as Germany, do it in specialized technical colleges of high standing.

So there are the cultural aspects of universities and the vocational aspects. As far as society is concerned these are important but rather humdrum activities. Research is what contributes directly to new ideas and to progress. But there is no real evidence that universities are still the best place for research. In the past most research has come from universities because that is where research was being done. Since corporations started doing their own research quite a lot has come from this direction. There are researchers who may not want to do any teaching and may not be good at it. There may be a case for specific research institutes, of which there are some already, such as the Princeton Institute of Advanced Studies.

Universities want their independence because they fear that as a direct arm of government they will be forced to follow government policy: 'Churn out more electronic engineers.' Yet independence may also mean ineffectual democracy. If every existing department has to vote about the establishment of a new department, it is not likely to happen. Cambridge University in England is such a place. The result is that Cambridge recognized mathematics as a fit subject for study only in about 1850 and even today does not have a business school.

Universities are very prone to the problem of apostolic succession. This means that the new appointees are chosen in the image of those who are already there. Universities are also bureaucracies in which the preservation of the existing direction is more important than anything else. They have a solid historic base and that is one of the reasons why it may be time to change the concept and to unbundle education, research and cultural continuation.

Universities do a good job, but the same resources applied in a different way might do a better job.

Communication

Language is probably the single most important barrier to progress. It is possible that we simply cannot progress any further because we have come up against the ultimate limit of language. In a previous section I have dealt with the deficiencies of language as a thinking system. In this respect it is much poorer than we suppose. We continue to mistake fluency for value.

For the majority of people communication is through the media of language: books, newspapers, radio, television, talking, political speeches, discussions, commentaries.

There are some excellent science journalists and economic journalists and even political commentators, but in the past the quality of persons going into journalism has not been very high. Entrepreneurs are busy being entrepreneurs and scientists are busy being scientists, so they have little time to communicate directly. Most communication passes through the intermediaries we know as 'journalists' in the broadest sense of that word.

The sheer ability of journalists to comprehend different fields is usually limited, so they have to fall back on three basics: the human angle; some gimmick aspect; attack. The prime purpose is not exposition of the subject but journalistic 'interest'. The ludecy is clear. Commercial democracy has its own ludecy. The larger the readership or the viewership the higher the advertising rates, so the search for the mass market is necessary. Clash and controversy are intrinsically more interesting than agreement, so disagreements have to be played up and emphasized. Scandals are fun, so personalities rate more than substance.

All these points are in addition to the limitations of the media in the 'truth' department. Just as there is no truth in perception, so there is no truth in the media. Partial perception and selectivity are inevitable. Perceptions are always from a particular point of view. A bloody scene on TV is of interest but may be a small sample of the whole scene, which may be very different – if one person in a crowd is hurt the cameras will, where possible, be on that person. To complain about partial perception is valid but unlikely to change anything. It is the nature of the medium and the nature of the game.

The media can set perceptions directly and that is a power for the good or the bad. The media played an important part in such crusades as: product quality, healthy food and exercise (with a significant health effect), Vietnam, ecology and conservation, racial attitudes, gender attitudes, the dangers of smoking. In all these instances there was the power of propaganda for good causes. In some areas the media are a power for change and new perceptions, in others they reinforce the old perceptions. The criterion is 'whatever makes the more interesting copy'.

Packaging

If advertising were to become really effective, society could no longer tolerate it. That is why we have not permitted subliminal advertising. It may be that in the future our understanding of perception will be so good that we can make advertisements that are so compulsive that the viewer will be forced to take action.

In politics the packaging of a political campaign or a candidate has become a very skilled operation. Feedback and polls predict exactly how people will respond to certain lines. The blandness of candidates in the 1988 presidential elections is as much due to this as to anything else. The message is 'don't upset people' and 'let them read into your utterances what they want to hear'. Journalists may clamour for hard-edged policy statements in order to have something to write about, but campaign managers know better. Reagan showed very clearly what every person who has ever been on television knows – no one listens to what you have to say, they react to you as a person. Campaign managers know that too.

These things are not new. Franklin Roosevelt used to ask George Gallup to go out and pre-test how people would react to a controversial speech. If the result was positive, the courageous speech would be made. It is just that we are getting so much better at it.

For the first time in history we are within reach of powerful perceptual tools. There is no need to attempt to appeal to people through logic. Emotional appeals are not necessary either. The battle of politics will become the battle of perception. That is why we need to pay a great deal more attention to the perception aspects of thinking – as I have attempted to do in this book.

Summary of Practical Outcomes

At this point we have reached the end of a progression which had the following stages:

1. A look at the self-organizing model of the brain and a contrast between self-organizing information systems and table-top systems.

2. A look at how the behaviour of perception arises directly from the behaviour of self-organizing systems.

3. A look at the impact of an understanding of perception on our traditional thinking habits and their defects.

4. A look at thinking in society and its institutions.

I would now like to pull together and summarize in this section some of the practical outcomes of this exercise. There are many, ranging from the very specific (such as creativity tools) to the more general (such as concern with the deficiencies of language). Some of the points are simple but others open up huge areas of further consideration. To repeat a point I have so often made in this book, I have not set out to provide all the answers but to indicate that these matters now need very serious attention. There are other points implicit in the book which I have not listed here but which individual readers will note and consider.

The practical outcomes fall into two broad areas:

1. Practical points arising directly from our understanding of the nature of perception.

2. Defects in our traditional thinking habits made visible by our understanding of perception.

Complacency

The most astonishing thing is our remarkable complacency and self-satisfaction with our traditional thinking systems. We are so locked into table-top logic that it has almost become a belief system. We can see the world only in these terms, so that what we see reinforces our way of looking. We are so bemused with the success of our thinking in technical matters that we account for its relative failure in human affairs by saying that these matters are simply intractable owing to the perversity of human nature.

The Need for More Effort and Attention

We need to pay far more attention to our thinking systems and the matters that have been considered in this book. This is the most fundamental of human concerns (the very nature of our thinking) and yet the most neglected. After many years I moved out of the academic area (Oxford, Cambridge, London, Harvard) because it was not possible to find a way of pursuing these matters. This is because they do not fit into psychology or philosophy or mathematics, but cut across many disciplines.

System Basis

For the first time in history we have a system model for the brain. This is the self-organizing model described simply in this book. This reopens the whole area of thinking and perception in particular. We can now see how the brain might be a simple mechanism that is capable of behaving in the complex ways we know as mental activity.

Traditional Philosophy Is Dead

Traditional philosophy can continue only as a word-game. Many philosophers had come to this conclusion anyway. In future philosophers will need to have a good understanding of systems behaviour and different models of information systems, in particular self-organizing systems. Anything else is just the exploration of the inadequate words we use to describe things we do not understand.

Perception

Our understanding of the difference of behaviour between passive information systems and active (self-organizing) systems allows us for the first time to explore perception, as I have been doing in this book. We can begin to understand the logic of perception. With an understanding of this logic we can look forward to big changes in human affairs.

Mental Illness

The self-organizing model of the brain can give us new insights into mental illness. For example in paranoia there is an 'excess of meaning'. In schizophrenia there is 'disorganized meaning'. In autism there is a 'lack of meaning'. In the model we can pinpoint the defects that could give rise to this type of behaviour. At any of these points a defect would give rise to what we see in that type of mental illness. For any type of aberrant behaviour there may be many possible points. And at any of these points a number of things might be wrong. But we can move from the purely descriptive to the hypothesis stage and begin to test different approaches.

Free-Will

We can begin to understand the physiological basis of such matters as free-will. We can begin to understand how it is possible to be free in a deterministic system. This has profound implications. For example it may sometimes make sense to punish offenders even if they could not help what they were doing. This is totally contrary to our ideas of justice.

Evolution for Change

We need seriously to reconsider our traditional model of evolution for progress. For many reasons this is grossly inadequate. For example, in order to go forward we may need to take to pieces existing concepts so that the elements may be recombined in different ways. Paradigm shifts also require this type of change.

Our complacency within the evolution model has made us rely on critical thinking, argument and problem-solving as methods of change. All these are flawed and limited in their effectiveness.

Argument

The argument process is central both to our traditional thinking system and also to such practical institutions in society as law, politics and scientific progress. We need seriously to reconsider the effectiveness of the method. If argument is intended as 'exploration' of the subject, there are much better methods – and we can devise even newer and better methods of exploration. The validity of argument depends on certain assumptions about absolutes and also on a lack of imagination. The polarizing, distorting and conflict-generating aspects of argument have long been self-evident.

Critical Thinking

We have always highly esteemed critical thinking because we have believed that a 'search for the truth' is what thinking is all about. As a result of this fallacy we have sadly neglected the generative, productive, constructive, creative and design aspects of thinking. New concepts, new perceptions, new hypotheses, new designs have to be created – they are not just discovered. We also need to realize that, far from being a difficult mental process, critical thinking is very easy because of the possibility of choosing your reference standard. We do need critical thinking but only as part of thinking along with the generative side, which is so much more important. We can also realize that the most effective critical thinking is actually creative thinking, because the ability to generate an alternative explanation is the most powerful way of destroying the uniqueness of a claim. Also the imagination to see the consequences is the best critique of action proposals.

Clash

Our belief in revolution through clash has limited us to concepts of negative revolution. This means: define the enemy, hate the enemy, attack the enemy. Because this is often impractical and often unsuccessful we do not have the revolutions that are needed. It is quite possible to design positive revolutions.

Analysis

We need to realize that the analysis of data is not enough. We can find in the data only reflections of the ideas we already hold. This arises directly from the nature of perception. So our reliance on analysis for decision-making is inadequate. We need to develop creative conceptual skills as well. In the scientific area the traditional belief in the most reasonable hypothesis is also faulty, because we are then restricted to viewing the data through that hypothesis. So other hypotheses are essential even if they are far less reasonable.

Problem-Solving

The major defect of this traditional method of surviving is that problem-solving will only get us back to where we were before. In business, politics and social progress this idiom of 'problem-solving' dangerously limits progress. Problem-solving needs to be contrasted with the process of 'design', which moves forward to a need. We must certainly stop using the term 'problem-solving' to cover all thinking, since this restricts us to one small aspect of thinking.

Truth and Absolutes

We need to re-examine carefully our concepts of truth. There is constructed truth, as in mathematics, and there is perceptual truth, as in belief. Then there is relative truth provided by authority, particular circumstances and the concept repertoire we have. Truth may best be described as a particular constellation of circumstances which will give a particular outcome. Our traditional concept of truth has led to our creation and use of absolutes. The rigidity of these and their independence from circumstance gives them a certain practical value but also makes them poor instruments for progress. We need to devise systems based on 'water logic' rather than 'rock logic'. This certainly does not mean 'relativism' or 'anything goes'. We need a pragmatism with integrity.

Description

We need to be very clear about our use of description. Some types of description are no more than fancy arabesques of language and ideas with a value that is only decorative. Other types of description have the value of allowing us to perceive differences and identities. Then there is description as an exercise in the design of possible hypotheses. So description can be very valuable or a misleading waste of time.

Obsession with History

We need to escape from our obsession with history, which mops up too much talent and resources. A high concern with history reduces the effort to look forward with 'design'. The concepts it has provided limit our perceptions and may actually be dangerous in circumstances that are now very different.

Intelligence Is Not Enough

The general notion that intelligence (analysis, logic, and argument) is enough is dangerous in many ways. The emphasis is on the logical rather than perceptual skills, which are so important in real-life thinking and doing. The ability of an intelligent person to avoid obvious errors and to put together a coherent argument often blinds that person to the need to develop deliberate thinking skills. The avoidance of error is certainly not enough in thinking.

Language

We need to be even more aware of the deficiencies and deceptions of language. The direct emotional appeal of value adjectives and the insidious effect of 'sneer' adjectives set the context for percep-tions and so determine the range of patterns that can be used. The phenomenon of the wide catchment of perceptual patterns, combined with the certainty, identity and categories of logic, allow logic to be used to support almost any case. In addition, language is an encyclopaedia of ignorance, since perceptions based on comparative ignorance are frozen into the permanence of words and so limit future thinking. We must realize that language is not a thinking medium at all but a communication medium. The ability of language to describe something adequately in hindsight by means of an assembly of words may actually prevent us from developing a richer code of language with which to perceive things in the first place (for example, the paucity of words to describe human relations).

Polarizations

The dichotomy habit of language (us/them, friend/enemy, tyranny/freedom) gives rise to crude and dangerous perceptions. This system has been essential to our traditional thinking habits in order that we may operate the principle of contradiction. In practice it may be the single most damaging aspect of that tradition. We need to explore the middle ground and create a whole spectrum of perceptions. We need to see that a categorization under one set of circumstances does not hold under other circumstances. We need to create new concepts that cut across dichotomies, for example 'friend/enemy' as one concept.

More Is Better

The traditional habit of fixed categorization causes problems with the Laffer or 'salt' curves. If something is good, more must be better. Table-top logic simply cannot cope with this problem and the result gives rise to serious inefficiencies in society (for example in the US legal system).

Limited Gate-Keepers

The gate-keepers for change in culture or thinking tend to be people in the literary tradition. Very often they are simply unable to comprehend other idioms. These other idioms are therefore ignored or inadequately represented. The result is that society is insulated from potential change and also steeped in the defective thinking of the language culture.

Understanding Perception

We have always been able to describe perceptions. We have always had a feeling that perception was a very important part of thinking. We have tried, with little success, to apply logic to perception and only found ourselves basing our logic on other perceptions. At last, for the first time, we can begin to understand perception. We can do this because we can now see perception as the natural behaviour of a self-organizing system. We can see that perception is not haphazard but has its own logic. The logic of behaviour is the inescapable behaviour of the underlying system.

Perception and Emotion

We can begin to understand how emotions can change perceptions. This is part of the general effect of context on perception and can have practical outcomes where efforts to change the context may change perceptions.

Perception and Belief

Circularity in a self-organizing system can very easily set up beliefs. We have the difficult task of realizing that beliefs are so easy to set up that they need only a slight basis in reality. At the same time the perceptual truth of a belief can be very strong indeed. Furthermore, a belief, even if false, can provide an organizing system, a value system and a meaning framework.

Perception and Truth

There can be no truth in perception except the circular truth of a belief. We should not expect truth or objectivity in the media, which are extensions of the perceptual system. It may be better to accept this rather than pretend otherwise.

Prejudice and Logic

Once we understand the basis of perception we can see why logic cannot alter prejudices, beliefs, emotions or perceptions.

Over the ages we have put a great deal of effort into this use of logic and been disappointed at the failure. We can now see how only perceptions and emotions can alter these things. Even experience may be powerless. That is why we need to give a high priority to the development of specific perceptual skills (for example with the CoRT programme in schools).

Time Sequence

The build-up of perceptions is highly dependent on the sequence of experience over time. The perception at any moment is highly dependent on the time sequence leading up to that moment. Consciousness can have a practical effect on instructions, announcements, presentations, negotiations, propaganda etc., etc. This effect is certainly already known, but the system base shows it to be even more important than we had supposed.

Reconstruction

The 'trigger' effect of perception means that we can construct or reconstruct matters which are not there at all. This is done with no element of dishonesty or fraud. So perception, no matter how honest, must always be suspect. We come to see what we think is there.

What We Are Prepared to See

When we think we are analysing data we are actually only looking at it through our existing paradigms and with a limited range of available concepts. In the future we may come back to the same data and see them very differently. There is therefore a practical reason for re-examining old data through new perceptions. There is also a practical reason for generating, and listening to, new concepts.

Innocence

The research tradition has insisted that you should read all available knowledge on a matter before starting work in that field. But if we become too aware of the existing concepts we shall only be able to view the field in exactly the same way. So there is a dilemma. Insufficient knowledge means duplication and also the inability to build on existing work. Too much knowledge means lack of originality. There are some ways around this. In any case the practical point is that too much research can have a negative effect.

Humour

We can see humour in a new light. Humour is not just an odd aberration of mind but an important behaviour of self-organizing systems. As such, humour is one of the best indications that the brain works (at least in perception) as a self-organizing system. The pattern-switching of humour is a good model for creativity and insight.

Poetry

We can see that the logic of poetry is the 'water logic' of perception in which meaning is not built up sequentially but layer by layer. Poetry works because of the 'sensitivity' or 'readiness' effect in the self-organizing system.

Stratal

The stratal is a new grammatical form that, like poetry, seeks to take advantage of the sensitivity behaviour of the self-organizing system. The meaning is built up by the layering of different statements between which there is no need of a logic connection. A convenient number of statements might be four or five.

Six Thinking Hats

This is a deliberate thinking device which builds directly on the sensitivity and 'context' behaviour of perception. Each of the six hats sets a new context in a way that is deliberate and artificial. Instead of just waiting for the context to change we can take steps to change the context.

Attention

The self-organizing model of the brain explains the important phenomenon of 'attention' and shows how attention can flow from area to area. The model also explains why attention is 'unitary'. From this understanding of attention we can move in several practical directions.

Perceptual Tools

The CoRT thinking tools that are being taught in a practical way to millions of schoolchildren are based directly on the self-organizing model. The tools provide simple attention directors. Instead of attention just flowing from 'point to point' as in most perceptual thinking, there are deliberate attention directors the effect of which is to give the thinker more control over attention. As a result attention is broader and deeper. Youngsters are able to look at the consequences of action, at other people's views, at alternatives etc.

Mechanics of Interest

Quite soon we shall be able to work out the basic mechanics of 'interest'. What makes something on television 'interesting'? This interest need not arise from the actual content. Such an understanding would be extremely useful to programme designers because it would give them a way of becoming architects of interest. It would also be of use to advertisers and propagandists.

Attention Flow in Art

We may find that successful art is a choreography of attention. That may be the basis of aesthetics. Where does attention flow? How long does attention stay there? How does attention loop back?

Manipulation of Perception

There is a danger that as we come to understand the logic of perception we shall become more and more powerful at manipulating perception for the purposes of advertising, political campaigns and media ratings. There is nothing new in this. Art, literature, political campaigns and advertising have been striving to do this for a long time. It is just that we may become so very good at the process that society will not be able to tolerate it. Logic and critical thinking will not protect us because they will work within some perceptual framework. That is why it is so extremely important that we develop skills of 'perceptual thinking' directly and seriously (such as the CoRT programme).

Zero-Hold

Our understanding of the behaviour of patterns in the self-organizing system of the brain suggests that we need a 'zero-hold' device which would allow us to put forward patterns which did not exist in experience (provocation) and which would delay our quick entry into existing patterns.

'Same as . . .'

We have a strong tendency to see new things as examples of things we already know. In general this is useful because it allows us to extend our existing patterns to cover new situations. The habit is dangerous, however, because it prevents creativity by treating an emerging new idea as something unworthy of attention because it is already known. The habit also prevents progress in general. The phrase 'the same as ...' is very easy to apply even if the resemblance is slight. Proper attention and examination of the new idea is thereupon halted. This is a danger to watch for.

Understanding Creativity

We know that creativity happens. We can describe it and even attempt to extract some features which seem to recur. All this is very weak. Now, for the first time, we can understand the 'logic' of creativity. The logic arises directly from the asymmetric patterns that inevitably form in a self-organizing system. So from the self-organizing model we can go directly to understanding creativity in a way which was never possible before.

The Logic of Provocation

In traditional logic systems provocation could never have a place. There could be no place for something which did not make sense and which was not related to what had come before. But in a self-organizing system provocation is not only logical but a mathematical necessity. The logic of provocation can be signalled by the word 'po', which I invented many years ago.

The Logic of Insight

If you enter a pattern at a certain point you may have to follow the long way round. If you enter the same pattern at a slightly different point the route may be very short indeed. This natural behaviour of patterns is what gives rise to the surprising phenomenon of 'insight' in which we suddenly see something differently.

Specific Tools of Lateral Thinking

From an understanding of creativity, from the logic of provocation, from the logic of insight, we can design specific creative tools. Instead of just waiting for inspiration we can use such tools deliberately in order to generate new concepts and ideas. These are the specific tools of lateral thinking, which have now been used effectively with practical success. These tools could not have been designed in our traditional thinking system. For example, in our traditional system the simple 'random-word' technique would be total nonsense. Yet in a self-organizing system this technique makes perfect sense. In practice it works very well.

Resistance to Change

Our understanding of perception helps us to see why there is such resistance to change. Our existing perceptions, concepts, models and paradigms are a summary of our history. We can look at the world only through such a framework. If something new comes along we are unable to see it. Or, if we do see it, we see it as a mismatch with our older perception so we feel compelled to attack it. In any case we can judge it only through the old frame of reference. For example the judgements and absolutes of 'rock logic' make it very difficult for us to see how 'water logic' can work. The other type of resistance to change is the dismissal of an idea with 'the same as . . .' response. This is all quite apart from those whose vested interests in the old idea make them actively hostile to the new one.

The Next Step

The next step we take is very much determined by where we are at the moment. Change may require that we step back several paces in order to move off in a new direction, and this is extremely difficult. Everything becomes locked in with everything else. There is a web of concepts and perceptions each of which

284 I AM RIGHT – YOU ARE WRONG

supports the others. This means that any successful strategy for change should provide an easy direction which can be taken but which does not require any backstepping. That is why our understanding of the self-organizing type of information system is such a key point that allows us to review our entire thinking system.

Education

Traditionally education has concerned itself with information, analysis and some critical thinking. This may have seemed sufficient in terms of the traditional thinking system. In the new perspective, education is doing less than half its job. There needs to be deliberate attention to perceptual thinking skills. Such skills are quite separate from a concern with art and literature. There is need for attention to operacy and the skills of doing. There is need for attention to design thinking in its broadest sense. There is need for attention to thinking that is productive, constructive, generative and creative. Reactive thinking and problem-solving will not equip people to improve society. Unfortunately education is so locked into its traditional concepts that the needed changes will not easily take place.

Universities

On the whole universities are not equipped, intellectually, to do the venture thinking that is needed. Universities absorb the bulk of human and financial resources available in any country for intellectual progress. Much of these resources are wasted on sheer continuity. Some of them could be more effectively used in 'intellectual venture units' where the emphasis was not on protecting tradition and anointing history but on new areas that were opening up. Usually such new areas cut across existing disciplines and are therefore unlikely to arise within them.

Compartments

Specialities get more and more specialized until everything is happening in small compartments which have little communication with each other. We need ways of having people communicate with each other across speciality boundaries. We need ways of overcoming the administrative boundaries that restrict movement of people. We need basic concept languages for communication. The perceptions and concepts that occur within a speciality should be easily available to everyone.

Short-Term Thinking

Eventually most structures in society will tend to shorten their thinking horizons. With increasing pressure on funds there is a need to show results. Showing results means responding to the needs of the moment. Such short-term thinking puts the emphasis on immediate problem-solving. There is less time for design, for speculation and for the larger issues. A journalist believes that the future can happen only one day at a time, so to look after this day is to look after the future. In exploration and design work it may be a long time before things reach a critical mass of sense and value. It is this critical mass which launches a new design or a new paradigm.

Ludecy

When a game is played as an end in itself we have what I have called 'ludecy'. It is almost like an action belief system: what is done is there to support what is being done. Unless there are ways of generating fresh ideas almost all organizations will settle down to this 'self-organized' steady state. Bureaucracies are only one example. This is another fault of our reliance on evolution for change.

Learning Backwards

Patterning systems strongly suggest that learning backwards should be more effective than learning forwards. This prediction needs to be worked out in practical detail. For example, what does learning backwards mean when applied to matters with levels of complexity? There is work to be done here.

New Language

I am currently working on a new language for thinking which will allow us a much richer perception without the baggage of our usual languages.

Water Logic

We need to clarify and develop water logic so that it becomes a practical, usable system. The 'hodics' system outlined in the appendix is a step in this direction.

Hope

If we felt that we were already operating at the limits of our thinking system, there would be little hope. We would look forward to a future in which the increasing problems would overwhelm us. With an emphasis on new thinking we can re-kindle hope for a much better future. Revolutions do not have to be negative. Positive revolutions can take place. And the first such revolution must be in our attitude to thinking. Thinking is not just being right and avoiding error. Thinking is exploration, new concepts and design for a better future.

Summary

For centuries we have worked within our traditional thinking system. We are convinced that this traditional thinking system is the only possible one. Surely truth and reason are absolutes for which there can be no alternative and beyond which it cannot be possible to go. Surely these are the absolutes demanded by the system itself. It is true and reasonable to have a system based on truth and reason.

As we begin to understand self-organizing systems we find that neural networks can work in this manner. The very simple model of a self-organizing neural network given in this book shows how a few interactions can give rise to complex behaviour. Should we just ignore the big step forward that this provides in understanding how the brain works? Should we choose to persist in dogmatic ignorance on the basis that such understanding might be disturbing?

The implications of self-organizing systems for perception and for our traditional thinking habits are very considerable. In this book I have tried to spell out some of these implications. In each case I have done no more than hint at an implication. There are two basic types of implication. The first type is an understanding of how perception works, which covers such things as humour, creativity, catchment, and circularity of beliefs. This gives us an understanding of why perception is so very useful and yet so distorted. The second type of implication covers the defects in our traditional thinking system, with its absolutes, categories, identities and contradictions. We can easily see how the imperfections of this system have both given rise to serious problems in human affairs (wars, racism etc.) and prevented us from making much progress in them.

At this point we have some choices. We can simply ignore completely what I have written or set out to prove that it is incorrect (at least in some aspect). This would be very silly, because the matter is so fundamental that it will return again and again with more force. We can simply never ignore self-organizing systems again, now that we know about them.

We can accept what is said at least in its broad terms even if not in all detail. We can accept it and then ignore it to continue with our existing system as if nothing had happened. But a thought once thought cannot be unthought. So at the back of our minds there will be some growing doubts about the arrogance and assurance of our traditional thinking.

We can take the view that this is indeed a useful description of how the mind works. We can take the view that this description shows up the messiness and unreliability of the human brain and then marvel at the achievement of classic Greek thinkers in giving us a thinking system (with its absolutes and logic) that gives such a practical way of proceeding. Most people will take this view but are then left to answer the original question: why have we been so unsuccessful in dealing with human affairs as compared with technical matters?

We can take the view that what has been described in this book deals with perception and is most valuable and useful for this purpose. Then we say that the second aspect of thinking is processing (logic, mathematics etc.) in which we construct artificial systems with which to process our perceptions. This is a satisfactory view, but it does mean that logic has to retreat. Because we have never understood perception we have tried to apply the logic of traditional thinking directly to the world. Once we acknowledge that perception must come first, we must spend a great deal more time working on the logic of perception because this is extremely important. We shall then find that a great deal of our thinking really takes place in this perception stage.

I would be very happy indeed if we did but acknowledge that perception was a very important part of thinking. Once we do this we soon find that the table-top logic habits of our traditional thinking system do not readily apply (as I have been showing in this book) and that we must develop a better understanding of perception and deliberate perceptual skills (as with the CoRT programme in schools). Perception becomes a new area that we must work within.

That has been the objective of this book: to shift the emphasis to the importance of perception.

Appendix: Water Logic

At several points in the book I have referred to 'water logic' as a contrast to the 'rock logic' of traditional thinking. The purpose of this naming of 'water logic' is to give an impression of the difference. At this point I shall spell out in more detail some of the points of difference.

A rock is solid, permanent and hard. This suggests the absolutes of traditional thinking (solid as a rock). Water is just as real as a rock but it is not solid or hard. The permanence of water is not defined by its shape.

A rock has hard edges and a definite shape. This suggests the defined categories of traditional thinking. We judge whether something fits that category shape or not. Water has a boundary and an edge which is just as definite as the edge of a rock, but this boundary will vary according to the terrain.

Water will fill a bowl or a lake. It adapts to the terrain or landscape. Water logic is determined by the conditions and circumstances. The shape of the rock remains the same no matter what the terrain might be. If you place a small rock in a bowl, it will retain its shape and make no concession at all towards filling the bowl. The absolutes of traditional thinking deliberately set out to be circumstance-independent.

If you add more water to water, the new water becomes part of the whole. If you add a rock to a rock, you simply have two rocks. This addition and absorption of water logic corresponds to the process of poetry, in which new images become absorbed in the whole.

It is also the basis of the new artificial device of the 'stratal'. With conditions and circumstances, the addition of new circumstances becomes part of the whole set of circumstances.

We can match rocks by saying this shape 'is' or 'is not' the same as another shape. A rock has a fixed identity. Water flows according to the gradient. Instead of the word 'is' we use the word 'to'. Water flows 'to' somewhere.

In traditional (rock) logic we have judgements based upon right/wrong. In perception (water) logic we have the concepts of 'fit' and 'flow'. The concept of 'fit' means: 'Does this fit the circumstances and conditions?' The concept of 'flow' means: 'Is the terrain suitable for flow to take place in this direction?' Fit and flow both mean the same thing. Fit covers the static situation, flow covers the dynamic situation. Does the water fit the lake or hole? Does the river flow in this direction?

Truth is a particular constellation of circumstances with a particular outcome. In this definition of truth we have both the concepts of fit (constellation of circumstances) and of flow (outcome).

In a conflict situation both sides are arguing that they are right. This they can show logically. Traditional thinking would seek to discover which party was really 'right'. Water logic would acknowledge that both parties were right but that each conclusion was based on a particular aspect of the situation, particular circumstances, and a particular point of view.

In the body of the book we saw the problem that traditional thinking had with the Laffer or 'salt' curve. 'If law is good, more law must be better.' 'If salt is good, more salt must be better.' This problem does not arise in water logic. The 'amount' of something is a condition for it to have value. The point is that water logic is highly dependent on defined circumstances or conditions, whereas the very essence of traditional rock logic is that it is circumstance-independent.

We must note that we are so immersed in our rock logic

system that water logic will at first seem so pragmatic that 'anything goes' and there is no way of making judgements or getting a decision. This is not so at all. Water will not flow uphill or against the gradient. The behaviour of water is well defined and so is the behaviour of water logic. The difference between rock logic and water logic will take a lot of getting used to.

Consider the following example of the difference between rock logic and water logic. A woman takes her electric kettle into a smart store and asks them to replace it because it does not work:

Assistant A: 'I am sorry but you couldn't have bought that kettle here because we don't sell that brand. So I can't replace it.'

Assistant B: 'Are you quite sure you bought it here? Do you have the receipt? I'm sorry I can't change it unless you show me proof that you bought it here.'

Both assistants A and B show traditional rock logic. They want to know what 'is' the state of affairs.

Assistant C: 'Yes, of course we'll change it. I'm so sorry you were put to this trouble.'

Now assistant C knows that the kettle could not have been bought in that store because the store does not sell that brand. Nevertheless the assistant perceives that the customer is genuinely mistaken. The assistant is also interested not in what 'is' but in what the situation leads 'to'. What the situation leads to is extraordinary customer service. This may seem absurd, yet research actually shows that for every dollar spent on customer service five dollars are returned in increased sales and customer loyalty.

What if this benevolence is abused? Then you deal with that abuse when it arises. Also the assistants are free to use their own perceptions as to whether it is a genuine mistake. If you have a piece of rock in a glass and you tilt the glass the rock is either in the glass or falls right out. There is an 'all or none' effect. That is not so with water. You may pour some water from the glass but still retain some water in it.

Hodics

The word 'hodics' is derived from the Greek word for road (*odos*). Hodics is the name I have given to a system of notation with which to handle the flow of water logic. I had intended to describe hodics in this book and have, indeed, promised this at some points in the book. On reflection, however, I have removed this section so as not to overburden the reader and also to avoid the risk of diluting the main theme. I shall return to hodics in a later (much shorter) book.